THE ONTOLOGICAL ARGUMENT FROM DESCARTES TO HEGEL

JHP BOOKS SERIES

THE
ONTOLOGICAL
ARGUMENT
FROM
DESCARTES
TO HEGEL

KEVIN J. HARRELSON

BOOKS SERIES
Published in Cooperation with the
Journal of the History of Philosophy

Humanity
Books

an imprint of Prometheus Books
59 John Glenn Drive, Amherst, New York 14228-2119

Published 2009 by Humanity Books, an imprint of Prometheus Books

Inquiries should be addressed to
Humanity Books
59 John Glenn Drive
Amherst, New York 14228–2119
VOICE: 716–691–0133, ext. 210
FAX: 716–691–0137
WWW.PROMETHEUSBOOKS.COM

13 12 11 10 09   5 4 3 2 1

Library of Congress Cataloging-in-Publication Data

Harrelson, Kevin J., 1976–
    The ontological argument from Descartes to Hegel / by Kevin J. Harrelson.
        p. cm. — (JHP books series)
    Includes bibliographical references and index.
    ISBN 978–1–59102–639–6 (hardcover)
    1. God—Proof, Ontological. 2. Descartes, René, 1596–1650. I. Title.

BT103.H37 2008
212'.1—dc22   2008016492

Printed in the United States of America on acid-free paper

Contents

CHAPTER TWO: REFUTATIONS OF ATHEISM: ONTOLOGICAL ARGUMENTS IN ENGLISH PHILOSOPHY, 1652–1705   79

CHAPTER THREE: BEING AND INTUITION: MALEBRANCHE'S APPROPRIATION OF THE ARGUMENT   101

CHAPTER FOUR: AN ADEQUATE CONCEPTION: THE ARGUMENT IN SPINOZA'S PHILOSOPHY 121

CHAPTER FIVE: ONTOLOGICAL ARGUMENTS IN LEIBNIZ AND THE GERMAN ENLIGHTENMENT 141

CHAPTER SIX: KANT'S SYSTEMATIC CRITIQUE OF THE ONTOLOGICAL ARGUMENT 167

PREFACE

This book provides a philosophical analysis of the several debates concerning the "ontological argument" from the middle of the seventeenth to the beginning of nineteenth century. My aim in writing it was twofold. First, I wished to provide a detailed and comprehensive account of the history of these debates, which I perceived to be lacking in the scholarly literature. Second, I wanted also to pursue a more philosophically interesting question concerning the apparent unassailability of ontological arguments. In pursuit of this latter problem, the driving question that my account addresses is "why has this argument, or kind of argument, been such a constant in otherwise diverse philosophical contexts and periods?"

As familiar as the ontological argument is, there have been no book-length studies in English about the historical development of the arguments of Anselm, Descartes, etc. A vast collection of articles and chapter-length treatments of the history of these arguments does exist, however; and in composing this work I have benefited from the labors of numerous scholars. Particularly helpful was the work of Bernardino Bonansea, Charles Hartshorne, Asnat Avshalom, and Oded Balabon. Even more influential were the many monograph-length studies that have long appeared in other Western languages, especially in German and French. In conducting the necessary research I accrued an enormous debt to the authors of these texts. I thus owe my sincere gratitude to Wolfgang Roed, Louis Girard, and Jan Rohls. My greatest debt in this regard, however, is to Dieter Henrich. My work is little more than an extended argument with him.

I conceived this project shortly after completing and defending my more narrowly focused doctoral dissertation entitled *Hegel's Defense of the Ontological Argument for the Existence of God* (University of Kentucky, 2004), and some of the content of that dissertation reappears here in chapters one, six, and seven. On the long road from that narrow treatment of Hegel's *Logic* to the broad chronological study here presented, I benefited from the assistance and advice of many individuals. First and foremost, I am indebted to James Force, Martha Bolton, and the editorial board at JHP Books for inviting me to complete this project. Ronald Bruzina, Brandon Look, Oliver Leaman, Michael Jones, and David Olster served previously on my dissertation committee, and their comments and suggestions were of considerable assistance in my initial conception of the present work.

Further acknowledgement is due to Reinhard Schaeffer and Michael Wladika, who conducted an enlightening seminar on the ontological argument at the University of Heidelberg in the summer semester of 2002. My thanks go to the many participants in that seminar. I hope they find the fruit of some of their insights herein. I am indebted also to two referees from JHP Books for their astute comments on an earlier version of the manuscript. In addition, I would like to thank my many friends and students who have discussed this material with me over the years, as well as the librarians from the University of Kentucky who retrieved the many necessary sources for me. Most of all I thank my advisor, Daniel Breazeale, for his years of generous guidance and support. I dedicate this book to him.

Muncie, August 2008

ABBREVIATIONS

1705   Samuel Clarke, *A Demonstration of the Being and Attributes of God*. Frommann Verlag Stuttgart, 1964 (1705 edition).

A   G. W. Leibniz, *Saemtliche Schriften und Briefe*, Berlin Academy, 1923.

AA   Immanuel Kant, *Kant's Gesammelte Schriften* (in 23 vols.), ed. Prussian Academy of Sciences, Walter de Gruyter and Company (Berlin), 1910–22.

AT   René Descartes, *Oeuvres de Descartes*, eds. Adam and Tannery, Paris/Vrin, revised edition, 1964–76.

Bonansea   Bernardino Bonansea, "The Ontological Argument: Proponents and Opponents," in *Studies in Philosophy and the History of Philosophy*, ed. John K. Ryan, Catholic University of America Press, 1973.

Censura   Pierre-Daniel Huet, *Censura philosophiae cartesianae*, Paris, 1689. English edition: *Against Cartesian Philosophy*, trans. Thomas M. Lennon, JHP Book Series, Humanity Books, 2003.

CSM   René Descartes, *The Philosophical Writings of Descartes*, ed. John Cottingham, Robert Stoothoff, and Dugald Murdoch.

Curley   Spinoza, *The Collected Works of Spinoza*, ed. Edwin Curley, Princeton University Press, 1985.

Dialogues   Nicolas Malebranche, *Dialogues on Metaphysics and on Religion*, trans. Morris Ginsberg, George Allen and Unwin, 1923.

EL   G. W. F. Hegel, *The Encyclopedia Logic*, trans. Geraets, Suchting and Harris, Hackett 1991.

G   G. W. Leibniz, *Die philosophischen Schriften von Gottfried Wilhelm Leibniz*, ed. Carl Immanuel Gerhardt, Berlin, Weidmann, 1849–55.

Hartshorne   Charles Hartshorne, *Anselm's Discovery*, Open Court Press, 1965.

Henrich   Dieter Henrich, *Der Ontologische Gottesbeweis*, Tuebingen, 1961.

HS   G. W. F. Hegel, *Lectures on the History of Philosophy*, trans. Haldane and Simson, London, 1892–96.

KrV   Immanuel Kant, *Kritik der reine Vernunft*. English edition: *Critique of Pure Reason*, trans. Allen Wood and Paul Guyer, Cambridge, 1997.

Loemker   G. W. Leibniz, *Philosophical Papers and Letters*, ed. Leroy Loemker, 2nd edition, Riedel 1969.

Metaphysica   Alexander Gottlieb Baumgarten, *Metaphysica*, Halle, 1779 (originally 1739).

Oeuvres   Nicolas Malebranche, *Oeuvres Completes de Malebranche*, ed. Henri Gouhier, J Vrin, Paris, 1958.

Opera   Spinoza, *Spinoza Opera*, ed. Gebhart, Heidelberg 1925.

Rel   G. W. F. Hegel, *Vorlesungen ueber die Philosophie der Religion*
               (in 3 vols.), ed. Walter Jaescke, Felix Meiner, Verlag (Ham-
               burg), 1993.

Rohls   Jan Rohls, *Theologie und Metaphysik: Der ontologische Gottes-
               beweis und seine Kritiker*, Guetersloh, 1987.

Sketch   C. A. Crusius, *Entwurf der nohwendigen Vernuft-Wahrheiten*,
               Leipzig, 1745, reprinted by Georg Olms, Hildesheim, 1964.

SL   G. W. F. Hegel, *Science of Logic*, trans. A. V. Miller, Humani-
               ties Press, 1959.

Suhrkamp   G. W. F Hegel, *Werke* (in 20 vols.), ed., Eva Moldenhauer and
               Karl Markus Michel, Suhrkamp Verlag, 1970.

True System   Ralph Cudworth, *True Intellectual System of the Universe*,
               First American Edition, Andover 1839 (originally 1678).

Wolfson   Harry Wolfson, *The Philosophy of Spinoza*, Harvard 1934.

"Je n'ai jamais vu personne mourir pour l'argument ontologique."

Camus

Introduction

AN EPISODE IN THE HISTORY
OF AN ARGUMENT

THE LEGACY OF ANSELM'S ARGUMENT

Ever since Anselm introduced his *unum argumentum* in the eleventh century this subtle and elusive piece of reasoning has met with either enthusiasm or scorn. To most who have encountered it in one form or another Anselm's argument is an instance of blatant sophistry. In apparent defiance of every conceivable rule of demonstration the conclusion asserts the existence of an object on the basis of a mere verbal definition. Accordingly, a long line of dissenters from Gaunilo to the present have believed themselves capable of exposing the simple fallacy in "the ontological argument." The success of these objectors, however, has been nothing if not fleeting. Time and again philosophers have resurrected Anselm's strategy, albeit in diverse contexts and with different premises. In many cases the proponents have succeeded in reducing the supposed objections to misplaced platitudes. The history of this process, like Anselm's argument, is without analog.

In both the middle ages and the modern era ontological arguments suffered disrepute as a result of attacks by the most influential philosophers of those respective epochs. Shortly after Anselm proposed his novel proof, Thomas Aquinas responded with a number of criticisms that seemed destructive to the argument.[1] Although the prominence of Thomism damaged the standing of the *ratio Anselmi*, and the nominalism of the later middle ages banished it to utter obscurity, the argument is not without an impressive list of medieval advocates. The names of Bonaventure and Scotus alone suffice to lend a certain degree of credibility and, at the very least, to remove the impression that there was ever a consensus of the wise against Anselm's proof.[2]

In the modern period it was Kant who gained the reputation of conqueror of the revised argument. Although most recognize that the seventeenth- and eighteenth-century champions of an a priori proof (Descartes, Spinoza, Leibniz, etc.) comprise an even more impressive cast than do Anselm's medieval supporters, it was and still is believed that those philosophers belong to a lost age of "dogmatic" rationalism. Kant appeared to have forever eliminated the possibility of proving the existence of God from the mere idea of such an entity. Nevertheless, the disappearance of the a priori proof in the wake of his *Critique of Pure Reason* was short-lived. The most renowned among Kant's successors in Germany, Hegel placed himself in the Anselmian tradition by defending and modifying the Cartesian proof. Other idealist philosophers in Germany in the middle of the nineteenth century, as well as their British and American turn-of-the-century descendents, also defended versions of the modern ontological argument.[3] The final scenes of this prolonged episode were not complete until the 1930s, when Gilbert Ryle publicly expressed his surprise that at such a late date in history R. G. Collingwood could still endorse a Hegelian version of the proof.[4]

If the idealist systems of Hegel and his anglophone followers likewise belong to a bygone age, the basic strategy common to Anselm, Descartes, and Hegel has nonetheless remained a part of the philosophical landscape. Although Frege and Russell imagined themselves to have forever eliminated *both* idealism and the possibility of an ontological proof (and Russell did associate these), early analytic philosophy put the latter in only a very brief respite.[5] The middle decades of the twentieth century in fact saw a remarkable renaissance of ontological arguments, sparked simultaneously by an increased interest in modal logic and some innovative treatments of Anselm's *Proslogion*. A mere two decades after the Collingwood-Ryle debate, Norman Malcolm and Charles Hartshorne initiated a movement in modal ontological arguments.[6] Alvin Plantinga subsequently furthered their arguments, and some level of support for this trend has persisted until the present day.[7] If there were an *obvious* and universal fallacy common to all these many sons of Anselm, belonging as they do to otherwise diverse traditions, this nine-hundred-year history would be hardly explicable.

It is a remarkable enough fact of the history of philosophy that such diverse philosophers over nine centuries have argued in ways so similar that a single name refers to their arguments collectively. Even more impressive is that these arguments have so often stood in opposition to the prevailing philosophical prejudices. Yet the basic objections raised against the various forms of the ontological argument are few in number, and the continuity to be found among the opponents of the argument is equally noteworthy. From Gaunilo to Aquinas, from Gassendi to Kant, and from Russell to the most recent publications, a small number of closely related objections reappear in only very modestly altered forms. The objections that appear in the journals of contemporary philosophy pose points similar to those that philosophers have disputed for the past millennium. An observer of this history can only find amusement at the sense of novelty with which these ancient quibbles are frequently raised: every time a scholar alleges to have uncovered a modal fallacy in a version of the ontological argument, or to have exposed the confusion of hypothetical for ontological necessity, that scholar merely assumes an old and repeatedly contested position. In many cases this occurs in entire ignorance of not only the history of the argument, which would be forgivable, but also the intentions of the particular proponent in question as well as the basic problems underlying the dispute. It should thus not seem astonishing when the defenders of an ontological argument refuse to surrender their cause in light of a newly exposed fallacy. The reemergence of an ontological proof in the face of any apparently novel objection will never surprise the perspicacious student of its history.

A convincing case can thus be made for the need for an acquaintance with that history, and it is the intention of the present volume to contribute to this. Since the history of Anselm's argument divides somewhat naturally into three considerably distinct phases (viz., medieval, modern, and contemporary), I have limited myself to just one episode of this long and varied story. The concern here is specifically with those versions of the argument that appear within the metaphysical systems of the seventeenth, eighteenth, and nineteenth centuries. The arguments common to this period are importantly different from those to be encountered in either medieval or contemporary philosophy, whereas the development of the a priori proof that stretches from Descartes to Hegel and his followers remains within a relatively uniform framework.

Definitive of the arguments of this period are both a commitment to a classical conception of God and an aggressive metaphysical program that situates the controversial inference to the existence of a deity.[8] At the outset of the so-called modern period in the history of philosophy, Descartes famously salvages the a priori proof from the scholastic scrapheap by placing it in the context of a subjective epistemology. He lends further support to the controversial inference in the form of theological doctrines that, in some cases decisively for the ontological proof, differ dramatically from those of the mainstream Catholic tradition. In the following century the epistemological and theological premises of the Cartesian proof undergo refinement in the ambitious rationalist systems of Malebranche, Spinoza, Leibniz, Wolff, and others. The general tendencies concerning the defense of the proof among these philosophers reach their most extreme formulation in Hegel's mature system.

In the following chapters I argue that the strategy for proving a priori the existence of God that remains in place during this period, from Descartes' initial argument in the *Discourse on the Method* (1637) to Hegel's final lectures in Berlin (1831), is both internally consistent and free of any easily identifiable error. More importantly, I try to show that the most common objections to the modern ontological proof, raised by the likes of Gassendi, Hobbes, Hume, and Kant, fail to identify any conclusive and universal fallacy. A careful analysis of the many supporting arguments suggests rather that the objections address shortcomings only in one or another particular presentation. In most cases there are to be found more consistent defenses of the argument that address and correct these shortcomings.

The modern period contains, to be sure, a number of instances in which the critics succeed in gaining the upper hand in the debate. In these cases, however, it is always a matter of local, rather than universal success. Descartes' interlocutors, for instance, manage to expose some unintended consequences of his presentations of the proof, and this is what drives the constant revision of his argument throughout the following century. Descartes' argument contains a series of at least apparently corrigible shortcomings, and the modern history of the argument consists mainly of efforts to provide the requisite corrections. Kant's criticisms represent a second and equally interesting case of local victory for the objectors. Although Kant claims, and has been too often believed, to have demonstrated the impossibility of *any* ontological proof, his objections in fact apply only to the markedly inferior versions of the proof that appear in eighteenth-century textbooks. The limited extent of his success, although for so long he was imagined to have had the last word, in part explains why ontological arguments reappear not only in Germany at the turn of the nineteenth century, but again among twentieth-century academic philosophers.

The conclusion to be drawn from this, however, is not that any of the philosophers from the modern period in fact offer a sound a priori demonstration of theism, and I do not intend for my analysis of this debate in modern philosophy to be an outright defense of the ontological argument. On the contrary, the ontological arguments of Descartes, Hegel, et al. stand and fall with a fairly well-defined set of metaphysical, psychological, and theological claims to which the arguments are wedded. My analysis suggests that the historical decline of what I designate as the "modern ontological argument" depends upon a very great number of factors, only part of which involve the apparent vulnerability of the argument to the familiar objections. Finally, I should note that it is not the intention of this text to provide a complete intellectual history of the ontological argument in modern philosophy, but rather only to clarify and analyze the important philosophical features of the relevant debates on a chiefly textual basis.

THE "MANY FACES" OF THE ONTOLOGICAL ARGUMENT I: FROM ANSELM TO DESCARTES

Although the name "ontological," which binds these arguments together, first appears only in the late eighteenth century,[9] there is a certain degree of appropriateness in this convention that thereby unites Descartes' argument from the *Fifth Meditation* to Anselm's notorious *Proslogion* argument. Both arguments depart from a definition of God as possessing supreme greatness or perfection; both allege to reveal a contradiction in the attempt to think of God as not existing; both arguments involve a modal distinction of the divine existence; both arguments hinge on the vast difference between God and any other conceivable entity; finally, it is an important feature of both arguments that the inference from essence or concept to existence is unique to the case of God.

Not only does Descartes' argument bear considerable formal similarity to Anselm's, but the modern versions of the ontological argument also include frequent and conscious references to their scholastic heritage. To some degree at least, the history of the ontological argument is a self-conscious one. Whether Descartes actually has Anselm's proof in mind at the time he composes his *Discourse on the Method* or *Fifth Meditation* is open to question.[10] What is undisputable is that he is aware of the similarity between Anselm's argument (if not with the name of this man) and his own as early as 1641, when Caterus accuses him of borrowing the proof from Thomas's *Summa theologiae*.[11] In the subsequent decades the argument is known simply as "Cartesian," and reference to the medieval tradition is indeed somewhat sparse.[12] Frequent comparisons between Descartes' argument and Anselm's are to be found, however, in Leibniz and other late seventeenth-century writers, and some level of awareness of a "history of the ontological argument," albeit without this title, is in play at least as early as the 1680s.[13]

Descartes nevertheless takes pains to distinguish his argument from the one that appears in Thomas's text, and the premises of the "Cartesian argument" are, to be fair, unique to his philosophical context. The distinction between Descartes' and the medieval ontological arguments is present as well to the consciousness of most other philosophers of early modernity. The arguments of this period differ from their scholastic antecedents chiefly due to the epistemological context of seventeenth-century philosophy. In Descartes' case, the distinguishing feature consists primarily in the importance he grants to the theory of "clear and distinct" ideas and his subjective criterion of truth. His rejection of the medieval argument accordingly takes the form of an accusation that the latter rests solely on the meaning of words, and thus receives no guarantee of the veracity of the definition of God. Although in subsequent seventeenth- and eighteenth-century formulations the epistemological premises of the Cartesian argument undergo considerable revision, the proponents nonetheless remain faithful to Descartes' commitments to the extent that they each provide a comparable epistemological background for the argument.

Anselm's precise line of reasoning from the *Proslogion* possesses only very indirect relevance for the history of the modern argument, and many twentieth-century philosophers were justified in claiming that both his critics and followers were unfaithful to his exact intentions.[14] In his now famous text he begins with the definition of God as "that than which no greater can be conceived," and constructs two closely related arguments.[15] The first argument (*Proslogion* II) concludes that "that than which no greater can be conceived" exists both "in reality" (*in re*) and "in the understanding" (*in intellectu*), while the second (*Proslogion* III) adds that the entity in question cannot be thought not to exist.[16] These arguments suffer the objections first of Gaunilo and subsequently of Thomas, while receiving extended defense both by Anselm (in open correspondence with Gaunilo) and Bonaventure. Due to the prominence of Thomas's *Summa theologiae*, however, as well as the relative obscurity of the Anselm-Gaunilo exchange, seventeenth-century philosophers are familiar with the proof primarily via Thomas's discussion of it. Consequently, it is a passage from the *Summa*, not the *Proslogion*, that serves as the backdrop for Descartes' explanation of his argument.

In the opening sections of the *Summa* Thomas considers a version of the ontological argument under the general heading of "whether there is a God," and specifically within the article concerning the self-evidence of that question. Anselm's reasoning is cited as the affirmative position in the debate about self-evidence:

> [A] proposition is self evident if we perceive its truth immediately upon perceiving the meaning of its terms. . . . Now once we understand the meaning of the word "God" it follows that God exists. For the word means "that than which nothing greater can be meant." Consequently, since existence in thought and fact is greater than existence in thought alone, and since, once we understand the word "God," he exists in thought, he must also exist in fact. It is therefore self-evident that there is a God.[17]

It is worth noting that Thomas not only restricts the discussion to the argument from *Proslogion* II, to the neglect of the argument from *Proslogion* III, but also substitutes *significari* for *cogitari* in the definition of "God."[18] Although the two objections that he then introduces do not depend entirely upon this last misconstrual, his phrasing nonetheless weighs the dispute slightly in his favor. His first objection asserts that, given the pseudo-Anselmian definition *id quo maius significari non potest*, "nothing thus defined would thereby be granted in the world of fact, but merely as thought about." In other words, it follows from Anselm's premises that God exists "in the apprehension of the intellect," to translate by the letter, but not in nature. This first Thomistic objection allows only that if we accept Anselm's definition we have to *think* of God as existing.

Thomas's second objection adds a skeptical dilemma: from the fact that we have to think of God as existing it does not follow that he "in fact" exists. Necessity for thought is not sufficient to establish existence. The conclusion of the argument, then, is only *true* if a corresponding object is given. Thomas thus continues: "Unless one is given that something in fact exists than which nothing greater can be thought—and this nobody denying the existence of God would grant—the conclusion that God in fact exists does not follow." The second Thomistic objection asserts that the Anselmian argument presupposes the existence of an entity corresponding to the definition of God.

More than five centuries later this passage reaches Descartes' desk at the prompting of a Dutch Thomist known as Caterus. This author of the *First Set of Objections* to Descartes' *Meditations* quite reasonably underlines the analogy between the argument from the *Fifth Meditation* and the above-cited argument from the *Summa*.[19] In his reply to Caterus, Descartes grants the relevance of the Thomistic objections to the argument found in the *Summa*, before eventually highlighting the important difference between the scholastic argument and his own.[20] To Thomas's objections he adds his own variation of the critique of the pseudo-Anselmian argument:

> In this form the argument is manifestly invalid. For the only conclusion that should have been drawn is: "Therefore, once we have understood *the meaning of* the word 'God' we understand that *what is conveyed* is that God exists in reality as well as in the understanding."[21]

This is the background against which Descartes formulates what I argue, in the following, is the most complete version of the Cartesian ontological argument. In the very next lines he attempts to distinguish his *Fifth Meditation* argument from Thomas's formulation of the medieval argument, and to accomplish this he highlights in particular the epistemological premises of his argument. He writes, "my argument however was . . ." and offers the following syllogistic version of the proof (hereafter the "*First Replies* syllogism"):

> Premise 1: That which we clearly understand to belong to the true and immutable nature, or essence, or form of something, can be truly asserted of that thing.

> Premise 2: But once we have made a sufficiently careful investigation into what God is, we clearly and distinctly understand that (necessary)[22] existence belongs to his true and immutable nature.

> Conclusion: Hence we can now truly assert of God that he does exist.

This argument possesses a number of elements that distinguish it both from the *Proslogion* arguments and the more abbreviated argument from the

Summa. Most striking among these differences is the inclusion of a major premise claiming that, under ideal epistemic conditions, what we attribute to a thing really belongs to that thing. If this premise (hereafter either the "major premise" or "predication thesis") is allowed, no objection of the Thomistic sort is possible. In other words, it could not be claimed that the argument shows only that we must think of God as existing, since it has been granted that what we must think of as belonging to a thing really belongs to that thing.

However controversial inferences from mere thoughts or definitions to realities may be, then, the premises of the *First Replies* syllogism warrant such inferences. Likewise, whatever validity Thomas's quibbles have as objections to Anselm or Bonaventure, epistemological considerations set the modern argument apart and safeguard the proof from any Thomistic attack. In a Cartesian context there can be no matter of a simple confusion of "existence in thought" with "real existence," since a dogma stipulating the reality of predicates serves as the major premise of his argument. Although his successors frequently reject the subjectivism of the Cartesian epistemology (and thus his predication thesis), in most cases they nonetheless adopt the strategy of beginning with an epistemological premise. Almost without exception they present some analogous epistemological realism (the analysis of possibility, absolute idealism, the theory of real definitions, etc.) that prefaces the inference in the ontological argument, and thereby discards the Thomistic objections in advance.

THE "MANY FACES" OF THE ONTOLOGICAL ARGUMENT II: DESCARTES AND LEIBNIZ

If, as I have suggested, the ontological arguments that appear in the remainder of the modern period demonstrate a good deal of faithfulness to the Cartesian syllogism, this is not to say that there are no important differences among the arguments in question. Putting aside for a moment the various revisions of the major premise, important differences remain between the arguments of the late seventeenth century (the proponents of which include Malebranche, Spinoza, and Henry More) and the Leibnizian arguments of the early eighteenth century (represented by the likes of Christian Wolff and Alexander Baumgarten). Two perceived difficulties with the Cartesian arguments occasion the eighteenth-century amendments, and in both cases Leibniz serves as the progenitor of the revisions. First, these philosophers understand the ontological argument to require a supplemental proof of the "possibility" or noncontradictory nature of God (hereafter the "possibility objection"). Second, they distinguish arguments based on the concept of necessity from those based on the concept of perfection.

The first objection Leibniz raises is one with a scholastic heritage of its own, and Leibniz's adoption of it represents a conscious alignment both with Duns Scotus and Mersenne.[23] Modern proponents of an ontological argument divide on this issue into those (mostly Leibnizians) who accept the objection and those (post-Cartesians) who reject the attribution of "possibility" to God. Leibniz's position has the oft-noted advantage that it leads to a more rigorous presentation of the ontological argument. The penalty to be paid for this rigor, however, is fatal to the proof. The drawback of the possibility objection, as well as Leibniz's supplemental arguments designed to meet it, is that the objection consists in a tremendous concession to those who reject the ontological argument outright: if the mere "possibility" of God can be subject to a separate and preliminary investigation, this is so only to the extent that we are indeed capable, in apparent contradiction to the central claim of any ontological proof, of at least mentally abstracting "existence" from the thought of God.[24]

The second problem is even more decisive for the history of the proof in the late seventeenth and early eighteenth centuries. Leibniz objects to what he sees as an unexplained connection between the notion of an *ens perfectissimum* and the concept of necessary existence. What the proponents of seventeenth-century arguments apparently fail to notice is that the minor premise conjoins two thoroughly distinct concepts (hereafter I refer to this claim as the "two-concept thesis"). In his very latest works Leibniz employs these diverse concepts to construct two distinct arguments for the existence of a God. The arguments purport to establish the existence of an *ens perfectissimum* and an *ens necessarium* respectively. Only as a supplement to these proofs does he draw the vital conclusion that a perfect being exists necessarily (i.e., that the two initial arguments in fact concern the same entity). The voluminous German natural theologies of the eighteenth century, from Wolff to Kant's early works, follow this procedure.

Analogously to the possibility objection, however, the two-concept thesis purchases demonstrative completeness at the expense of contradiction to some of the theological implications of the conclusion. Another key point of disagreement between the post-Cartesians and the Leibnizians concerns the appropriateness of the distinction of "necessity" from "perfection." Since the underlying assumption of any ontological argument is that the essence (perfection) and existence (necessity) of God are indistinct, most of the seventeenth-century proponents reject the claim that the minor premise contains diverse concepts. On this point these philosophers are merely following a long tradition in European philosophical theology of identifying "God" with his "existence." If God is indeed identical to his own existence, then it could only represent a shortcoming of human reason to distinguish the notion of a "perfect being" from that of "necessary existence." In that case, then, the appearance of the two-concept thesis already signals a terrible misapprehension of the insight alleged to lie at the heart of the ontological argument. In eighteenth-century Germany, on the other hand, an importantly different set of metaphysical prejudices prevails, and this conditions the defense of Leibniz's two-argument strategy.

Although the seventeenth-century position is quite clearly more amenable to the ontological argument, this fact does not speak unequivocally in the favor of that position. The following problem represents just one consequence of the view: the peculiar identification of "God" and "necessary existence" renders misleading all theological statements about the existence of the deity. The best that can be said for the philosophers in question is that, in most cases, they accept this apparently unpalatable consequence. When Kant later writes that the expression "God exists" does not fit the form of a predicative proposition (i.e., it does not represent a synthetic connection between a subject and its predicate), he is thus not making a point destructive to all forms of the ontological argument.[25] In early modern philosophy we find rather that theological propositions are understood to be akin to identical statements, and the philosophers in question fall just short of claiming that "perfect being" and "necessary existence" have the same meaning.[26] "Necessary existence," like God's other predicates, is identical with God's whole nature. This identity of subject and predicate would seem to exempt theological statements from the rules governing normal attributive statements.

These problems highlighted by the two-concept thesis are of considerable historiographical significance. Since eighteenth-century theologians were prone to distinguish two lines of "ontological" argument, some scholars have organized their histories around the thesis that there are precisely two ontological arguments from this period (hereafter the "two-argument thesis"), one argument based on the notion of perfection, the other argument limited to the concept of necessity.[27] The distinction between the starting points of these arguments, however, designates only one plausible yet contested position among early modern proponents of the ontological proof. In order to give a more balanced account of the modern ontological argument, then, I consider the two-argument hypothesis to represent just one possible interpretation of the key premise that it belongs to the nature of a perfect being to exist necessarily.

DESCARTES' TRIANGLE AND THE PROBLEMS OF ANALOGY AND EXPLANATION

Common to these distinctions between the seventeenth- and eighteenth-century forms of ontological argument is that, despite considerable improvement of the argumentative basis of the proof, the eighteenth-century developments result in a sacrifice of consistency with both the conclusion and the underlying theological assumptions of the proof. This apparently peculiar historical fact stems from the central problem of the modern ontological argument, one that reappears in various contexts throughout the following: the conclusion of the argument stands in conflict with the attempts to explain and justify that conclusion.[28] This problem is evident, in outline, even in Descartes' initial expositions of his argument, and it unfolds gradually over the subsequent century. In Descartes' case, the problem stems from the fact that while he rightfully insists that the assertion of God's existence is thoroughly unique, at the same time he attempts to explain this conclusion by analogy with a geometrical claim about a triangle.[29]

The major objections to his argument aim principally at the triangle analogy, and in most cases the objections prevail to whatever extent the analogy remains crucial to the proof. Accordingly, the tendency to underplay the importance of analogy pervades the defense of the argument by Descartes and his more immediate successors. The chief means of such defense is to emphasize the vast difference between God and finite entities, the idea of God and every other idea, the ontological argument and every other argument, etc. The success of a particular defense against the objections is thus a direct correlate of the degree to which the given philosopher has succeeded in clarifying these distinctions while simultaneously reducing the role of analogy. The difficulty in this endeavor, however, is that some analogy seems necessary to any presentation of the proof, just as it typically seems necessary to explain the obscure by the familiar. Many of the various formulations of the ontological argument, I try to show, are only so many ways of negotiating this tension between the means of communicating the alleged insight and the claim at the heart of the argument.

The philosophers of the seventeenth and eighteenth centuries are not of a mind concerning how strongly the triangle analogy is to be taken. The post-Cartesian rationalist systems of the seventeenth century reflect a more consistent and complete rejection of the analogy, whereas the eighteenth-century proponents of the ontological argument make some noteworthy concessions in this regard. A small set of disagreements between the philosophers of these periods in ontology and theology condition the consistency conferred upon the respective ontological arguments. These disagreements concern, first, the ontological status of "God" in relation to any analysis of entities in general. Second, the philosophers in question diverge with respect to the theory of divine predication.

The entire Cartesian terminology (*ens perfectissimum*, idea of God, etc.), if not also the spirit of Descartes' defense of his argument, lends itself to the analogical interpretation of the argument that prevails in the eighteenth century. In the first place, the expression "supremely perfect being" suggests that even a God is merely one among many entities in existence (i.e., a particular entity subsumable under the species "entity"). On this reading, God would of course be subject to all the general rules applicable to "any being whatsoever" (i.e., all the rules enumerated in the division of metaphysics later called "ontology")[30], and these include a number of rules that would preclude the deduction of existence from a definition, concept, or essence. In this context it seems reasonable to attribute the general properties of entities to this (apparently) particular entity, God, a supremely perfect being, etc.

The seventeenth-century proponents of the ontological argument evade this dilemma by defining God in contradistinction to entities in general, thereby precluding the subsumption of God under the general laws of ontology. Malebranche and Spinoza, for instance, develop metaphysical terminologies that aim at distinguishing God absolutely from all finite things. Since these philosophers manage to avoid subsuming "necessary beings" and "contingent beings" under the more general category "beings," they thereby more successfully discourage the analogy between God and creatures. Malebranche achieves this by defining God as "*l'etre sans restriction*" and emphasizing that God is not any particular thing. Spinoza, on the other hand, considers God to be the only thing, and reduces every other "thing" to a mere modification of this one and only substance. These claims represent two concerted efforts at expressing the absoluteness of the difference between God and everything else. In the context of these philosophical systems, the misunderstanding that a rule for things in general can apply also to God becomes less probable.

Of no less importance is a divergence regarding the important scholastic theological dispute over divine attribution. Many of the philosophers of the seventeenth century, however surprising this may seem, reject the Thomistic tradition and follow instead Maimonides and the Hebrew tradition in disallowing any analogy between divine predicates and finite predicates.[31] Nothing we attribute to God (knowledge, power, existence, etc.), they argue, is predicable of him "in the same sense" in which we otherwise employ these terms. God's existence thus has little or nothing in common with finite existence.[32] In the following century, however, the Thomistic theory of theological analogy reenters the arena, a development that plays no small role in the critique of the ontological argument that prevails in the latter part of that century.

Since the fate of any ontological argument seems to rest on the relative analogy or disanalogy between, for instance, God and any other entity, many of the most famous disputes reduce to simple disagreements over whether the claims of a given ontological argument are subject to the same type of analysis as the purportedly analogous claims (e.g., the geometrical claims about the triangle). The most prevalent objections to ontological arguments consist specifically in the assertion that a particular ontological argument violates a given general rule governing a class of statements (e.g., rules about definitions, existential claims, etc.). The assumption of the objectors, then, is that theological statements are to a very great degree analogous to other kinds of scientific statements, such as the propositions of geometry. Conversely, the proponents of the ontological argument are frequently rather steadfast in their denial of analogy. What becomes clear is that if the ontological argument is to be successful, the appearance of analogy must be diminished.

Characteristic of the debates over these objections, unfortunately, is that the participants fail to clarify that the debate concerns mainly (and sometimes only) whether theological claims fall under the general rule in question. More often than not the combatants in these battles have badly missed their targets, the objectors naively asserting a given general rule while the proponents baldly deny its applicability. Too frequently both sides have nonetheless found reason to declare victory. In the following section I will outline a few of the more common objections in the interest of bringing to light by a few instances the problem I just described. These instances are important, however, not only because they highlight this central problem, but also because they constitute so much of the content of historical debate over the ontological argument.

Objections and Replies

The following is a short list of those objections, other than the possibility and Thomistic, that are prevalent in the modern period. After each objection I give a caricature of the kind of reply that is frequently found among proponents of the modern argument. I also give a brief explanation of the debate, in which I try to indicate, very roughly, the historical contexts in which the respective objections and replies appear and reappear. The terms here used to refer to the objections, some of which are adopted from the existing literature, remain in use for the remainder of the text.[33] For the reader's convenience, a brief glossary including summaries of these and other objections, as well as description of various other positions of importance, appears at the end of the volume.

    1. The modal objection: The premise of the argument asserts existence hypothetically or conditionally, whereas the conclusion asserts existence absolutely. Alternatively: the necessity in the premise is hypothetical, whereas the necessity in the conclusion is absolute.

    Reply: The objection mistakes a rule that regulates the definitions of finite things, viz., that they imply existence only hypothetically, for a rule applicable to all definitions. The very claim in the ontological argument is precisely that in this one unique case a definition implies existence absolutely.

    Explanation: This objection was the subject of much discussion in England in the seventeenth century. Considered in light of Descartes' exposition of the proof, especially in the *Discourse on the Method*, but also to some extent in the *Meditations*, the modal objection is not without validity. Descartes' reliance upon the analogy with geometrical truths in his exposition of the key premise (the premise that "necessary existence belongs to God's nature") indeed lends his argument to the misconception that the absolute or ontological necessity asserted in the conclusion of the proof is supposed to be analogous to the hypothetical or relative necessity of the propositions of geometry. The Cambridge proponents of the ontological argument, however, were quick to recognize the misleading nature of the analogy, and they therefore specify that the existential claim in the ontological argument is a unique one. Subsequent champions of the Cartesian proof likewise reduce the role of the analogy with geometry and instead emphasize the uniqueness of the claim in the conclusion. Most importantly, the consistent defense of the argument involves the denial of the general rule that all definitions assert existence merely hypothetically.[34] If there is any hope for the a priori demonstration, the rule in question must apply to everything *except* God.

2. The empirical objection: The proof makes illicit use of "existence" as a predicate. Existence is not a "perfection," or is not among the properties that can belong to the definition or essence of a thing.

Reply: Although "existence" is not, in the usual case, a predicate of an entity, there is exactly one case in which "necessary existence" belongs to the nature or essence of something. This case, and this case only, is at issue in the argument.

Explanation: In this objection the rule in question concerns the nature of existential claims. Whether "existence" can belong to the nature of an entity is indeed an issue that has received considerable attention since Kant issued his famous (or infamous) proclamation that "being is obviously not a real predicate."[35] The common perception that this objection, which belongs originally to Gassendi, constitutes an *independent* refutation of the ontological argument represents a misunderstanding of the highest rank. Even Descartes' exposition of the argument in the *Fifth Meditation* anticipates this specious contention; a basic assumption of the argument is that there is one exceptional case in which existence belongs to the nature or essence of a thing.[36] To reiterate a general rule about the predication of existence would thus not only be to ignore the crux of the argument, but also to state a trivial claim that even the proponents of the proof accept. In other words, no defender of the argument has ever denied that existence *in general* cannot belong to the essence of things. On the contrary, the very novelty of the argument lies in the fact that only God's existence is subject to a priori argumentation.

The initial fortification of the argument against this objection consists in the modal distinction of "existence" and the interpretation of this distinction in terms of the relation of "essence" to "existence." Descartes asserts that it is only necessary existence that it is at issue in the ontological proof,[37] and he interprets this concept as inseparability of essence and existence. Hegel later makes this point more explicit by frequently repeating that the separation of "essence" and "existence" is the definition of finitude.[38] On this reading, then, the claim that "existence is not a predicate of a thing" amounts only to the application of the definition of finitude to a proof about God. To assert that "being is not a predicate," and to make pretense that this should be relevant to the ontological argument, is thus to assume that laws governing statements about finite entities should apply also to theological claims.

3. Clarke's objection: The argument turns on the conflation of a subjective idea with a "real idea," or of the idea (of God) with the object of that idea. Alternatively: the conclusion follows only if the "thing" whose existence is asserted is the same as the idea "in my mind."

Reply: Since the human mind, to some extent at least, participates in the divine intellect, the object of the idea (in this unique case) is not something distinct from the idea.

Explanation: Here the objection derives not so much from an explicitly stated rule, but from a very general assumption about human perception and thought. It seems as if we can always distinguish that about which we think from our actual thought about the thing in question. There is thus plainly a difference, the objector reasons, between any idea and the object of that idea. True as this may be, the context of modern metaphysics brings about a qualification of this assumption for the case of the idea of God. Metaphysicians like Spinoza, Malebranche, and Hegel translate into philosophical doctrine the religious tenet that we participate in God's nature: the human mind, for these philosophers, is an actual part, expression, or mode of the divine mind. In the unique case of the idea of God, then, the object of the idea is not something (entirely) external to the idea. More caution is therefore needed also in applying the distinction between "idea" and "object of the idea" to theological arguments.

One of the earliest to raise this objection in the modern period is Samuel Clarke, who indicates a shortcoming in the traditional presentation of the argument when he claims that the proof confuses a nominal definition for a "real idea." Three quarters of a century later Kant expresses the point more clearly when he accuses his opponents of conflating the idea of God with the object of that idea (viz., God himself). Like many other objections, this claim is indeed relevant to certain forms of the argument considered in isolation from their context. Moreover, most formulations of the argument from the modern period lack an explicit premise that would seem to address this objection. In many other cases, however, the wider metaphysical context in which the argument appears includes some form of response to the objection I call, for lack of a more descriptive term, Clarke's objection.

The rationalist philosophy of the seventeenth century, at least in its post-Cartesian varieties, shares with the idealisms of the nineteenth century, in addition to the ontological argument, this obscure doctrine of the inclusion of the human intellect in the divine. Such a doctrine is to be found, not only in the pantheism of Spinoza, but also in the relative orthodoxy of Malebranche, Arnold Geulincx, Ralph Cudworth, and others. If, as these philosophers argue, the human mind exists only within the mind of God, then the object of the idea of God is not utterly distinct from the "merely subjective" idea. God's existence would indeed be accessible without appeal to experience, since that existence is, to some extent, internal to our thought. This last, of course, does not mean that God's existence is limited to *my* thought in particular.

4. The transition objection[39]: The idea of God is a construction developed by analogy or transition from the ideas of other objects. Alternatively, the ideas of the attributes of God are formed by transition or indefinite extension from finite and genuinely intelligible qualities (e.g., the notion of "omniscience" is a mere extension or multiplication of the idea of human knowledge).

Reply: The idea of God belongs originally to the human mind, which is incapable of inventing the idea of such a perfect thing. Variations of the reply refer to doctrines of innate ideas, "vision in God," etc.

Among epistemological objections to the ontological argument the most prevalent is the claim that the idea of God comprises an analogy ("transition") from or infinite extension of ideas derived from experience. In the Cartesian defense of the argument the theory of innate ideas plays the principal role in establishing that the concept of God (or his attributes) is not a construction whose derivation is empirical. Descartes has recourse also to his celebrated a posteriori argument from the *Third Meditation* in order to protect him against the possibility that the concept of God is a human invention.[40] Although Descartes' successors frequently accept neither his theory of innate ideas nor his causal argument for the existence of God, they do share with him a commitment to some kind of realism about ideas, in particular about the idea of God. The theory of theological equivocation is of assistance here as well: "Omniscience," to take just one example, is not a mere extension of "knowledge," as this is applicable in other contexts. The terms are in no way analogous, so that there can be no transition from the latter to the former.

THE DEMISE OF THE CARTESIAN ARGUMENT

The suggestion of the foregoing comments is that these common objections to ontological arguments are each insufficient as independent criticisms. By no means does it follow that the *argumentum cartesianum*, or any related proof, is a sound demonstration of theism. The conclusions to be drawn are rather (1) that in the history of modern philosophy the Cartesian ontological argument receives an intelligent and consistent defense against the popular objections and (2) that the history of this argument warrants closer scrutiny. If the seventeenth-century successors of Descartes indeed provide a relatively consistent context within which the common objections meet with the above-mentioned replies, some other explanation must be sought for the disappearance of these arguments.

In the first place, the consistency of the defense of the argument wanes in the eighteenth century, and this occurs to a large extent independently of the objections like the Thomistic, modal, empirical, or transition. In that century, both the epistemological underpinnings of the proof and the theory of theological equivocation begin to fade from philosophical consciousness, and the role of analogy in supporting the conclusion increases considerably. The Leibnizian possibility arguments signal the beginning of the demise of the modern ontological argument. The "school philosophers" of the subsequent decades develop his arguments without recourse to previously held positions, eventually providing a complete philosophical background for the analogy between the existence of God and other philosophical truths. Kant ultimately demolishes the arguments establishing this analogy, as these arguments are passed to him through Wolff and Baumgarten. The degree to which the critique of the ontological argument in the eighteenth century possesses relevance and importance, then, is a correlate of the degree to which the history of rationalism, from Descartes to Baumgarten, undergoes a consistent development in respect to philosophical theology.[41]

The seventeenth-century defense of the argument is not without its own problems, although the extent to which these contribute to the actual historical collapse of the modern argument is open to question. In England, the ontological argument falls victim to an objection regarding the persuasiveness of the proof. In that country, the role of philosophical theology is more practical than in the post-Cartesian environment in France; More, Cudworth, Locke, and Clarke endeavor to abate the spread of atheism. The inutility of ontological proofs to this end is apparent even to the most ardent proponents such as Malebranche and, to a lesser degree, Descartes.[42] The ontological proof, on any account, is a subtle and esoteric argument that is useless for convincing "common people." This fact provides enough motivation for Cudworth, Locke, and Clarke to strike the argument also from the philosophers' book.

On the Continent, the ontological argument traverses a path that is more difficult to retrace. If (as I suggest) the most consistent defense of the Cartesian proof appears within the works of Spinoza and Malebranche, respectively, the decline of that argument is probably tied to the decline of those philosophies. This occurs, in the first place, largely for reasons not immediately connected with the ontological proof. Malebranche's philosophy, for instance, is defeated by Leibniz's, not due to the latter's revisions to the Cartesian argument, but largely because of the untenability of the system of occasionalism. Spinoza's case is another story altogether. As is well-known, his philosophy suffers neglect for reasons that are not properly philosophical. That a Leibnizian form of the argument wins the public battle in the early part of the eighteenth century, then, is not *necessarily* a product of a consistent and indisputable philosophical advance.

In any case, the arguments of even the most consistent proponents are ridden with philosophical difficulties. Chief among these is the problem that many ontological arguments from Descartes to Hegel concern not only the existence of God, but also our experience and/or intuition of that existence. The nearly ubiquitous reference to a theological intuition or perception inhibits, in many cases, the communication and exposition of the alleged "insight" into the unity of God's essence and existence. The Cartesian ontological argument, like the various rationalist systems that support and elaborate it, suffers from a corresponding shortage of credibility, which likely would have been enough to bring about its downfall in the absence of any other objections.

NOTES

1. According to Bernardino Bonansea ("The Ontological Argument: Proponents and Opponents" in *Studies in Philosophy and the History of Philosophy*, ed. John K. Ryan, Catholic University of America Press, 1973) Aquinas's arguments from the *Summa theologiae* (1a, qu. 2) are directed at Bonaventure. Bonaventure proposes an ontological argument in his *Commentary on the Sentences* of Peter Lombard (4 vols. Quaracchi, 1934–39).

2. See Bonansea's "Duns Scotus and the Ontological Argument." Scotus discusses the proof in his *De primo principio*. A bilingual edition of this work is available in *The* De primo principio *of John Duns Scotus*, ed. and trans. Evan Roche (St. Bonaventure, 1949). For a thorough discussion of the argument in the Middle Ages, see Jan Rohls' *Theologie und Metaphysik: Der ontologische Gottesbeweis und seine Kritiker* (Guetersloh, 1987, hereafter "Rohls"), pp. 35–164. For a briefer discussion in English see Charles Hartshorne's *Anselm's Discovery* (Open Court Press, 1965, hereafter "Hartshorne") pp. 137–64.

3. Among the German proponents of the argument after Hegel, one of the more notable was Christian Hermann Weisse. See his *Die Idee der Gottheit* (Dresden, 1833) and the analysis thereof in Dieter Henrich's *Der ontologische Gottesbeweis* (Tubingen, 1960, hereafter "Henrich"). In the English speaking world Robin George Collingwood, writing a century later, was the chief defender of the Hegelian form of the ontological proof. See both his *Essay on Philosophical Method* (Oxford, Clarendon Press 1933) and his *Essay on Metaphysics* (Oxford, Clarendon Press 1940).

4. See Ryle's "Mr. Collingwood and the Ontological Argument," E. E. Harris's reply on Collinwood's behalf ("Mr. Ryle and the Ontological Argument") and Ryle's "Back to the Ontological Argument." The entire debate is reprinted in *The Many-Faced Argument: Recent Studies on the Ontological Argument for the Existence of God* (eds. John Hick and Arthur C. McGill, MacMillan, 1967), pp. 246–75.

5. See, for instance, "General Propositions and Existence" in Hick and McGill, pp. 219–25. For a balanced introductory analysis of the consequences of Russell's theory of descriptions for the ontological argument, see Graham Oppy's *Ontological Arguments and Belief in God* (Cambridge, 1995), especially pp. 32–38.

6. See Malcolm's "Anselm's Ontological Arguments" (in *The Philosophical Review* 69 (1), 1960, pp. 41–62) and Hartshorne's "What Did Anselm Discover?" (in *Union Seminary Quarterly Review* 17, 1962, pp. 213–22). These and other key early essays of the modal movement are also reprinted in *The Many-Faced Argument*, ed. John Hick and Arthur McGill, Macmillan, 1967, pp. 301–56. For a lengthier treatment that also includes discussion of Anselm, see Hartshorne's *Anselm's Discovery* (Open Court Press 1965).

7. See especially *God and Other Minds* (Cornell, 1967) and *The Nature of Necessity* (Oxford, 1974).

8. I refer here to Hartshorne's notion of "classical theism" in order to distinguish, after him, the modern from the contemporary arguments. Classical theism is simply the denial of contingent states within God. The defenders of contemporary arguments deny classical theism and its many metaphysical implications, so that they are arguing about a vastly different conception of God than is to be found anywhere from Anselm to Hegel.

9. Kant is the one who coins this term. Many of his immediate predecessors have

no term by which to refer to the argument, despite the fact that the argument had become so common. Throughout much of the seventeenth and eighteenth centuries, however, the argument is widely known as the Cartesian argument. Kant uses the title "Cartesian argument," which appears also among other earlier authors, both in England and Germany.

10. Although Descartes enjoyed feigning ignorance, it is highly probable that he had already encountered the medieval ontological argument in some form.

11. See the *First Replies* (in *Oeuvres de Descartes*. Adam and Tannery, eds. Paris/Vrin, revised edition 1964–76, hereafter "AT," v. VII pp. 97–100) and *The Philosophical Writings of Descartes* (ed. John Cottingham, Robert Stoothoff and Dugald Murdoch, Cambridge 1984, hereafter "CSM," v. II, pp. 70–72).

12. In the seventeenth century Malebranche and Cudworth were among those who employ this name, while in the following century Crusius and Kant also refer to the ontological argument as the "Cartesian argument."

13. Leibniz's gives brief sketches of the history of the argument in, among other places, the *New Essays* (*New Essays on Human Understanding*, trans. Remnant and Bennet, Cambridge, 1981) and "Meditations on Knowledge, Truth and Ideas" (*Die philosophischen Schriften von Gottfried Wilhelm Leibniz*, ed. Carl Immanuel Gerhardt, Berlin, Weidmann, 1849–55, hereafter "G," IV, pp. 422ff. A translation appears in *Philosophical Papers and Letters*, ed. Leroy Loemker, 2nd ed., Riedel, 1969, hereafter "Loemker," pp. 292–93). Clarke refers to it in one place ("The answer to a sixth letter being part of a letter written to another gentleman . . ." which is reprinted in the Cambridge edition of *A Demonstration of the Being and Attributes of God and Other Writings*, ed. Ezio Vailati, Cambridge, 1998 [originally 1705]) as the "scholastic way" of proving God's existence. Authors like Cudworth (*True Intellectual System of the Universe*, First American Edition, Andover, 1839 [originally 1678], v. 2, p. 141) refer to the "many disputes" over the argument, which is suggestive of a deeper history.

14. To take just one example, in *Anselm's Discovery* Hartshorne is especially vigilant in his attacks on the entire tradition regarding their interpretation of Anselm.

15. On the relationship between these arguments, see Malcolm's "Anselm's Ontological Arguments," in *The Philosophical Review* 69 (1), 1960, pp. 41–62 (reprinted in Hick and McGill, pp. 310–20).

16. *A New, Interpretive Translation of St. Anselm's Monologion and Proslogion* (ed. Jasper Hopkins. The Arthur J. Banning Press, Minneapolis 1986, pp. 224–28).

17. *Summa theologiae*, vol. 2. McGraw Hill, 1963, p. 5. In most cases, I cite the translation from this text with only minor alterations.

18. If Thomas is indeed thinking of an argument from Bonaventure rather than from Anselm, this fact may explain any minor departures from the wording of the *Proslogion*.

19. AT VII 98; CSM II 71: "But now please tell me if this is not the selfsame argument as that produced by M. Descartes . . ."

20. AT VII 115; CSM II 82: "... on this issue I do not differ from the Angelic doctor in any respect. St. Thomas asks whether the existence of God is self-evident as far as we are concerned (*per se notum secundum nos*), that is, whether it is obvious to everyone. And he answers, correctly, that it is not."

21. Ibid. (my italics)

22. Although his initial formulation does not specify existence modally, in the following pages (AT VII 118; CSM II 84) Descartes clarifies that "it is only necessary existence that is at issue here."

23. Although it is probable that Leibniz was familiar also with Scotus's discussions of the argument, he was at the very least familiar with the following passage from the *Second Replies* (AT VII 127; CSM II 91): "This comes down to an argument which others have stated as follows: 'If there is no contradiction in God's existing, it is certain that he exists; but there is no contradiction in his existing.'" Although Scotus is not mentioned by name, the referent of "others" is likely, if not Scotus, some follower of his. Cf. Scotus's *Ordinatio* I, part I, question 2. A summary of Scotus's views appears in Bernardino Bonansea's "Duns Scotus and St. Anselm's Ontological Argument" (in *Studies in Philosophy and the History of Philosophy*, ed. John K. Ryan, Catholic University Press, 1969, pp. 128–41).

24. We confront here the obvious temptation of distinguishing between thinking of God without considering whether he exists and thinking of God *as non-existent*. This distinction is, however, not of overwhelming significance in the case of the ontological argument. A number of proponents of that argument, including Descartes, require the former also to be impossible (upon sufficient reflection and training). Whoever can think of "God" without thinking that he exists, Descartes holds, has not liberated himself/herself from preconceived notions. In any case, it would be an evasion of the central problem to try to seek solace in some distinction "in our thought" between the essence and existence of God. No one denies that it is, at some elementary level of metaphysical education, possible to so distinguish. The question concerns only whether the distinction is a mistake. The early modern defenders of the ontological argument solve this problem by limiting the relevance of the ontological argument to those who have overcome such epistemic tendencies. In Descartes' case, it belongs to the minor premise that "we" perceive existence along with God, so that this premise is factually false for anyone who insists in thinking of an *ens perfectissimum* without also thinking that there exists such a thing. The premise adds only the *ad hominem* stipulation that upon "sufficient(ly) careful investigation" it is impossible even to think of God without thinking that he exists.

25. *Kritik der reine Vernunft* (hereafter "KrV") B 625 and 629–30 (in *Kant's gesammelte Schriften*, ed. Prussian Academy of the Sciences, Walter de Gruyter 1926, hereafter "AA," volumes 3–4). English translations from this work are, with some revision and exception, *Critique of Pure Reason*, trans. Paul Guyer and Allen Wood, Cambridge, 1997.

26. On the exceptional nature of the proposition of the existence of God in regard to both Descartes and his predecessors, see Jorge Secada's *Cartesian Metaphysics* (Cambride, 2000).

27. Dieter Henrich's excellent book (*Der ontologische Gottesbeweis*, Tuebingen, 1960) is the preeminent example of this. His research has provided much of the inspiration for the present volume, which is largely an argument with his work. In the interest both of concision and, more importantly, of preventing such argument from providing a distraction from the primary sources, I have restricted my many disputes with him to the notes.

28. The cause of this problem is seen easily enough: the ontological argument claims (in any case) that it belongs to the essence of God to exist, and in most cases what drives the inference is the observation that God cannot be thought except as existing. Establishing a proof of the existence of any given entity, however, requires that what the entity is (i.e., its essence) becomes the subject of some preliminary discussion. This, however, suggests that we consider the essence before concluding existence, which is exactly what the conclusion rejects as impossible.

29. See, for instance, AT VI 36; CSM I 129 and AT VII 65; CSM II 45–46.

30. Wolff (*Ontologia*, ed. Jean Ecole, Georg Olms 1978 [originally Leipzig 1736] #1) defines "ontology" or "first philosophy" as "the science of beings in general insofar as they are beings." Baumgarten (*Metaphysica*, Halle, 1779 [originally 1739] #4) defines it as "the science of the general predicates of things."

31. It is worth citing by way of introduction two key texts on this issue. Descartes discusses this in reply to Mersenne (*Second Replies*) at AT VII 137; CSM II 98. Spinoza states his position on the matter in, among many passages, the Scholium to Proposition 17 of the *Ethics* (*The Collected Works of Spinoza*, ed. Curley, Edwin. Princeton University Press, 1985, hereafter "Curley," p. 426; *Spinoza Opera*, ed. Gebhart, Heidelberg, 1925, hereafter "*Opera*," II 62). On the history of this problem in Jewish thought, see David Kaufmann's *Geschichte der Attributenlehre* (Amsterdam, Philosophical Press, 1967).

32. Hence Spinoza insists in the *Cogitata Metaphysica* that the existence of God "differs entirely from the existence of created things (*Ghodts wezendlijkeit van de wezendlijkeit der geschape dingen geheelijk verschilt)*" (Curley 315, *Opera* I 249).

33. Dieter Henrich (*Der ontologische Gottesbeweis*, Tubingen, 1960) and Paresh Chandra Debnath ("The Ontological Argument and Leibniz's Formulation," in *Indian Philosophical Quarterly* 12, no. 4, October–December, 1985) both offer similar divisions of the objections. I borrow the expression "empirical" objection from Henrich.

34. The claims in question hold only of the seventeenth-century proponents of the argument and serve to distinguish these philosophers from their eighteenth-century successors. Leibniz, for instance, treats the definition of God according to general rules for definitions; Baumgarten goes as far as to actually assert that the necessity of God's existence is analogous to the hypothetical necessity of geometric claims. For the relevant references, consult the notes to chapters five and six.

35. KrV B 626.

36. See AT VII 66; CSM II 45–46: "At first sight, this is not very clear, but has the appearance of being a sophism. Since I have been accustomed to distinguishing between existence and essence in everything else, I find it easy to persuade myself that existence can also be separated from the essence of God, and hence that God can be thought of as not existing."

37. AT VII 118; CSM II 84.

38. The following passage from the *Science of Logic* is one of many such comments by Hegel: "Although it is nonetheless correct that being is distinct from the concept, God is even more distinct from the hundred dollars and other finite things. It is the *definition of finite things*, that concept and being are distinct in them ... the abstract definition of God is, on the contrary, precisely that his concept and his being are not separate and are inseparable." All Hegel citations are from the Suhrkamp edition of his works (20 vols., ed., Moldenhauer and Michel, 1970, hereafter "Suhrkamp") and are my own translation. I will provide page numbers to English translations where possible. This passage is from *Wissenschaft der Logik*, Suhrkamp 5, p. 92 (*Science of Logic*, trans. A. V. Miller, Humanities Press, 1959, hereafter "SL," see pp. 84–90)

39. I take the name for this objection specifically from the following passage in Huet's *Against Cartesian Philosophy* (JHP Books, 2003, p. 163, hereafter "Censura" [originally *Censura philosophiae cartesianae*, Paris, 1689]): "It is clear that the idea and likeness of God is conceived and extracted Kata Metabasin, that is, by transition, as Cicero calls it, from the confused thought of ourselves and of other things."

40. This does not place the Cartesian ontological argument (as a proof of God's existence) in a relation of dependence to the *a posteriori* argument. The former does not borrow the conclusion "God exists" from any prior argument, but only the proof of the innateness of the idea of God. Further, the *Third Meditation* argument supplies only one of several Cartesian proofs that conclude that the idea of God is not a fictitious construction. For others, see the *Fifth Meditation* (AT VII 68; CSM II 47).

41. Recognizing this, while at the same time wedded to the popular view concerning the status of Kant's *Critique of Pure Reason*, Dieter Henrich was forced to try to explain how the ontological argument did in fact develop consistently in the period under consideration. His conclusion is appropriate to his aim: Baumgarten was the greatest philosopher before Kant. Anyone who is unwilling to accept this (rather bizarre) consequence is forced to reconsider the relationship between Kant and his predecessors.

42. Malebranche offers the most emphatic statement of this view when he admits in his *Search after the Truth* that "it is rather useless to propose these arguments to common men" (*Oeuvres Completes de Malebranche*, ed. Henri Gouhier "Oeuvres," J Vrin, Paris, 1958, p. 103; English translations from this work are from *Search after the Truth*, trans. Thomas Lennon and Paul Olscamp, Ohio State University Press, 1980).

Chapter One
PROOF AND PERCEPTION
The Context of the
Argumentum Cartesianum

Although the a priori proof for the existence of God that Descartes provides in his *Discourse on the Method* is soon recognized as a "revival" of the controversial scholastic argument, the novel approach to philosophy undertaken in that work does not fail to bear on the form of the argument in question.[1] The concerns of the *Discourse* are methodological and epistemological, and our author ventures into theological reflection in part four only in explanation of certain facts about his own mind.[2] When he reaches the argument that so closely resembles Anselm's proof, the topic under discussion is the status of geometrical knowledge.[3] Almost as if by accident, we discover that the relation of "existence" to God's nature is analogous to the relation between a triangle and its properties. This initial formulation of the modern ontological argument is entirely dependent upon the analogy in question: we can be certain of the existence of God precisely because we perceive the similarity between "God exists" and a familiar claim about a triangle.

A few years later Descartes writes his *Meditations*, the stated goals of which are more metaphysical than epistemological.[4] Even in this work, however, the proofs of God's existence arise at least partly in response to questions concerning the veracity of ideas in general.[5] Although Descartes admits that his proofs of the deity from the *Discourse* had been incomplete, the analogical basis of the a priori proof remains unchanged.[6] The same triangle analogy appears also in the *Fifth Meditation*, and the theological argument he proposes therein derives from a discussion of the mind-independence of geometrical entities.[7] Due in no small part to the popularity of this text, Descartes' analogy indeed remains in discussion for over a century, and it serves to place atheism in the most unwelcome of quandaries: if the assertion of the existence of God is as certain as basic mathematical truths, then the only conceivable atheism is extreme skepticism. The analogy is one way of trying to make the theistic proof look very convincing, since it situates the conclusion in a vital place within the account of the human mind.

The triangle analogy nonetheless sees its role reduced in later Cartesian formulations of the argument. In the *Principles*, for instance, it becomes clearer that the analogy does not contribute to the actual inference from the idea of a perfect being to the necessary existence of that being.[8] To be sure, the inference in question is conducted "in the same way" as the inference from the triangle to the sum of its angles, and Descartes never softens his statement of this point. The analogy, however, factors now only in the explanation of the proof, and no longer seems central to the inference. Even in the much earlier *Second Set of Replies*, the triangle had been only one of several analogs to the relation between the *ens perfectissimum* and necessary existence. In that text Descartes succeeds in identifying the common characteristic that would justify the analogy: both the geometrical and theological claims represent instances of clear and distinct ideas of some characteristic "belonging to the nature" something.[9] There is nothing in particular, it would seem, about the relationship between "God" and "existence" that suggests a similarity to the relationship between "a triangle" and "three angles equal to two right angles," other than the very extrinsic fact that in each case Descartes clearly and distinctly perceives the respective characteristic to belong to the thing in question.

This of course begs the question of how Descartes wishes to justify the attribution of necessary existence to God. As Gassendi remarks in the *Fifth Set of Objections*, geometers possess a precise and unobjectionable demonstration of the proposition about the triangle, whereas Descartes provides no strictly analogous argument for "a perfect being necessarily exists."[10] Descartes seems even to concede the weakness of his analogy when he, in two instances, conducts his a priori proof without reference to it.[11] The analogy is, at the very least, dispensable, and all that remains in its absence is the assertion of a clear and distinct perception that necessary existence belongs to the nature of a perfect being. Some additional passages from the *Replies* bring further uncertainty upon this issue, and in these texts Descartes assumes theological positions that impose impassable limits on the analogy. The properties of a triangle, one would presume, are not *the same* as the triangle, and are not distinguishable from one another "merely by a defect of our understanding."[12] Yet Descartes accepts the traditional doctrines of the sameness of God and his existence, as well as of the inseparability of his attributes.[13]

These apparent inconsistencies have engendered some disagreement both among Descartes' contemporaries and among his many later commentators. In particular, the ambiguous role of the analogy has brought into question whether the ontological "argument" involves a reference to intuition or whether it is a demonstration in some more proper sense of this term.[14] The formulations of the ontological argument that we find in the *First Set of Replies* and "Geometrical Demonstration" attribute "necessary existence" to the "supremely perfect being" solely on the basis of our purportedly clear perception. In other words, in these texts Descartes appeals neither to an analogy nor to the axiom that "existence is a perfection," and the argument that remains is, for that very reason, more consonant with certain of his theological commitments. Descartes, however, never completely renounces either the analogy or the claim that existence is a perfection, and the importance of these to his popular expositions of the ontological argument, as well as to the pedagogical value of that argument, is indisputable.

However this problem may admit of resolution with reference to Cartesian texts alone. The mere appearance of ambiguity on this point remains important for the history of the ontological argument: seventeenth-century followers of Descartes develop his argument in multiple directions, and in several cases they claim affiliation with Descartes. Even if the triangle analogy and the claim that "existence is a perfection" are ultimately indispensable to Descartes' ontological argument, some of his followers indeed dispose of these points, all the while taking their lead from Descartes and purporting to be preserving the crux of his argument. At the same time, on the other hand, there are contemporaries of Descartes who seek to highlight both the argument from perfection and the triangle analogy. In the following we will thus pay particular attention to these points of contention, in order to trace the various trajectories that the argument takes throughout the subsequent two centuries. My own belief is that Descartes wavers between these two interpretations of his argument. Even if the case were to be decisively argued in favor of just one interpretation, however, this would not change the historical importance of his apparent ambiguity on this issue.

THE *FIRST REPLIES* SYLLOGISM
AND THE PERFECTION ARGUMENT

Any confusion over the form and context of the Cartesian ontological argument is compounded by the frequently overlooked fact that Descartes formulates two arguments in the *Fifth Meditation* that address the existence of God.
The first argument begins with a discussion of the Cartesian "rule for truth"[15];
the second argument concerns the concept of perfection.[16] Of these it is the
former to which Descartes and his interlocutors devote the majority of their
attention in the *Objections and Replies* to the *Meditations*. That argument
appears in a more concise form in three important discussions from the
Replies. Descartes condenses the argument initially in *The First Set of Replies*[17];
in *The Second Set of Replies* he articulates a very similar proof[18]; finally, in the
"Geometrical Demonstration" he offers the same argument once more.[19] The
first of these formulations includes one clause omitted by the other two,
namely, the subordinate clause of the minor premise. As the most thorough
formulation, then, this passage from the *First Set of Replies* (hereafter the "*First
Replies* syllogism") enjoys some authority as an interpretation of the argument
from the *Fifth Meditation*. The proof runs:

> Premise 1: That which we clearly understand to belong to the true
> and immutable nature, or essence, or form of something, can be
> truly asserted of that thing.

> Premise 2: But once we have made a sufficiently careful investigation
> of what God is, we clearly and distinctly understand that (nec-
> essary) existence belongs to his true and immutable nature.[20]

> Conclusion: Hence we can now truly assert of God that he does
> exist.

Although Descartes makes it explicit in the above-mentioned passages that
an argument like this is the principal argument from the *Fifth Meditation*, it is
the second argument from that text upon which subsequent philosophers
confer the title "Cartesian argument," this label eventually giving way to the
more infamous appellation "ontological argument." That argument appears a
few pages after the initial discussion of the existence of God. While considering

a possible objection to the minor premise of the above-cited syllogism, Descartes puts forth the following line of reasoning: God is a being that possesses all perfections; existence is a perfection; therefore, God possesses existence.[21]

Readers of the *Meditations* overestimate the importance of this argument (hereafter the "perfection argument") as early as 1641, although the public nature of his defense of that work enables Descartes to discourage, at least temporarily, the several misunderstandings that ensue. Caterus attacks the perfection argument in the *First Set of Objections* by comparing it to Anselm's argument and citing Thomas's objections to the latter.[22] In his reply, Descartes refuses to acknowledge the alleged resemblance; he instead shifts the discussion to the above-cited argument, prefacing the syllogism with the claim "my argument however was ..."[23] This provides a clear sign that he does not consider the perfection argument to be the chief theological argument in the *Fifth Meditation*. In subsequent discussions of that text, Descartes again defends only the first argument, which fact provides further evidence that the argument from perfection is, if not a subsidiary to the first, at best of secondary importance.[24]

Having read the *First Objections and Replies*, the subsequent objectors, as well as other seventeenth-century philosophers like Clauberg, Spinoza, Malebranche, and Henry More, avoid repeating Caterus's error.[25] The entire dispute over the a priori argument that takes place from 1641 until around 1676 concerns chiefly the *First Replies* syllogism. In the few cases in which the perfection argument actually appears it serves only as an alternative demonstration of the minor premise of that syllogism.[26] It is not until near the end of the seventeenth century that the perfection argument regains prominence, and this occurs mainly as a result of Leibniz's attempt to salvage it. Leibniz's revised perfection argument influences most eighteenth-century proponents of the a priori proof and thus indirectly Kant, Hegel, and most others after them.[27] One result of this long history is that the confusion of the perfection argument for the main a priori proof subsequently becomes a commonplace of philosophical consciousness. In recognition of the fact that this confusion occurs only in the eighteenth century and after, the syllogism from the *First Set of Replies* will receive greater consideration throughout the following.

The priority of the *First Replies* syllogism has consequences for the old debate over the relative importance of the context of Cartesian philosophy for the ontological argument.[28] Unlike the perfection argument, the *First Replies* argument contains explicit reference to a number of Descartes' other doctrines. Although this fact becomes clearest only in the extended discussions of the minor premise, a first glance at the major premise offers an immediate suggestion of the deeper context of the argument. The premise reads: "that which we clearly understand to belong to the true and immutable nature, or essence, or form of something, can be truly asserted of that thing." Descartes justifies this "predication rule" by appeal to the more general rule that "what is distinctly and clearly perceived is thereby true."[29] In this form, at least, the ontological argument assumes epistemological rationalism as a premise.[30]

While the major premise of the argument incorporates one controversial doctrine, a full elaboration of the minor premise proves the argument to presume an even broader philosophical context. Descartes attempts to justify the minor premise at length in the *Fifth Meditation* as well as in the *First* and *Fifth Sets of Replies*, and in doing so he designates a series of other philosophical doctrines as auxiliary conditions of the argument. The ontological argument ultimately becomes the conclusion of an entire philosophical system. The objectors to the argument are aware of this, and the earliest disputes over the Cartesian proof are essentially disputes over the philosophical context of the central insight expressed in the minor premise.

References to the doctrines in question appear in response to the many objections that Descartes' contemporaries raise against the proof. For the most part, these objections are the same ones that reappear in the eighteenth and nineteenth centuries. The result of this is twofold. First, the Cartesian argument anticipates most, if not all, of the relevant objections to it. Second, the argument addresses the objections only to the extent that it is thoroughly embedded in Cartesian philosophy. A remark addressed to Gassendi from the *Fifth Set of Replies* provides a pertinent warning regarding this last point:

> This obliges me to point out that you have not paid sufficient attention to the way in which what I wrote all fits together. I think this interconnection is such that, for any given point, all the preceding remarks and most of those that follow contribute to the proof of what is asserted. Hence you cannot give a fair account of what I have to say on any topic unless you go into everything I wrote about all the other related issues.[31]

In the following we will by no means "go into everything" Descartes "wrote about all the other related issues." It will suffice merely to underline which issues are the relevant ones and how they serve as conditions for his ontological argument. The principal objections to the argument are voiced by his contemporaries Caterus, Gassendi, Hobbes, Arnauld, and Mersenne; Descartes' own views on the objections, and thus his complete defense of his ontological argument, appear in his *Replies* to these interlocutors.

THE ROLE OF THE MAJOR PREMISE: DESCARTES' REPLY TO CATERUS

Given the relatively loose structure of the *Meditations*, it is unsurprising that Descartes' immediate audience mistakes the perfection argument for the entire a priori proof of the deity. It is no more surprising that an apparently very learned theologian such as Caterus notices the resemblance between the perfection argument and the scholastic arguments of Anselm, Thomas, and Scotus.[32] It is fortuitous, though, for the early history of the Cartesian argument that this otherwise unknown Catholic priest gives Descartes occasion to correct the relevant misunderstandings in the very first round of discussion of the work. In his reply to Caterus, Descartes highlights the importance of the predication rule qua major premise, and he thereby offers advice on how we should understand the presentations of his argument as they appear elsewhere in his corpus. If the perfection argument were to be abstracted from the *First Replies* syllogism, Descartes admits, Caterus would be entirely justified in raising Thomas's two objections to the former argument.[33]

Although this fact is less than obvious, the *First Replies* syllogism accurately reflects the structure of the remaining Cartesian formulations of the proof. While the *Fifth Meditation* fails to make unmistakably explicit the inclusion of Cartesian epistemology as a premise in the ontological argument, the structure of the opening passages of that text does correspond to the syllogistic argument.[34] The emphasis during the subsequent discussion is rather on the necessity of the *thought* of God's existence (viz., the minor premise), and the major premise of the complete argument serves merely as an antecedent condition. Divorced from the predication rule, however, the notorious subarguments for the minor premise establish only facts about the human mind; from these arguments Descartes concludes nothing more than that "*I* am not free to *think* of God without existence …"[35] The entire discussion of the minor premise aims only at necessity in thought, it being already (and separately) established that certain characteristics of thought are sufficient to guarantee actual existence. The fact that the predication of necessary existence (viz., the minor premise) receives greater attention in the *Fifth Meditation*, however, makes it easy to overlook the contingency of the proof as a whole upon the preceding epistemological reflections (i.e., upon the major premise).

The analogy with geometry serves as further evidence that the arguments for necessary existence demand only hypothetical necessity, and it thereby strengthens the case for the importance of the predication rule: if the minor premise has the same level of certainty as the truths of mathematics, then it, like those truths, is contingent upon the results of *Meditations Two, Three*, and *Four*. In other words, if mathematical truths are dubitable, and only the Cartesian rule for truth secures their objectivity, then the minor premise should likewise stand in a relation of dependence to that rule. The analogy to the triangle thus serves as a kind of nod to Thomistic reasoning: arguments like the perfection argument suggest only that God exists "in the apprehension of the intellect," as Thomas allows in his *Summa*.[36] That necessary existence belongs to God's nature is indeed, for Descartes, as certain as mathematical theorems, but *all* such truths require the rule to which the major premise alludes.[37] If the premise in question were overlooked we would indeed have to join Caterus in proclaiming the success of the Thomistic objections.

Although the placement of the argument in *Principles* I.14 lends the argument an appearance of independence from the major premise, that passage considered alone likewise does not establish actual existence: ". . . simply on the basis of its perception that necessary and eternal existence is contained in the idea of a supremely perfect being, *the mind must* clearly conclude that the supreme being does exist" (my emphasis).[38] Descartes is again concerned only with the subjective certainty of the idea (i.e., with the necessity of our perceiving "necessary existence" within the essence of God, or of our thinking that God exists). Only much later in that work do we receive assurance of the reality of perception, and it is only then that we become certain of the actual existence of God (i.e., that what we perceive in the idea really belongs to the corresponding entity).[39]

As these passages show, the tendency of Descartes' exposition is not merely to leave the argument vulnerable to the Thomistic objections, but rather to circumvent the problem altogether by proceeding entirely according to the necessity of the mind. It is only the *Reply* to Caterus and the "Geometrical Demonstration" that explicitly supply the missing premise and thereby assert existence *outside the intellect*. In the two more popular texts (the *Meditations* and the *Principles*), the ultimate truth of the conclusion is contingent upon other discussions. The veracity of our perceptions, including our perception of God's existence, requires the independent confirmation that the major premise supplies.

THE MINOR PREMISE: DESCARTES VERSUS THE MATERIALISTS

The elaboration of the premise in the First Replies

While the major premise is important both in situating the argument within Cartesian philosophy and defending it against the Thomistic objections, the minor premise of the *First Replies* syllogism becomes the subject of a more extended and historically important discussion. Although the complete defense of the premise appears only in his subsequent disputes with the leading materialists of his day, Pierre Gassendi and Thomas Hobbes, Descartes offers a kind of preface to those discussions in his reply to Caterus. At issue is the key claim in Descartes', or any, ontological argument, namely, the inclusion of "necessary existence" in the notion of a "supremely perfect being." Descartes' justification for this inclusion has been subject to great controversy from 1641 to the present, and this uncertainty receives little help from the lengthy version of the premise offered in the *First Replies*: "once we have made sufficiently careful investigation of what God is, we clearly and distinctly understand that existence belongs to his true and immutable nature."[40] The ensuing discussion of the premise, however, provides some conditions that enable interpretation of his position.

In the lines immediately following his formulation of the syllogism Descartes admits two apparent difficulties with the minor premise, the first of which addresses the relative inaccessibility of the insight expressed in the main clause of that premise: "we are so accustomed to distinguishing existence from essence in the case of all other things that we fail to notice how closely existence belongs to essence in the case of God...."[41] The problem is that the attribution of God's existence is unique, so that some danger remains of our failure to recognize how this existence relates to God's nature. Descartes attempts to avoid this danger first by a discussion of the modal distinction of the existence of God with respect to "everything else," then by adding a kind of methodological caveat for the argument as a whole.

That the existence of God differs modally from the existence of every-thing else is enough, in Descartes' mind, to discourage any possible confusion of God with other things. Some such distinction between necessary and pos-sible existence thus accompanies nearly all subsequent formulations of the argument.[42] His interpretation of this distinction, however, varies both among his several formulations of the proof and from contemporary understanding of the distinction. Regarding the latter point, Descartes does not understand "necessity of existence" to mean only "existence in all possible worlds," but rather the conjunction of "actual existence" with the other properties of the thing in question.[43] That God exists "necessarily" means, for Descartes and for other early modern philosophers, that his existence belongs to his essence in the same way that his other attributes belong to it.

Regarding the first point, viz., the discrepancy among Cartesian formula-tions of the possibility/necessity distinction, Descartes seems to waver on the meaning of "possibility" and whether this can rightfully be ascribed to God. In the *First Replies* he allows that God is possible, although later he seems to retreat from this position, a matter that is of considerable importance for the history of his argument.[44] In the "Geometrical Demonstration" he excludes mere possible existence from God's nature, writing that "possible or contin-gent existence is contained in the concept of a limited thing, whereas neces-sary and perfect existence is contained in the concept of a supremely perfect being."[45] In this case "possibility" has a sense closer to that of "contingency," and this is the sense that predominates throughout the following decades of discussion of the existence of God.[46]

Regardless of the precise meaning of the modal distinction, Descartes' intention is clear enough: he is worried that the unique nature of the assertion "God exists" will limit the pedagogical effectiveness of his argument. This sig-nals his first recognition of what comes to occupy later proponents of the ontological argument; namely, that the argument hinges on the emphasis of the disanalogy between its claim and any claim about "creatures," a fact that calls for revision of a number of metaphysical and theological dogmas. Descartes' immediate concern in this passage, however, lies only with a pos-sible psychological confusion: it lies with our remembering what this modal distinction asserts. God, namely, is essentially different from limited or finite entities, and this difference concerns also the modality of his existence. Since this qualification is important to the second premise of the ontological argu-ment, it is also important to that argument that we do not fail to remember this distinction. A precondition of our analyzing the argument is that we "attend to this difference between the idea God and every other idea" and do not ascribe to the idea of God properties that are relevant only to other ideas.

This caveat becomes commonplace among rationalists of the seventeenth century, and the constant attention it calls to the difference between God and everything else leads them ultimately to adopt a controversial position on the scholastic problem of divine predication; namely, the doctrine of equivocal attribution. Although in the *First Set of Replies* Descartes does not yet arrive at this doctrine, a number of later passages suggest that he considers some version of it. This is one point, however, on which Descartes does not appear to have achieved the same level of clarity that we find later in, for instance, Spinoza or Malebranche.[47]

The subordinate clause of the *First Replies* formulation of the minor premise appends yet a third auxiliary condition to the claim that existence is a predicate of God. The proviso "once we have made sufficiently careful investigation of what God is" suggests that there is an *ad hominem* precondition for the argument. Descartes thereby acknowledges his proof to be contingent upon our knowledge of the metaphysical conception of God, with the result that the argument is not intended to be evident to everyone.[48] It is not simply the case that the uninitiated will fail to understand an objectively valid premise; rather, the premise asserts that upon sufficient training "we" have a very specific perception. In other words, that we perceive the necessary existence of God is written into the premise, so that the conclusion of the argument is irrelevant to anyone who does not have the perception in question. This fact undoubtedly speaks against the utility of the argument as a pedagogical device, a situation that Descartes claims inspired in him some hesitance concerning its appearance in the *Meditations*.[49]

These three conditions of the minor premise (metaphysical sophistication of the arguer, modal distinction of existence, and attention to the difference between God and creatures, i.e., to the doctrine of equivocal attribution) stand in the background of Descartes' entire dispute with the materialists, and any assessment of Gassendi's objections should take account of them. Reference to these theological, logical, and psychological doctrines suggests that the dispute over the premises of the proof becomes increasingly a matter of larger philosophical context, so that ignorance of this context would lead to fatal misunderstandings. Although Gassendi is by no means ignorant of the context of Descartes' argument, his attack on it consists mainly in a consideration of the premises in light of a very different set of philosophical assumptions.

Gassendi's Triangle and the Empirical Objection

An important passage from the *Fifth Set of Objections* reveals that it is no small injustice of philosophical historiography that has attributed the objection "being is not a predicate" (hereafter the "empirical objection") primarily to Kant. Several paragraphs of the latter's chapter "On the impossibility of an ontological argument"[50] are nearly verbatim repetitions, however unknowingly, of the *Fifth Set of Objections.* The author of these objections, Pierre Gassendi (1592–1655), ranks not only as an important critic of the ontological argument, but also as perhaps the chief competitor to Cartesianism in mid-century France. His philosophical contributions range widely, from an early, skeptical attack on scholastic philosophy to his later defense of atomism.[51] As a critic of the a priori argument his significance consists both in the insightful manner in which he introduces the empirical objection into the discussion and in his admirable attempt to clarify the notion of "existence."

Just as Kant would later do, Gassendi begins his assault on the minor premise by challenging the analogy between the existence of God and the angles of a triangle:

> It is quite all right for you to compare essence with essence, but instead of going on to compare existence with existence or a property with a property, you compare existence with a property. It seems that you should have said that omnipotence can no more be separated from the essence of God than the fact that its angles equal two right angles can be separated from the essence of a triangle. Or, at any rate, you should have said that the existence of God can no more be separated from his essence than the existence of a triangle can be separated from its essence.[52]

Gassendi indicates here, quite rightly, that the compared properties are incongruent. "Existence" is not normally a property like "having three angles equal to two right angles," so that the analogy fails to render the argument persuasive. For his part, Gassendi makes no bald assertion, but rather refers the analogy to a specific, albeit circular, definition of "existence." "Existence," he writes, is "that without which no perfections can be present" or "that in virtue of which both the thing itself and its perfections are existent."[53] Existence is thus *not* a perfection (or "predicate") in the same sense as the property of the triangle.

In a final reflection on the analogy, Gassendi concludes against the inclusion of existence in the definition of God:

> Thus, just as when you listed the perfections of the triangle you did not include existence or conclude that the triangle existed, so when you listed the perfections of God you should not have included existence among them so as to reach the conclusion that God exists.[54]

"Existence," according to Gassendi, is not included in the definition of a triangle, but is rather a precondition for the existence or real inherence of the other properties. The same observation, he assumes, should hold in the case of God. The problem indicated here, however, does not represent a mere oversight on the part of the proponent of the proof. The text of the *Fifth Meditation* anticipates this discussion by insisting on the difference between God and all other entities. The ontological argument, Descartes admits, has "the appearance of being a sophism" because we are "accustomed to distinguish between existence and essence in everything else."[55] It is not the intention of the argument to deny the difference between "essence" and "existence" in the case of any other entity (such as a triangle). An inference from the latter to the former is by all accounts impossible in any instance *except* that of God. A general analysis of existence as distinct from essence, then, clearly begs the question at the heart of the argument.[56]

Gassendi, like Kant after him, recognizes the intention of the Cartesian argument to involve this difference between God and other entities concerning the relation of essence to existence. In other words, he is aware that Descartes is not ignorant of the empirical rule, but instead wishes only to cite an exception to that rule. Gassendi in turn denies the exception in question on nominalist grounds:

> You say that existence is distinct from essence in the case of all other things, but not in the case of God. But how, may I ask, are we to distinguish the essence of Plato from his existence, except merely in our thought? Suppose that Plato no longer exists: where now is his essence? Surely in the case of God the distinction between essence and existence is just of this kind: the distinction occurs in our thought.[57]

This passage represents a continuation of Gassendi's nominalist critique of Descartes' innatism.[58] Presumably he understands Descartes' innatism to imply a real distinction of essence and existence in finite things. The Cartesian argument indeed seems to presuppose such a position, since this would allow God to differ from creatures in this regard. Such a position would draw attention specifically to the real unity of God's essence and existence. In truth, Descartes takes a more subtle approach to this problem, although he does not address the issue until several years after the debate with Gassendi.[59] In the *Fifth Set of Replies* he merely insists on what has been denied; namely, the difference between God and finite things as concerns the distinction between essence and existence: "the relation between essence and existence is manifestly quite different in God from what it is in the case of the triangle."[60]

Although this difference hardly suffices to justify the analogy with the triangle, it at least qualifies the critique of that analogy: "Hence the existence of a triangle should not be compared with the existence of God."[61] It is Gassendi, as well, not only Descartes, who suggests the comparison of unlike things: the existence of God is something entirely different from the existence of a triangle.[62] In the *First Set of Replies*, among other places, Descartes specifies this difference modally, and Gassendi's objection consists in an apparent denial of that distinction. A position like Gassendi's requires that "existence" be considered in the same way with regard to both God and creatures. While Gassendi is not ignorant of the fact that Descartes intends for the modal distinction to imply a difference here, he offers no real objection to the Cartesian version of that distinction. In any case, Gassendi needs to explain how the meaning of "existence" in the conclusion of the ontological argument is analogous to the meaning of this term when applied to finite entities. His position at this point consists in nothing more that the bald assertion that there is such an analogy.

The related assertion of subsequent empiricists that "existence" cannot belong to the nature of an entity, a claim later associated with both Hume and Kant, by no means constitutes an *independent* refutation of Descartes' or any other ontological argument. The empirical objection presupposes definite positions on both modal logic and divine predication, and the objection is effective only if these positions prevail. Specifically, the objection assumes a single, unequivocal notion of existence and a certain relation of this to "essence." Taken in isolation, Gassendi's objection is patently question-begging. Its undue celebrity rests largely on an ignorance of what the ontological proof actually asserts, viz., that there is one and only one instance of warranted inference from an essence to (a unique species of) existence.[63] The myth that the empirical objection, as voiced by Kant, alone reveals the error in the ontological argument nevertheless persisted throughout much of history. The prevalence of that myth was probably partly responsible for the revival of the ontological argument in the middle of the twentieth century.[64]

Hobbes on "Essence" and "Existence"

Gassendi's attack on the inclusion of existence in the definition of God stems from two considerations. First, in the *Fifth Objections*, he outlines a concept of "existence" that foreshadows what Kant later contributes to this discussion: existence is "position," or the precondition for predicating anything of a subject, rather than something that is itself predicable of that same subject. Later, in his *Counter-Objections*, Gassendi offers a critique of the Cartesian minor premise based on logical considerations: the attribution of existence as a property of things amounts to a kind of category mistake and leads to absurdities. If existence were a property, then no other properties would exist, since no property is attributable to other properties.[65]

Although irreconcilable assumptions underlie this encounter between Gassendi and Descartes, and neither discussant ever comes close to conceding any important points, there is nonetheless sufficient understanding between them to allow for a relatively fruitful discussion. Even the joke that they mutually indulge by addressing one another respectively as "flesh" and "mind," besides providing entertainment, occasions some illumination.[66] The same cannot easily be said of Descartes' exchange with an even more radical materialist, Thomas Hobbes (1588–1679). The latter raises objections that stem from premises so dramatically opposed to Descartes' own assumptions that they rarely manage to solicit a serious response.

As a philosopher Hobbes needs little introduction, since his later political writings bring him fame equal to that of any of his contemporaries. Although he has not yet written his most important works, he seems cognizant of the basic plan for his theoretical philosophy at the time he composes the *Third Set of Objections*: he is a materialist ambitious enough to begin applying his principles in the realm of both ethical and political philosophy. As a critic of Descartes he is, again, too little sympathetic to shed any real light on the shortcomings of that philosopher's arguments, and the exchange between these philosophers is a lesson in stubborn misunderstanding.

A number of Hobbes's epistemological objections to the *Second* and

Third Meditations do merit discussion, and we will consider these below. In reference to the *Fifth Meditation*, however, Hobbes's comments are briefer and less significant, and Descartes' patience with the "celebrated English philosopher" has, by this point in the debate, almost completely diminished. The importance of this discussion lies only in that it brings both the nominalism and materialism implied by Gassendi's criticisms to their most extreme consequences. In so doing, Hobbes makes explicit a concept of "existence" that reappears among a number of objectors to the ontological argument in the modern period. A similar view appears in Germany a century later, and does not fail to have an influence on Kant.[67]

Hobbes wastes no time in drawing the ultimate consequence of nominalism for theology. The very first line of his objection reads: "If a triangle does not exist anywhere, I do not understand how it has a nature."[68] Here, Hobbes is merely repeating a point that he elaborates more fully in his objections to the *Second Meditation*.[69] What is more important for the current discussion is the rationale for this nominalism as stated in the next clause: "for what is nowhere is not anything (*quod enim nullibi est, non est*)." For Hobbes, then, to be is to be somewhere. For the remainder of his career, Hobbes consistently rejects immaterial existence on a definitional basis. In his work on Thomas White, for instance, he equates *ens* with *corpus*, excluding as a matter of principle the possibility of any entity that is not physical.[70] In the *Leviathan* he claims that the expression "incorporeal substance" is a contradiction in terms.[71] The popularity of this doctrine in the following century has a fatal consequence for the ontological argument: if "to exist" means primarily or exclusively "to exist somewhere," then it will be easier to object to the premise that existence belongs to God's nature. The definitional presentation of this doctrine, however, as it appears in the *Third Set of Objections*, is even more overtly question-begging than Gassendi's empirical objection.[72]

NECESSITY AND POSSIBILITY: DESCARTES IN RESPONSE TO MERSENNE

As is the case with the previous objections, Descartes and his interlocutors do not fail to consider another line of reasoning that would later gain widespread acceptance; just as Gassendi anticipates Kant with astonishing accuracy, so does Mersenne anticipate Leibniz. In this case, the objection has a scholastic antecedent, and Marin Mersenne (1588–1648) probably appeals to his knowledge of Duns Scotus or related figures in formulating his objections to Descartes' argument.[73] Although Mersenne's repute stems chiefly from his work in mathematics, he spends many years as a teacher of theology and philosophy, and the *Second Set of Objections* provides much evidence of this background (if indeed the text is Mersenne's own work).[74] Mersenne considers the premises of the syllogistic Cartesian argument and claims that they unwarrantedly presume the non-contradictoriness of the idea of God:

> The conclusion should have been: "hence, once we have made a sufficiently careful investigation of what God is, we can with truth affirm that existence belongs to the nature of God." Now it does not follow from this that God in fact exists, but merely that he would have to exist if his nature is possible, or non-contradictory. In other words, the nature or essence of God cannot be conceived apart from existence; hence, granted the essence, God really exists. This comes down to an argument which others have stated as follows: "If there is no contradiction in God's existing, it is certain that he exists; but there is no contradiction in his existing."[75]

According to Mersenne, the minor premise of his proposed argument, "there is no contradiction in his existing," is open to doubt. Knowledge of God's essence seems requisite in order to claim that this essence is not contradictory. The objector appeals, however, to what he knows Descartes already to allow: we do not know God's essence, since we are finite whereas God is infinite. It would seem, then, that we could not be sure that God's essence does not contain a contradiction, so that the given argument would falter.

Mersenne's position here is complicit with both Leibniz's and one that Kant later attributes to his potential opponents.[76] All recognize the Cartesian claim that existence belongs to the essence of God, or that in the case of God existence and possibility are inseparable. The completion of the argument thus seems simple: establish possibility and existence follows immediately. Leibniz, for at least much of his career, will wrestle with arguments for God's possibility, viz. non-contradictoriness.[77] Descartes, however, diverges sharply from Mersenne and Scotus on this issue. His view asserts, to the contrary of the possibility arguments, that the assurance of God's possibility or non-contradictoriness does not precede but rather *follows from* our knowledge that God exists. Although Descartes shortly changes his position on the ascription of possibility to God, his stance on the priority of our knowledge of God's existence is revealing. The argument seems to suggest that we are aware of this existence more or less immediately, viz., that this awareness is not mitigated by a prior analysis of the concept of God in terms of the mere logical consistency of this concept.

In the same passage Descartes attempts to ease Mersenne's worry about our knowledge of God's essence; full knowledge of God's essence, Descartes argues, is not necessary. We need only be certain that existence belongs to the essence of God, and this does not imply that we perceive this essence fully or that we know each of God's attributes. The argument from the *Second Set of Replies* reads:

> All self-contradictoriness or impossibility resides solely in our thought, when we make the mistake of joining together mutually inconsistent ideas; it cannot occur in anything which is outside the intellect. For the very fact that something exists outside the intellect manifestly shows that it is not self-contradictory but possible. Self-contradictoriness in our concepts arises merely from their obscurity and their confusion: there can be none in the case of clear and distinct concepts. Hence, in the case of the few attributes of God which we do distinctly perceive, it is enough that we understand them clearly and distinctly, even though our understanding is in no way adequate. And the fact that, amongst other things, we notice that necessary existence is contained in our concept of God (however inadequate that concept may be) is enough to enable us to assert both that we have examined his nature with sufficient clarity, and that his nature is not self-contradictory.[78]

Descartes' position, in this passage at least, is clear enough: knowledge of non-contradictoriness is not a condition for but rather a result of the ontological proof. The argument Mersenne considers, then, is far from anything to which Descartes could have assented. As I have already twice suggested, Descartes does not consistently offer this same view of the attribution of possible existence to God. In the above argument he allows that God is possible, and he objects to Mersenne's suggestion only to the extent that the latter confuses the inferential order of the propositions in question. In other texts, however, the implication is rather that possibility is a property unique to creatures and only inappropriately ascribed to God. The remarks appended to the minor premise of the ontological argument from the "Geometrical Demonstration" suggest this interpretation. God's existence is necessary; possible existence, by contrast, belongs only to the nature of a "limited being." In this text Descartes even seems to equate possible existence with contingent existence.[79]

To attribute possibility to God, then, would be to think of God as if he were a creature, and thus to disregard the difference between the idea of God and the idea of any other thing. Mersenne, on this reading, is guilty of confusing God with finite things, the chief crime in theological matters, to the extent that he proposes to inquire into the mere possibility of the idea of God.[80]

In neglecting these preconditions of the minor premise, the possibility arguments anticipate the empirical objection, and the prevalence of the former eventually contributes to the repute of the latter. The empirical objection, like the possibility objection, consists in a generalization of the distinction between "essence" and "existence." To the essence or nature of a thing, the view runs, belongs only possibility; consideration of the thing's possibility, then, should rightly precede inquiry about its existence.[81] Such a rule, Descartes seems to conclude, holds in all cases *except* that of God. God does not possess "possible existence" in the sense that all other entities possess it, since to consider possibility in advance of existence amounts to considering the essence in isolation from its existence. This last is inappropriate in the one case in which the essence is supposed to include existence.[82]

A further metaphysical doctrine compounds the confusion here; God is said to be the *same* as his existence, and this claim serves as part of the basis for the traditional argument. Descartes raises this point only tangentially in his reply to Gassendi, leaving it to successors like Malebranche and Spinoza to place it at the center of the dispute over the ontological argument.[83] God is not "something," not a particular being, that could be considered apart from his existence, and this is part of what the predication of "necessary" existence implies. "Possibility," by contrast, is attributed to any entity only to the extent that it is considered in abstraction from its existence.[84] Neglect of these points by Mersenne, Leibniz, and others ultimately made the argument susceptible to a number of criticisms of Kant's.

Descartes shoulders much of the blame for this confusion. Since he does not consistently reject the attribution of possibility to God's nature, he leaves it to others to debate the propriety of the possibility arguments. Even in the text from the *First Set of Replies* in which he issues his first warning against confusing the idea of God with the idea of anything else, he writes as if necessary existence and possible existence are compatible with one another.[85] In the *Second Set of Replies*, Descartes first allows that they are compatible, and then, just a few pages later, writes as if they are mutually exclusive properties.[86] On this issue, as on several others, we find Descartes torn between his early arguments that encourage analogy (the possibility objection, etc.) and the many metaphysical and theological doctrines (equivocation, immediate knowledge of God, identity of God with his existence, etc.) that address the implications of those arguments.

THE EPISTEMOLOGICAL BACKGROUND: THE VERACITY OF THE *IDEA DEI*

True versus fictitious ideas

Accompanying the minor premise in the *First Set of Replies* are two warnings regarding potential objections to the claim that necessary existence belongs to the idea of God.[87] The first of these, as discussed above, represents an anticipation of the empirical objection and consists in the modal qualification of existence together with a reminder of the absolute difference between God and all other entities. The second difficulty pertains to the assurance that our idea of God is not fictional, and this anticipates the fourth kind of objection to the ontological argument, viz., the attack on the notion of God presumed in the premises.

In the discussion of this second difficulty, Descartes reminds the reader that we are accustomed to overlooking another distinction: "we do not distinguish what belongs to the true and immutable essence of a thing from what is attributed to it merely by a fiction of the intellect."[88] The argument thus proves to be contingent upon yet another major trope of rationalist epistemology: before proceeding in philosophy we must distinguish intellection from imagination, true ideas from fictional ones, etc. Our text elaborates this point concisely enough:

> To remove the second part of the difficulty, we must notice a point about ideas which do not contain true and immutable natures but merely ones which are invented and put together by the intellect. Such ideas can always be split up by the same intellect, not simply by abstraction but by a clear and distinct intellectual operation, so that any ideas which the intellect cannot split up in this way were clearly not put together by the intellect.[89]

Our ideas of "true and immutable natures," of essences, are distinguishable from fictional ideas insofar as we can divide the latter but not the former.

The idea of an "existing lion" (Caterus's example) is thus at least possibly fictional to the extent that I can clearly distinguish its components (i.e., I can imagine the lion also as not existing). The idea of God's existence, however, is analogous to the idea that the sum of three angles of a triangle is equal to two right angles. Just as we cannot separate the idea of that property from our idea of the triangle (*under the condition that we are aware of the rule in question*), so we also cannot separate the idea of necessary existence from the idea of God, provided that we have "sufficiently investigated" the idea of God. The point is psychological rather than logical. Anyone sufficiently schooled in geometry will be unable to think of a triangle without also recognizing that the degree of the angles adds to the given sum. Similarly, any sufficiently well trained metaphysician will be unable to think of God without also recognizing that it pertains to his nature to exist. In both cases our perception of the given property follows with a kind of necessity from our consideration of the initial idea.

It is appropriate to interpose into this discussion an objection mentioned by Gassendi.[90] Perhaps Descartes' observation holds in respect to the experience of the metaphysician. The latter, assuming he is also a competent geometer, perceives the attribute "necessary existence" when he thinks of "God" just as unavoidably as he thinks of certain properties of the angles when he thinks of a triangle. The perceptions are analogous also to the extent that they require a degree of training in the relevant sciences. One important difference remains, however, that jeopardizes the Cartesian analogy: the geometer learns *by force of demonstration* to attribute a certain quantity to the angles, and this same demonstration allows him to persuade any dissenters. Descartes offers no analogous demonstration for his attribution of "necessary existence," and this lack prevents him from convincing his opponents. It thus seems plausible for an opponent to claim that Descartes is fabricating this idea, while no one can make the analogous objection to the geometer.

The guarantee that the ontological argument is not based on a fictional idea receives various formulations among Descartes' works. The *Principles* addresses this dilemma only by appealing to the uniqueness of the property of necessary existence. From the fact that the mind can find no other ideas that contain necessary existence it "understands that the idea of an *ens perfectissimum* is not an idea which was invented by the mind."[91] Descartes' intention is, presumably, that we could not have borrowed our representation of "necessary existence" from any other idea. This argument is significant for the history of the ontological proof, since much of the eighteenth-century critique of that proof stems precisely from the allegation that the idea of "necessary existence" is borrowed from other arguments.[92]

In the *First Set of Replies* Descartes offers an interesting argument to this same end, one that has merited considerable attention from scholars.[93] In response to Caterus's contention that the idea of a "necessarily existing God" is analogous to the idea of an "existing lion," Descartes sets out to give further evidence that the former idea is not complex, and thus also not fictional. He assumes only a simple concept, that of a "supremely powerful being" and proposes a deduction of the concept of existence from this concept. An entity whose power is unlimited, he reasons, can exist by its own power. Further, "it is evident by the natural light" that whatever can exist by its own power always exists.[94] The attribute of "necessary existence" thus belongs demonstrably to the notion of a "supremely powerful being."

The *Fifth Meditation* cites a plurality of assurances that the idea is not fictitious, although it neglects to provide detailed arguments for them.[95] In that work, however, any intricate proof of the non-fictional nature of our idea of God would be superfluous for a very obvious reason. In the *Third Meditation* Descartes provides what he considers to be his "principal argument"[96] for the existence of God; namely, the proof that only God is capable of causing our idea of him. The idea, Descartes insists, contains more perfection than he himself is capable of putting in the idea, and this alone is enough to ensure that the idea is not fictitious. The argument from the *Fifth Meditation* thus leans on a point established by the a posteriori argument, viz., that we have an innate (or non-fictitious) idea of God.[97]

The transition objection and the a posteriori argument

If the ontological argument from the *Fifth Meditation* is not entirely independent of the a posteriori argument, then the primary objections to the latter serve also as objections to the former.[98] In fact, many of the modern period's most prevalent objections to the ontological argument first appear among the *Objections* to the *Third Meditation*. These objections concern neither the explicit premises of the Cartesian syllogism nor the inference involved. They address instead the epistemological status as well as the origin of the idea of God. It is indeed one of the most effective means of attacking the ontological proof to criticize our ability to think of anything like God.

Two lines of objection predominate the critique of the idea of God: the critics argue either that we possess no such idea or that the idea is a construction by analogy or "transition" from empirical concepts. Both Mersenne and Hobbes pursue each line, despite the apparent incompatibility of the two objections.[99] Of the two objectors it is predictably Mersenne who supplies the more relevant form of the first, more extreme objection, and it is only he who elicits an elaboration of Descartes' view. Mersenne wants to assert that we cannot really have an idea of God, while at the same time he wishes to avoid any merely linguistic dispute over what it means to have an idea. For that reason he qualifies his denial that we have an idea of God by allowing that we can perhaps have ideas of impossible natures. His claim is thus that either we have no such idea, or it is a spurious one: ". . . in fact you do not have the idea of God, just as you do not have the idea of an infinite number or an infinite line (even if you may have the idea, the number is still impossible)."

Mersenne's quibble here is similar to his objection to the *Fifth Meditation*; he is afraid either that the definition of God is contradictory, or at least that Descartes has not proven otherwise. He suggests that a contradiction may lie hidden in the notion of a highest being, just as the notion of a highest number is contradictory. Descartes' reply does not attack the cogency of this analogy. Rather, he denies that we have reason to consider the concept of a highest number to be contradictory, thereby implying that we likewise cannot directly perceive any contradiction in God's nature. In other words, Descartes concludes from Mersenne's analogy (1) that both analogs are evidence only of the limitation of our minds, and (2) we cannot prove such notions to be contradictory[100]:

> Now in my thought or intellect I somehow come upon a perfection that is above me; thus I notice that, when I count, I cannot reach a largest number, and hence I recognize that there is something in the process of counting which exceeds my powers. And I contend that from this alone it necessarily follows, not that an infinite number exists, nor indeed that it is a contradictory notion, but that I have the power of conceiving that there is a thinkable number which is larger than any number that I can ever think of . . .[101]

Hobbes's attack on the purported idea of God is both more sweeping and less interesting. As with Mersenne's objections, there is a direct correspondence in Hobbes between the objections to the *Third* and *Fifth Meditations*. Just as Hobbes is definitional in limiting "being" to "being in a place," so is he definitional in claiming that we have no idea of God. He points out that our ideas of, for instance, both "men" and "angels" consist of visible qualities such as shape and color. It is clear, however, that we have no analogous idea of God. Therefore, it follows for Hobbes, that we have no idea of God.[102]

While Hobbes does not actually state that an "idea" is by definition an image of visible qualities, Descartes astutely perceives something like this to serve as a suppressed premise in the above argument: "Here my critic wants the term "idea" to refer simply to the images of things which are depicted in the corporeal imagination; if this is granted, it is easy for him to prove that there can be no proper idea of an angel or of God."[103] Impatient with such question-begging objections, Descartes simply restates his own, broader definition of "idea" with which he quickly terminates the discussion: "I am taking the word "idea" to refer to whatever is immediately perceived by the mind."

Outright denial of the idea of God is a strategy too extreme to serve as a relevant criticism of the ontological argument. In the first place, such a denial brings the discussion to an immediate end; one who claims he has no such idea can no longer deny that it entails necessary existence.[104] For both Mersenne and Hobbes, this tactic is accordingly a short-lived one. Both devote more energy to the contention that the idea of God develops by transition or by analogy from empirical concepts (i.e., to the denial of the innateness of the idea). In this regard, Mersenne proposes that we can indeed discover within ourselves all the elements that comprise the idea of God.[105] These include a number of perfections (e.g., omnipotence, omniscience, etc.), with which we are already acquainted in their finite manifestations. It seems plausible, then, that we arrive at the ideas of God's limitless power and knowledge by abstracting our familiar ideas of power and knowledge and "adding to infinity."

Hobbes offers a more thorough version of this same objection. His "Tenth Objection" consists in a relatively careful discussion of the idea of God in which he isolates a number of the more common attributes.[106] His intention is to show (1) that many of these attributes are not appropriately attributable to God and (2) that in any case we arrive at the notions by analogy with sensible qualities. For each attribute that he considers, Hobbes provides a brief explanation of the source of the concept in question and whether the ascription of it to God is appropriate. Independence and infinity, for example, derive from our experiential notions of dependence and finitude. The attribution to God of certain other characteristics (e.g., power and intelligence) is inappropriate, since these are patently human virtues. Lastly, the concept of God as creator serves as the clearest example of the *analogical* nature of the idea of God: "I can construct for myself a sort of image of creation from what I have seen. . . ."

Descartes replies to these arguments with a revealing ambivalence. On the one hand, he concedes to Hobbes and Mersenne that the philosophical notion of God develops by indefinite extension from experiential notions. The concept of omniscience, for instance, represents such an extension of the idea of knowledge that we find within ourselves.[107] On the other hand, however, Descartes denies that any of the individual attributes at which we arrive in this way are genuinely attributable to God "in the same sense" in which we understand them.[108] Descartes is not a proponent of theological analogy, although he does not seem to establish an alternative to this Thomistic doctrine. He allows that attributes such as "knowledge" exist formally in God's nature, but he also recognizes that God's "immensity, simplicity, and unity" (which have no "copy" in us) affect the manner in which God possess these.

An obvious consequence of Descartes' position here is that he both affirms and denies knowledge of God. On the one hand, we do clearly perceive a number of God's attributes, such as existence, knowledge, and power. On the other hand, God possesses an altogether different kind of existence, as we have already seen, as well as a different kind of knowledge, etc. It is just as true, then, that we do not understand God's attributes as they actually inhere in his nature. This paradox results from the fact that Descartes at once affirms the finitude of our minds and the inconceivability of God, while at the same time he claims philosophical certitude about God. He resolves this ambiguity only by distinguishing between clarity and adequacy. This is one of several points upon which later proponents of the ontological argument improve. The most notable of them, Malebranche, Spinoza, and Hegel, each in their own way seek to resolve the difficulties inherent both to the position that finite intellects participate in knowledge of the infinite and to the problem of divine attribution.

THE LIMITS OF ANALOGY
AND THE PROBLEM OF INTUITION

If Descartes offers a relatively consistent version of the ontological argument and has a degree of success in defending this against the Thomistic, empirical, possibility, and transition objections, a notable difficulty in the argument nonetheless remains. As Gassendi notes, the explanation of the argument rests almost entirely on an analogy that is in essence misleading; while geometrical propositions are in fact "clearly perceived," this is so as a result of demonstration.[109] The claim that necessary existence belongs to the nature of God has not been supported by any demonstration analogous to a proof of the properties of a triangle. The crucial claim in the ontological argument, then, consists of what appears to at least some philosophers to be a bald and unsubstantiated assertion.

In the *Fifth Set of Replies* Descartes does not honor Gassendi's request for a demonstration. Instead, he suggests that the connection between the concepts of a "supremely perfect being" and "necessary existence" has already been the subject of adequate proof.[110] As is the case with other objections, however, Descartes seems to offer several, perhaps in some instances mutually exclusive, arguments establishing the point in question. In the *Fifth Meditation* the perfection argument appears to play this role. The concept of an *ens perfectissimum* or God contains all possible perfections; (necessary) existence is a perfection; the concept of God thus contains existence. If the ontological argument ultimately rests on this inference then there is some small justice to the common error of mistaking the perfection argument for the full Cartesian proof. This celebrated argument, however, does not reappear within Descartes' corpus, a fact that speaks against its fulfilling such an important function. Moreover, since it suggests that "existence" is a particular attribute of God's nature, among which there are other, presumably distinct, attributes, the perfection argument is incompatible with the doctrines that God is the same as his existence.[111]

Descartes instead poses other arguments that verify the desired connection. The omnipotence argument from the *First Set of Replies*, for example, achieves the same goal. The concept of "necessary existence," the argument runs, is deducible from the concept of omnipotence, since it is assumed that any entity with the power to bring about its own existence would do so. Descartes also claims that such an entity would grant itself all perfections of which it could conceive,[112] so that an omnipotent being would possess all conceivable perfections.[113] The concepts of "necessary existence" and of a "supremely perfect entity," then, are derivable from the single, simple concept of omnipotence.[114]

Dieter Henrich rests his interpretation of the entire history of the ontological argument on the importance of this deduction.[115] This is the one instance, it seems, in which Descartes provides an objective argument aimed at connecting the two constituent concepts from the conclusion of his ontological argument. Like the perfection argument, however, the omnipotence argument portrays the relationship between God and his existence in a very misleading fashion. Both arguments promote the deception that "existence" is one among many properties of God's nature, when the claim in question is that God's existence is the same as his nature.[116] Further, neither argument is consonant with the fact that the minor premise does not claim an objective connection between these concepts, but rather only a perceived connection; overemphasis of the importance of these arguments makes it difficult to explain why some versions of the minor premise refer only to our perception. What requires explanation is not that an *ens perfectissimum* contains necessary existence, but rather why we perceive this to be the case.[117]

The Cartesian ontological argument is not merely about God, but rather about our perception of God. The formulations of the minor premise in the *First Replies, Second Replies*, "Geometrical Demonstration," and *Principles of Philosophy* make this point evident enough. What Descartes needs to demonstrate, then, is not an objective connection, but only the veracity of a certain perception. The major premise does not alone accomplish this. The minor premise is defended independently by a metaphysical elitism: whoever does not perceive the desired connection simply has not rid themselves of "preconceived notions."[118] While the *First Replies* offers this explanation only tangentially, the *Principles* supplies a separate paragraph devoted exclusively to this point.[119]

A few consequences of this problem persist throughout the subsequent history of the argument. First, from the fact that our perception is incorporated in the premise of the argument it follows that the conclusion is not true for everyone. In other words, whoever does not actually perceive the connection between "a supremely perfect being" and "necessary existence" cannot assent to the claim in the minor premise, in which case the conclusion remains undemonstrated.[120] It is not the case that these individuals fail to grasp a premise that is objectively true; rather, their perceiving a certain "truth" is itself part of the premise. The premise is *in fact* false in any instance in which the perception is lacking. The ontological argument is thus unsound in those cases. Regardless of whether the ontological argument is ever sound, then, it will sometimes be unsound. The objectors will always be, in some sense, in the right, despite their inability to discover an internal flaw in the argument.[121]

Second, the dependence on the perception that God necessarily exists stands in conflict with the entire effort of establishing a proof. Descartes provides a deductive syllogism as well as extended arguments for the premises; the aim of any such endeavor, it would seem, is to convince others of the truth of the conclusion. Descartes himself asserts the same when he lists the refutation of atheism among his goals in the *Meditations*.[122] The ontological argument, however, cannot independently achieve this goal. A person simply cannot be forced to have a certain perception. The "argument" is either a proof or a perception; it cannot successfully be both.[123]

Among the subsequent proponents of ontological arguments some seek to improve the quality of the demonstration, and thereby reduce or eliminate the appeal to intuition. Others instead emphasize the role of intuition, in which case the importance of demonstration is reduced, if such demonstration is not entirely abandoned. Henry More and Leibniz are two of the more significant philosophers who pursue the former path. Both provide objective, nonintuitive versions of the minor premise, which they justify with perfection arguments. Malebranche, and to a certain degree both Spinoza and Hegel, opt for the second course. In these cases, the role of the perfection argument is either reduced or entirely eliminated, and the emphasis is rather on the intuition of the unity of God with his existence. These philosophers place the intuition of God's reality at the center of a philosophy to which they attempt to lend greater consistency than they find in Descartes, often resigning themselves to the fact that the central insight of the argument, and hence of philosophy as they conceive it, is not apparent to everyone.

NOTES

1. While Caterus was the first to notice the resemblance to the arguments of Anselm and others, it was probably Leibniz who made this observation a lasting one. See, among other places, C. I. Gebhardt, ed., *Die philosophische Schriften von G. W. Leibniz*, 7 vols., Berlin, 1875–90 (hereafter "G"), IV, 401.

2. Citations from Descartes are taken, with only occasional alteration, from *The Philosophical Writings of Descartes* (3 vols., trans. Cottingham, Stoothoff, and Murdoch, Cambridge, 1984, hereafter "CSM"). Page numbers to the edition by Adam and Tannery, *Ouvres de Descartes*, Paris/Vrin, revised edition, 1964–76, are indicated by "AT." AT VI 33; CSM I 128: "I decided to inquire into the source of my ability *to think* of something more perfect than I was."

3. AT VI 36; CSM I 129.

4. Although epistemological concerns seem to dominate the discussion, the aim of the Meditations is to establish "demonstrative proof" of the existence of God and the immortality of the souls (see AT VII 1–5; CSM II 3–5).

5. The ontological argument in the *Fifth Meditation* appears (AT VII 65; CSM II 45) in consequence to an epistemological discussion: "But if from the mere fact that I can produce from my thought the idea of something that entails that everything which I clearly and distinctly perceive to belong to that thing really does belong to it, is this not a possible basis for another argument to prove the existence of God?"

6. From the "Preface to the Reader" (AT VII 7; CSM II 6): "my purpose (in the *Discourse*) was not to provide a full treatment, but merely to offer a sample . . ."

7. AT VII 65; CSM II 45–46: "And my understanding that it belongs to (God's) nature that he always exists is no less clear and distinct than when I prove of any shape or number that some property belongs to its nature . . . it is quite evident that existence can no more be separated from the essence of God than can the fact that its three angles equal two right angles be separated from the essence of a triangle."

8. Part one #13 (AT VIIIA 10; CSM I 197–98).

9. AT VII 150; CSM II 106–107.

10. AT VII 324–25; CSM II 225–26.

11. *First Replies* (AT VII 155–56; CSM II 82–83), "Geometrical Demonstration" (AT VII 166–67; CSM II 117–18).

12. See the passage at AT VII 137; CSM II 98–99.

13. On the latter point, consult the passage referenced in the previous note. On the former, see AT VII 383; CSM II 263.

14. For a defense of the "intuitive" thesis, see Martial Gueroult's *Descartes' Philosophy Interpreted According to the Order of Reasons* (trans. Roger Ariew, Minnesota, 1985), p. 253. M. V. Dougherty ("The Importance of Cartesian Triangles: A New Look at Descartes' Ontological Argument," in *International Journal of Philosophical Studies* 10 (1), 2002, pp. 35–62) has recently argued against this view by emphasizing the role of the triangle analogy. Dougherty writes of the intuitive interpretation that it must allow that "the ontological argument is devoid of a proper *argument*."

15. The argument is introduced at AT VII 65–66; the rule in question is the claim that "everything I clearly and distinctly conceive is true."

16. AT VII 67; CSM II 46–47

17. AT VII 115–16; CSM II 83. The syllogistic argument from the *Replies* actually omits one premise from the *Fifth Meditation* argument. The latter has three premises, one of which is that "I have an idea of God" (See Willis Doney, "Did Caterus Misunderstand Descartes' Ontological Proof?" in *Rene Descartes: Critical Assessments, Volume II*, Routledge, 1991 (Hereafter "Doney"), pp. 344–53). This premise would be superfluous in the *Replies* arguments, since they refer to what I perceive to belong to God's nature, rather than to the idea I have of him.

18. AT VII 150; CSM II 107.

19. AT VII 166–67; CSM II 117.

20. Although Descartes does not, in the *First Replies*, add the word "necessary"

to this premise, he explains in the ensuing discussion of the argument (AT VII 118; CSM II 84) that "it is only necessary existence that is at issue here." In the "Geometrical Demonstration" (AT VII 166–67; CSM II 117) he does specify existence modally in the minor premise. See Axiom X and the Demonstration to Proposition I.

21. AT VII 67; CSM II 46–47

22. AT VII 97–99; CSM II 70–72. Caterus omits the premise of the perfection argument and attributes to Descartes only the claim that "a supremely perfect being includes existence, for otherwise it would not be a supremely perfect being."

23. AT VII 115; CSM II 83

24. Doney argues that the argument from perfection is independent of the *First Replies* syllogism, although it appears as a defense of the minor premise of the latter. Even if he is right (I think he is not), the lack of subsequent reference by Descartes to the perfection argument should serve as an indication of its relative insignificance. Bonansea (Bernardino Bonansea, "The Ontological Argument: Proponents and Opponents," in *Studies in Philosophy and the History of Philosophy*, ed. John K. Ryan, Catholic University of America Press, 1973), Wolfson (*The Philosophy of Spinoza*, Harvard, 1934), and Oppy (*Ontological Arguments and Belief in God*, Cambridge, 1995) are some of the few scholars of the ontological argument who do not place undue emphasis on the perfection argument. All three seem to consider the argument to serve only as attempted defense of the minor premise of the *Replies* argument.

25. Both Mersenne (AT VII 127; CSM II 91) and Arnauld (AT VII 208; CSM II 146) refer to the *Reply* to Caterus in the appropriate places. Spinoza and Malebranche defend only the *Replies* syllogism and lay little or no importance on the perfection argument. More advocates a perfection argument but only as an interpretation of the minor premise of the full Cartesian proof. For details consult the relevant chapters below.

26. More, *An Antidote Against Atheism*, ch. 8 (in *The Philosophical Writings of Henry More*, ed. Flora MacKinnon, Oxford University Press, 1925, hereafter "*Antidote*," pp. 23ff.); Spinoza, *Descartes' "Principles of Philosophy,"* Lemma 1.

27. Leibniz, *New Essays on Human Understanding* (trans. Remnant and Bennet, Cambridge, 1981), p. 438; Kant, *Nova dilucidato*, prop. VI, Scholum; Hegel, *Vorlesungen ueber die Philosophie der Religion*, 3, Felix Meiner, 1995, p. 272.

28. Martial Guerolt (*Descartes selon l'ordre des raisons*, English: *Descartes' philosophy interpreted according to the order of reasons*, trans. Roger Ariew, Minnesota, 1985) made famous the view that the Cartesian ontological argument is entirely dependent upon its context. This view is at least as old as Kuno Fischer's *Geschichte der neuern Philosophie* (Heidelberg, 1867–78), and is still shared by many European commentators like Wolfgang Roed (*Der Gott der reinen Vernunft*, C. H. Beck, Munich, 1992, pp. 69–71). Henri Gouhier and Dieter Henrich, among others, have opposed the contextualist view. For an English-language introduction to the classic literature on the

debate, see Donald Cress's, "Does Descartes' 'Ontological Argument' Really Stand on its Own?" in *Studi Internazionali di Filosofia* 5 (1973), pp. 127–36.

29. See AT VII 116; CSM II 83 and the discussion thereof below. Descartes and Leibniz clearly see these rules as, if not equivalent, closely related; the introduction of the ontological argument in the *Fifth Meditation* also strongly suggests this equivalence. Spinoza distinguishes them in the *Principia* by using the predication rule as a definition, although he does not establish the rule for truth until proposition 14.

30. This point holds, not only for the proof structure of the *Meditations*, but for all presentations of the ontological argument. Cress argues, to the contrary, that the argument from both the *Principles* and the "Geometrical Presentation" is independent of the doctrine that what is clearly and distinctly perceived is thereby true. The reason for his view, it seems, is that he does not consider the premise asserting the reality of predication (i.e., Definition IX of the "Geometrical Demonstration") to be a version of the doctrine of the reality of clear and distinct perception, as Descartes clearly does.

31. AT VII 379; CSM II 261.

32. AT VII 98–99; CSM II 71–72. The *First Set of Objections* is abundant with references to classical literature as well as to ancient and medieval philosophy.

33. Caterus cites Thomas's two objections and then repeats them in his own words: ". . . all that follows is that the concept of real existence is inseparably linked to the concept of a supreme being. So you cannot infer that the existence of God is anything actual unless you suppose that the supreme being actually exists."

34. The discussion of minor premise in *Meditation V* begins (AT VII 65; CSM II 45) with the claim that the first premise provides the "basis" for the argument: "But if the mere fact that I can produce from my thought the idea of something entails that everything which I clearly and distinctly perceive to belong to that thing really does belong to it, is this not a possible basis for another argument to prove the existence of God?"

35. AT VII 67; CSM II 46

36. For a summary of Thomas's arguments, see the introduction to this volume.

37. Descartes writes in the *Fifth Meditation* (AT VII 65–66; CSM II 45) that "even if it turned out that not everything on which I have meditated in these past days is true, I ought still to regard the existence of God as having at least the same level of certainty as I have hitherto attributed to the truths of mathematics."

38. AT VIIIA 10; CSM I 198.

39. At book I, proposition 30. Cress assumes that since in the *Principles* the discussion of the minor premise, which he mistakes for the entire ontological argument, precedes the discussion of clarity and distinctness, the former must independently prove God's actual existence. His error is that he overlooks the fact that I. 14 asserts only that the mind must perceive that God exists, not that God actually exists.

40. *First Set of Replies*, AT VII 115–17; CSM II 83.

41. AT VII 116; CSM II 83.

42. A version of Descartes' point is prevalent also in contemporary modal arguments. See Hartshorne's "What did Anselm discover?" in *Union Seminary Quarterly Review* 17, 1962, pp. 213–22 (reprinted in Hick and McGill, eds. *The Many Faced Argument*, Macmillan, 1967, pp. 321–34).

43. See AT VII 117; CSM II 83.

44. In reply to Caterus Descartes writes that "it must be noted that possible existence is contained in the concept of everything that we clearly and distinctly understand." In the *Second Replies* and in the "Geometrical Demonstration," however, he seems to exclude God from this. This discrepancy is easily explained: prior to reading the *Second Objections*, it seems, Descartes had not considered that his argument, on the first reading of "possible," could be taken to conclude only that "God exists, if he is possible."

45. AT VII 166; CSM II 117.

46. Spinoza, for instance, treats "contingency" and possibility as nearly interchangeable, and Malebranche vehemently denies that possible existence can be ascribed to God.

47. In his exposition of the *Principles* (P5 Scholium) Spinoza draws the connection between this passage from the *First Replies* and the doctrine of equivocation. The decisive Cartesian text on divine attribution is from the *Second Set of Replies* (AT VII 137; CSM II 98–99). This passage can at least be read as suggesting an equivocist position. Of course, the fact that I have an idea of God and an idea of other things suggests that God has at least some relative attributes in common with everything else, such as "being an object of my thought." Reference to God as an *ens* is also suggestive of a degree of analogy between God and creatures. Both Spinoza and Malebranche defend Descartes' position on these points more consistently than Descartes defends himself.

48. Although Descartes takes the proof to be self-evident, he would agree with Aquinas and Boethius that "certain notions are self-evident and commonplaces only to the learned" (*Summa*, pp. 6–7). Hence the frequent warning, in the context of the proof, that "its conclusion can be grasped as self-evident by *those who are free of preconceived opinions*" (AT VII 167; CSM 117–18. Cf. AT VII 68; CSM II 47).

49. AT VII 120; CSM II 85: "As I readily admit, it is the kind of argument which may easily be regarded as a sophism by those who do not keep in mind all the elements which make up the proof. For this reason I did have considerable doubts to begin with about whether or not I should use it; for I feared that it might induce those who did not grasp it to have doubts about the rest of my reasoning."

50. *Kritik der reinen Vernunft* (hereafter "KrV") B 620–31.

51. On Gassendi's changing career, see Barry Brundell's *Pierre Gassendi: from Aristotelianism to a new natural philosophy* (Kluwer, 1987).

52. AT VII 323; CSM II 224.

53. Ibid.

54. AT VII 323; CSM II 225.

55. AT VII 66; CSM II 46.

56. Oded Balabon and Asnat Avshalom ("The Ontological Argument Reconsidered," in *Journal of Philosophical Research* 15, 1989–90, p. 286) state this point nicely: "Regarding (the empirical objection) modern empiricists, in attacking the argument, are trying to beat down an open door."

57. AT VII 324; CSM II 225.

58. In the *Fifth Meditation* (AT VII 64; CSM II 44–45) Descartes writes: "When, for example, I imagine a triangle, even if perhaps no such figure exists, or ever has existed, anywhere outside my thought, there is still a determinate nature, or essence, or form of the triangle, which is immutable and eternal, and not invented by me or dependent on my mind." Gassendi (AT VII 321; CSM II 223) takes issue with exactly this example: "The triangle is a kind of mental rule which you use to find out whether something deserves to be called a triangle. But we should not therefore say that such a triangle is something real, or that it is a true nature distinct from the intellect. For it is the intellect alone which, after seeing material triangles, has formed this nature and made it a common nature...."

59. See his letter to an unknown addressee (AT IV 348; *Descartes: Philosophical Letters*, trans. Anthony Kenny, Oxford, 1970, pp. 186–88), which dates from around 1645. Descartes does admit of a merely conceptual distinction between essence and existence even in creatures, but this does not change the fact that the relationship between essence and existence is different in God than in creatures. For a lengthy analysis of this very complex problem, see Jorge Secada's *Cartesian Metaphysics* (Cambridge, 2000).

60. *Fifth Replies*, AT VII 383; CSM II 263.

61. Ibid.

62. The empirical objection in the eighteenth century, including in Kant's writings, also presumes that existence is attributed either univocally or analogically, rather than equivocally.

63. Both the objectors and the proponents of the ontological argument agree upon the same rule. The only difference is that the proponents claim to cite an exception to this rule. To reiterate the rule in response to this claim, as the empirical objector does, is to engage in an entirely spurious kind of argumentation.

64. It was inevitable that the myth in question was exposed for just that. Hartshorne and Malcolm (see Hick and McGill, pp. 301–56) achieved this primarily by reinterpreting Anselm's *Proslogion*. The argument from *Proslogion* II, they claimed, is not Anselm's chief argument. Rather, the modal argument from *Proslogion* III comprises Anselm's real proof for God's existence, and this argument is not subject to the empirical objection. In making this claim, however, they and others attempt to distinguish Anselm's argument from the modern argument. Although these are in fact different arguments, both Anselm and the moderns agree on the importance of modality.

The fact that the argument from perfection was frequently mistaken for the decisive modern ontological argument propagated the opinion that the moderns, Descartes in particular, made errors that Anselm did not. Hartshorne occasionally acknowledges that Descartes' argument is modal, but he does not recognize that this is true even of the argument in the *Fifth Meditation*.

65. *Disquisitio metaphysica, seu dubitationes et instantiae adversus Renati Cartesii Metaphysicam et responsa* (*Counter-Objections*), ed. Bernard Rochot, J. Vrin, Paris, 1962, pp. 491–93. An English translation of this section appears in *The Selected Works of Pierre Gassendi*, ed. Craig B. Brush, Johnson Reprint Corporation, New York, 1972, pp. 258–60.

66. Gassendi introduces the joke at AT VII 266; CSM II 186. Descartes indulges him, beginning at AT VII 348, CSM II 241: "I shall address you not as a discerning philosopher but rather as one of those men of the flesh whose ideas you have presented."

67. See the discussion of Crusius in chapter 5. I am not aware of any real, historical connection between Crusius and Hobbes regarding the definition of "existence."

68. AT VII 193; CSM II 135.

69. AT VII 178–79; CSM II 125–26.

70. See *Thomas White's* De mundo *examined*, trans. Harold Whitmore Jones, Bradford University Press, 1976, chs. 28–30. For a discussion of this text, see Yves Charles Zarka's "First Philosophy and the Foundations of Knowledge," in the *Camridge Companion to Hobbes*, Cambridge, 1996, pp. 62–85.

71. *Leviathan*, ch. 4, para. 21; on this, see Edwin Curley's "Hobbes versus Descartes" (in *Descartes and his Contemporaries*, ed. Roger Ariew and Marjorie Greene, University of Chicago Press, 1995, pp. 97–105) and his "'I durst not write so badly' or, How to Read Hobbes' Theological-Political Treatise" (in *Hobbes e Spinoza*, ed. Daniela Bostrenghi, Naples, 1992, pp. 497–593). See also A. P. Martinich's *The Two Gods of "Leviathan,"* Cambridge, 1992.

72. The proponent of the Hobbesian definition of "existence" might claim either that God is corporeal (Hobbes, later Crusius) or, in the context of Newtonian science, that he is space itself (e.g., Henry More). For an interesting discussion of this see Rohls, pp. 221ff.

73. See Scotus's *De primo principio* and Bernardino Bonansea's "Duns Scotus and St. Anselm's Ontological Argument" (in *Studies in Philosophy and in the History of Philosophy*, ed. John K. Ryan, Catholic University Press, 1969).

74. The editors of the Cambridge edition (CSM II 64) suggest that Mersenne is the author, and I will throughout attribute authorship of the *Second Set of Replies* to him, mainly for the sake of convenient reference. For a detailed discussion of the question of authorship of these *Replies*, see Daniel Garber's "J. B. Morin and the *Second Objections*," in Ariew and Grene, pp. 63–82.

75. AT VII 127; CSM II 91. The "others" mentioned in the argument are prob-

ably Duns Scotus and his followers. On this, see Bonansea (p. 152) and Rohls (pp. 121–50).

76. Leibniz, *New Essays*, p. 438; Kant, *Critique of Pure Reason* (hereafter "KrV") B 624–25. Kant is likely thinking of Baumgarten.

77. On these arguments see, among many other competent essays, Adriano Bausola's "Die Moeglichkeit des vollkommensten Wesens und der ontologische Gottesbeweis: die Position von Leibniz" in *Studia Leibnitiana* 13, 1981, pp. 1–24.

78. AT VII 152; CSM II 108.

79. "*nempe continetur existentia possibilis sive contingens in conceptu rei limitatae . . .*" (AT VII 166).

80. The confusion is further complicated by the fact that neither Descartes nor Mersenne seem to distinguish "possibility" as a modal characteristic from the logical characteristic of "non-contradictoriness."

81. In the eighteenth century, particularly in Germany, the terms "essence" and "possibility" are interchangeable. In the *New Essays*, bk. 3, ch. 3, #15, Leibniz writes that "essence is fundamentally nothing but the possibility of a thing under consideration."

82. This is exactly the point Kant will make in reference to an argument like Mersenne's: see *KrV* B 625 and its discussion below in chapter six. Of course, Kant is unaware that his objection ultimately serves as a defense of the ontological argument, since he is insensitive to the difference between the seventeenth- and eighteenth-century forms of the argument.

83. See Descartes, *Fifth Replies*, AT VII 383; CSM II 263. Although Descartes makes this point only once, it is something of a commonplace in philosophical theology. See, for instance, Aquinas' *Summa* and Spinoza's *Ethics* I, P22.

84. Part of the difficulty in assessing Descartes' view on the possibility of the idea of God is that Descartes does not lend any consistent meaning to this term. On this point, consult the entirety of his *Second Set of Replies*.

85. AT VII 116; CSM II 83. In this passage, the only requirement given for possible existence is clear and distinct perception, and the idea of God does in fact meet this criterion.

86. The passage at AT VII 163; CSM II 115 is inclusive: "they should reflect on the fact that . . . whereas the idea of God contains not only possible but wholly necessary existence" ("*et inter caetera considerent . . . in Dei autem idea non possibilem tantum, sed omino necessariam contineri*"). But, again, AT VII 166; CSM II 117 suggests exclusion rather than inclusion: "Possible or contingent existence is contained in the nature of a limited thing, whereas necessary and perfect existence is contained in the concept of a supremely perfect being."

87. AT VII 116–17; CSM II 83.

88. Ibid.

89. AT VII 117; CSM II 83.

90. *Fifth Set of Objections*, AT VII 325; CSM II 226.

91. AT VIIIA 10; CSM I 198.

92. This is the gist of Kant's criticism. Kant derives his understanding of the onto-logical argument from philosophers (Leibniz, Wolff, etc.) who indeed made the ontolog-ical argument dependent upon the cosmological (see chapters five and six below).

93. Willis Doney has written a very helpful essay on this argument, "Descartes' Argument from Omnipotence," in Moyal, ed., *Rene Descartes: Critical Assessments*, pp. 371–80. Henrich (pp. 14–22) even considers this to be the most important among the Cartesian ontological arguments. His preference for this argument, however, stems rather obviously from his prejudice for reading the entire history of the argument from the perspective of Kant's "Transcendental Dialectic." In other words, it is not based on a serious reading of Descartes on the latter's own terms.

94. AT VII 119; CSM II 85; See also *Meditation Three*.

95. AT VII 68; CSM II 47; the first argument from that text foreshadows the passage from the *Principles*.

96. AT VII 14; CSM II 10.

97. Hence the inclusion of this point as a premise in the *Fifth Meditation* argument. Descartes avoids the problem altogether in the *First Replies* and elsewhere by discussing God's nature or essence rather than our idea of him. On this, see Doney 1. It could be con-jectured that among Descartes' many objectives in the *First Replies* and the "Geometrical Demonstration," as well as in the *Principles*, is to present the ontological argument inde-pendently of the a posteriori proof. In denying the independent validity of the ontological argument, Martial Guerolt focuses mainly on the proof structure of the *Meditations*, in which case his claim is more evidently correct. Guerolt's point nonetheless holds of the other texts at least indirectly; i.e., although Descartes offers a syllogistic argument that pos-sesses a semblance of independence, the extended defense and explanation of the syllogism eventually incorporates most of the doctrines from the *Meditations*. In any case, it should be noted that the *Fifth Meditation* argument borrows from the *Third Meditation* only the proof that the idea of God is not fictitious, and *not* the conclusion that God exists.

98. Wolfson (I 169) opposes the Guerolt/Fischer thesis of dependency on the a posteriori argument, but at the same time recognizes the importance of Cartesian epis-temology for the proof. The fact that so many objectors claim that the idea of God is fictitious, however, makes the a posteriori argument important to the defense of the ontological argument. Although it is not Descartes' only means of proving that the idea of God is innate or non-fictitious, it is his primary means of so doing.

99. Mersenne is playing devil's advocate, so that he has no need to formulate a consistent position. Hobbes, on the other hand, is still developing his ideas at the time he writes the *Third Objections*, and he appears to have no consistent position on the nature of ideas at this time. See Tom Sorrel's "Hobbes's Objections and Hobbes's System," in Ariew and Grene, pp. 83–96.

100. It is only later in the *Second Replies* that Descartes adds the point, already discussed here, that an actual proof of God's non-contradictoriness is unnecessary.

101. AT VII 139; CSM II 99–100. This passage is of particular interest since Leibniz typically uses the example of a "highest number" (assuming this is contradictory) in order to express his worry over whether the notion of a perfect being might be contradictory.

102. AT VII 179–80; CSM II 126–27.

103. AT VII 181; CSM II 127; Hobbes actually allows that we have an idea of angels, but that we imagine them to be corporeal.

104. Probably because their defense of the argument is primarily a response to Hobbes, both Cudworth and More consider this point prior to completing their versions of the ontological argument.

105. AT VII 123; CSM II 88.

106. AT VII 186–88; CSM II 130–31.

107. AT VII 188; CSM II 132.

108. AT VII 137; CSM II 98: ". . . we recognize that, of all the individual attributes which, by a defect in our understanding, we assign to God in a piecemeal fashion, corresponding in the way in which we perceive them in ourselves, none belong to God and to ourselves in the same sense."

109. AT VII 325; CSM II 226.

110. AT VII 383–84; CSM II 263.

111. Of course, there is also only one passage (AT VII 383; CSM II 263) in which Descartes endorses this doctrine. One is thus left with the following problem: Descartes endorses *both* a deduction of existence as a property *and* the intuition of the sameness of God and his existence. His successors rightly make a choice where he does not. Malebranche opts for the latter, Leibniz the former. Spinoza attempts to make the two positions compatible by clarifying the relationship between intuition and rational demonstration; in this, his position is perhaps in agreement with the position of Descartes' *Regulae* (see the appropriate places below). Descartes writes only that there are different ways of elaborating the argument to correspond to the different mental habits of individual readers.

112. AT VII 119, CSM II 85.

113. Descartes obviously assumes that a supremely powerful being could conceive of all conceivable perfections. (See the *Third Meditation* at AT VII 48.)

114. Descartes introduces the omnipotence argument in the *First Set of Replies* in reference to the perfection argument from the *Fifth Meditation*. The former is one way of defending the latter, and both arguments correspond to a single method of defending the minor premise.

115. Henrich reads the eighteenth-century history of the ontological argument, specifically the two-argument thesis, back into the seventeenth century. The omnipo-

tence argument, despite its marginal place in the Cartesian corpus, thus naturally assumes a special importance for his account.

116. Descartes discusses this point concerning the identity of God and his existence in, of all places, his demonstration of the omnipotence argument.

117. Wolfson (*The Philosophy of Spinoza*, Harvard 1934, vol. I, pp. 180–81, hereafter "Wolfson") takes the omnipotence argument to be compatible with the reference to intuition, which corresponds, in the context of Spinoza's philosophy, to the compatibility of the second and third kinds of knowledge.

118. *Principles* I, 16; *First Replies*, AT VII 120 (CSM II 85).

119. *Principles* I, 16.

120. See Wolfson I, 172.

121. Henrich (p. 218) expresses a similar point when he writes (in Hegelian terms) that the objectors could only be persuaded if they were forced to occupy the "absolute" standpoint.

122. See the dedicatory letter to the *Meditations* (AT VII 3; CSM II 4).

123. Among scholars of the ontological argument, some (e.g., Wolfson, Earle) consider the proof to be an elaboration of an intuition, while others (e.g., Garrett, Dougherty) seem to find this notion repellent to their more contemporary sensibilities. Both views are a bit simplistic, since support for both sides is easily found among traditional proponents of ontological arguments.

Chapter Two

REFUTATIONS OF ATHEISM

Ontological Arguments in English Philosophy, 1652–1705

Atension concerning the persuasiveness of the ontological argument pervades Descartes' writings on the proof. On the one hand, he presents his argument in the form of a syllogism demonstration, and for that reason it appears to demand universal assent. The syllogistic presentation offers a simple deduction from purportedly indubitable premises, and as such it should be sufficient to silence any opponent. On the other hand, we find frequent admission of the obscurity of the ontological inference. Descartes allows that the argument is not likely to win assent from all parties, and he even suggests that it may bring discredit upon his other doctrines. One reason for his hesitation involves the intuitive nature of the minor premise. That premise may be indubitable from the standpoint of Cartesian philosophy, but those who are not free from preconceived ideas are unable to perceive that "necessary existence belongs to the nature of a supremely perfect being."

Two solutions to this dilemma appear among those contemporaries of Descartes who consider the argument to be valid. The first option is to remove the reference to the private intuition of the philosopher. In this case the argument stands in need of considerable formal improvement; the premises require justification not limited to vague reference to what is intuitively evident to the Cartesian philosopher but to no one else. The second alternative is to accept the intuitive nature of the argument and to eliminate the misleading appearance of logical inference that results from the syllogistic formulation of the Cartesian argument.

Many Cartesian philosophers on the Continent pursue the latter course. For them the aim is to develop Descartes' ideas into a more consistent, systematic philosophy, a trend that culminates in the philosophies of Malebranche and Spinoza. Malebranche is the first to accept without reservation both that the argument involves an appeal to intuition and that it is not likely to gain universal assent. His philosophical system accordingly provides a more suitable context for the intuitive nature of the argument than does Descartes' philosophy. He admits that our knowledge of God's existence is immediate, and hence he limits his employment of the misleading Cartesian analogy. His concern is rather to modify those Cartesian doctrines that lend an appearance of inconsistency to the argument. In this regard he emphasizes, both more radically and more consistently than Descartes, the difference between God and creatures. Even more importantly, he, like Spinoza, offers a sophisticated account of the relation between the finite intellect and the infinite being that it perceives. Our third and fourth chapters will trace these developments in the systems of Malebranche and Spinoza respectively.

The first alternative finds its most notable representative in the Cambridge philosopher Henry More. A mere eleven years after the appearance of the *Meditations*, More publishes a detailed and insightful exposition of the Cartesian argument in his *An Antidote against Atheism*.[1] Unlike Malebranche, More's immediate aim, as his title indicates, is to prevent the spread of atheism. Although he employs various forms of philosophical apparatus to this end, his first and chief argument is ontological.[2] His emphasis on the Cartesian argument displays an unusually deep conviction in the effectiveness of that argument; perhaps no philosopher in the history of the argument from Anselm to the present has had a comparable faith in the ability of the proof to confute infidelity. The current chapter will recount the fortune of this endeavor in More and his successors.

THE FATE OF DEMONSTRATION: MORE'S *ANTIDOTE*

Most accounts of the history of the ontological argument treat More only in passing, mentioning him as an influence of his better-known successor, Ralph Cudworth.[3] Although the prevalent historiography places these philosophers in the same school of "Cambridge Platonism," their formulations of the ontological argument differ greatly. They therefore play distinct roles in the history of the argument. Both Henrich and Hartshorne show greater esteem for Cudworth's contribution for reasons appropriate to their respective accounts. Cudworth distinguishes the concept of "necessary existence" very carefully from the concept of a "most perfect being," and attempts to offer a deduction of the former from the latter (hence Henrich's approval).[4] He also, more explicitly so than either Descartes or More, underscores the modal nature of the argument (hence his laudatory mention by Hartshorne).

If Cudworth's contribution is important in that it anticipates those eighteenth-century changes in the argument, More's formulation is equally important as a representation of the seventeenth-century argument. More's *Antidote* is, in both its logical structure and the date of its appearance, the closest to Descartes' *Meditations* among the noteworthy presentations of the ontological argument. Unlike most subsequent philosophers, More understands the systematic context of the Cartesian argument, and he attempts to present this context even more thoroughly and persuasively than his French contemporary. His presentation of the argument follows the same strategy found in the *Meditations* and *Discourse*: he argues first that the ascription of "necessary existence" to God is analogous to mathematical truths; he proposes a defense of the innateness of both the theological and mathematical ideas; lastly, like Descartes, he tries to show that refusing this version of the ontological argument leads inevitably to extreme skepticism (i.e., to doubt about both God's existence and the veracity of simple mathematical claims).

Despite spending his entire career at Cambridge, Henry More (1614–1687) manages to participate in many of the key philosophical controversies of his day. As a philosopher he is important for his defenses of doctrines like the immortality of the soul, the innateness of ideas, etc.[5] His knowledge of Descartes is extensive, and he conducts a brief correspondence with that philosopher in the late 1640s, which addresses topics such as the equation of extension and space, the distinction between "infinite" and "indefinite," etc.[6] The two philosophers do not broach the ontological argument in this correspondence, and the evidence points towards More's unqualified acceptance of the argument as he finds it in the *Meditations*. He incorporates this argument into his *Antidote against Atheism*, the intended opponent of which is probably Hobbes. The big event in English philosophy at this time is the appearance of the latter's *Leviathan*, which is published in 1651, or just prior to the composition of More's *Antidote*. The "atheism" More is combating in this text is thus likely the new materialism, which explains why he begins with an ontological argument that makes appeal to the innateness of ideas.[7]

The importance of the *Antidote* to the history of the ontological argument lies in the concise but thorough manner in which More reconstructs the *First Replies* syllogism. His argument actually has much to recommend it over Descartes' arguments from the *Meditations* and the *Discourse*: More defends without any ambiguity the Cartesian analogy between mathematical and theological knowledge. Because of this, the problems inherent to that analogy are more apparent in the *Antidote* than in the *Meditations*. The ultimate failure of More's use of this analogy, and his reproduction of the *First Replies* syllogism, is not specific to More. In other words, its shortcomings are not due to his presentation. The flaw in his version of the syllogistic argument is endemic to that argument. To be more specific, More inadvertently demonstrates how the syllogistic form and the mathematical analogies conflict with the conclusion of the ontological argument.

More accepts the role of the Cartesian premise that clarity and distinctness are the indicators of truth, and he provides a version of this doctrine that is in some respects superior to Descartes' version. Unlike Descartes and Malebranche, however, he allows that the premise is dubitable. His presentation begins with an amusing statement of an inverted Cartesian rule, one that gives a sense of the charm and wit that pervades his writings: it is possible "that there has been in the world time out of mind such a being as we call man, whose essential property it is to be most of all mistaken, when he conceives a thing most evidently true."[8] The ensuing ontological argument thus does not seek to convince an extreme skeptic. Allowing that the inverted Cartesian rule is conceivable, More's argument is instead hypothetical: a skepticism of the evil-demon sort notwithstanding, the ontological argument is entirely demonstrable. In other words, his claim is that the argument is dubitable only to the extent that our intellective faculties may be systematically misleading. Anyone who insists on this last possibility will remain unaffected by this or any other argument.

More accordingly directs the greater part of his attention to the minor premise and the several objections to it. His intention is to justify the analogy with geometry asserted in the elaboration of that premise. That God exists, for More, is as evident as that there are only five regular bodies. The only reasonable means of doubting the former, viz., denial of the Cartesian rule, leads also to skepticism regarding the latter.[9] His aim is thus to force the atheist into universal skepticism. That there is no God "is no more possible than that the clearest mathematical evidence may be false."[10]

His more modest claim in regard to skepticism, by comparison with

Descartes, accompanies his more ambitious goal in establishing theism. Descartes condemns himself to persuading only those who can navigate a very subtle chain of reasons, accepting the fact that anyone who has not, in a very specific manner, eliminated all preconceived notions, will not assent to his conclusion. More, by contrast, aims at winning over all except those who are stubbornly intent upon a universal skepticism. His argument, he proclaims, shall "win full assent from any *unprejudiced* mind."[11]

More's innovation regarding the role of the major premise signals a significant improvement in the presentation of the argument. If Descartes' procedure of hyperbolic doubt is unappealing, the rule that allows him to escape that doubt may appear unnecessary. A derivative of that rule serves as the major premise of the ontological argument, so that this last remains inaccessible to anyone who does not entertain the starting point. More begins rather with a disjunction: either the clear and distinct ideas are reliable or they are not. A consequence of opting in favor of the latter disjunct, however, is universal skepticism. Since More's goal is to persuade everyone except the extreme skeptic, he considers the former disjunct (i.e., the major premise, to be conceded). In this case, anyone who does *not* engage in exaggerated skepticism should be compelled to consider the argument.

This reference to skepticism in the second chapter of the *Antidote* serves as a kind of preface to subsequent discussion of the idea of God (chapters 3–8). If not read in light of the Cartesian texts, the remarks may appear dispensable. More's familiarity with the full Cartesian argument, however, is recognizable enough. His remarks on the skeptic replace the justification of the major premise. The following five chapters provide a more concise and direct defense of the minor premise than Descartes offers. The eighth chapter then professes that the conclusion is inevitable. The structure of the opening eight chapters of the *Antidote* thus clearly comprises an elaborate reproduction of the *First Replies* syllogism.

By prefacing the ontological conclusion with five short chapters on the idea of God, More also makes the systematic nature of the argument even more explicit than it is in the *Meditations*. In More's text, the replies to at least some of the objections appear within the presentation of the proof itself, whereas with Descartes the replies are dispersed throughout various texts. The contribution of these replies to the ontological proof is thus more apparent in the *Antidote* than in the *Meditations*. Descartes' ontological argument indeed arises in the appropriate context, since it follows a proof of the innateness of geometrical ideas. The actual arguments for God's existence, however, appear tangential, and for this reason many have denied the importance of their context.[12] Such a misinterpretation is less likely in the case of More's *Antidote*.

Like the *Fifth Meditation*, the *Antidote* first treats the major premise, and then inserts the additional premise that we have an idea of God (chapter three).[13] More takes the opportunity to address some of the relevant objections to this premise, such as the suggestion that this idea is formed by transition from sensible ideas. His reply is appropriate to his concern for establishing the cogency of the analogy to geometry: whatever might be objected to the idea of God in this regard could hold equally of geometrical ideas. The problem with the transition objection is that it commits its proponent to nominalism universally; the full reply to this objection accordingly consists in the establishment of innatism. More's observation holds true at least of the most prevalent objectors (i.e., those, like Hobbes, who attack the ontological argument in this way, are indeed nominalists with respect to geometrical ideas).

The fourth chapter discusses the properties of the idea of God as an absolutely perfect being. In this endeavor his presentation again proves to be more thorough than Descartes." Whereas the latter often merely lists the properties that he perceives in the idea,[14] More offers a number of arguments, however humble, deriving those same properties from axioms. The most notable among these arguments appears in section six, in which More finally arrives at the deduction of the property relevant to the ontological argument, viz., necessary existence. His argument is simple and unconvincing: "it is more *perfection* that all this be *stable, immutable* and *necessary,* than *contingent* or *but possible.*" Since necessity is more perfect than mere possibility, it is the former modality that belongs to the idea of an absolutely perfect entity.[15]

However unsatisfying it is for a proponent of the ontological argument to claim simply that necessity is more perfect than contingency (since the connection between "perfection" and "necessity" is precisely what stands in need of explanation), this premise nonetheless marks an important development in the ontological argument. Descartes' deduction is merely psychological; he perceives that he has the idea of God and he lists the qualities that he associates with this idea. The relationship between the idea and its properties finds justification only in the fact that Descartes perceives precisely those properties to belong to his idea, hence his frequent reminder that *the mind perceives* necessary existence to belong to the nature of an *ens perfectissimum*. More eliminates this need to refer to private experience, and although he relies on an argument borrowed from Descartes, he employs it with greater consistency than the latter had done.[16] He relates the properties to the idea of God only logically, never psychologically; he proposes a more straightforward argument intended to show that the property of "necessary existence" belongs to the idea of an absolutely perfect being. The result is that he increases, at least in spirit, the pedagogical value of the argument. Anyone who accepts the premise (that necessity is more perfect than contingency) will accept the conclusion (that a perfect being is necessary), and there is no need to appeal to the privileged standpoint of the Cartesian philosopher.

Chapters five through seven of the *Antidote* supply the arguments for innateness. Since the concern is ultimately to strengthen the analogy to geometry, these arguments do not initially treat the idea of God. More had already referred to the analogy in his defense against the transition objection: if the idea of God is merely nominal, so are the ideas of geometrical figures. His strategy is to prove the latter to be innate and mind-independent, and then to show that the same arguments apply also to the idea of God. The arguments he proposes in this vein are philosophical commonplaces, echoing Platonic texts as much as the *Fifth Meditation*.[17] "Material subjects," More argues, fail to convey to the mind the geometrical properties of the triangle.[18] The latter properties are more exact than are anything acquired through perception. Some theory of innateness or recollection is thus necessary to explain our geometrical knowledge.[19] In the subsequent chapter More lists a second characteristic of innate ideas: assent to them is involuntary. He then hastens to the conclusion that any ideas to which we involuntarily assent "must therefore be concluded not fortuitous or arbitrary, but natural to the soul."[20]

With the criteria for innateness now determined, More proceeds to apply these to the idea of "a Being absolutely perfect." Since our idea of God is involuntary, it must be natural to the soul, rather than invented by us. His conclusion in this case is stronger than is warranted, since he supplies no evidence that involuntariness alone is a *sufficient* condition for innateness. The third section of chapter seven nonetheless draws the conclusion of a relatively thorough, if not entirely flawless, proof of the minor premise:

> Wherefore now to re-assume what we have for a while laid aside, the idea of a Being absolutely perfect above proposed; it being in such sort set forth that a man cannot rid his mind of it, but he must needs acknowledge it to be indeed the idea of such a being, it will follow, that it is no arbitrary or fortuitous conceit, but necessary, and therefore natural to the soul at least, if not ever actually there.

The deliberations in chapters three through seven conclude with this assertion that the idea of a perfect being as necessarily existent is a "true" idea. With this much conceded, the conclusion to the argument, it appears to More, follows immediately. The opening passage of chapter eight proclaims that the matter is complete: "For if this idea or notion of God be true, as I have undeniably proved, it is also undeniably true that he doth exist."[21] The fact that More concludes the ontological argument at this point reveals his conviction that the epistemological objections to the idea of God are the only truly threatening objections to the ontological argument. Once these are defeated, the argument is complete. Here is further evidence that More is concerned chiefly with an opponent like Hobbes.

The discussion nonetheless concludes with a refutation of two other traditional objections. These appear to More to be something of an afterthought, and he discards them as if they were entirely unreasonable misunderstandings. His formulation of the second Thomistic objection serves only to remind of the role of the major premise in discarding that scholastic dithering: anyone who concedes the minor premise (that necessary existence belongs to the notion of God) but asserts that it does not follow that God exists "in fact" engages in "a palpable contradiction as much as respects us and our faculties, and we have nothing more inward and immediate than these to steer us by."[22]

His remarks in response to a related objection, however, reveal the flaw in his entire presentation. The fatal blow to his argument occurs when he reminds an imagined objector that essence and existence are indistinguishable in the case of God. This appeal is in reply to the following statement of the modal objection:

> Nor is it sufficient ground to diffide to the strength of this argument, because our fancy can shuffle in this abater, viz., that indeed this idea of God, supposing God did exist, shows us that his existence is necessary, but it does not show us that he doth necessarily exist.[23]

The proposed objection rests on the distinction between hypothetical and absolute necessity. The fact of God's existence, the objector suggests, is independent of our (hypothetical) idea of his necessary existence. More responds to this by repeating, nearly verbatim, a Cartesian caveat concerning the separation of essence and existence[24]:

For he that answers thus, does not observe out of what prejudice he is enabled to make this answer, which is this: he being accustomed to fancy the notion or nature of everything else without existence, and so ever easily separating essence and existence in them, he unawares takes the same liberty, and divides existence from that essence to which existence itself is essential. And that's the witty fallacy his unwariness has entangled him in.[25]

The modal objector asserts that our idea of the necessity of the divine existence does not imply its actual existence; the existence of a thing is always a fact independent of our idea of that thing. More correctly observes, however, that in the case of God essence is inseparable from existence. Our consideration of the essence, then, is already proof of the existence in question. In the unique case of God, existence is not a fact separable from his essence or idea. More's conclusion here is, with certain qualifications concerning our intellectual faculties and the relation of these to reality, justified, and he is right to point out that anyone who objects to the ontological argument by distinguishing hypothetical from absolute necessity has begged the central question of the argument. That distinction, the proponent of the ontological argument asserts, is valid in all cases *except* that of God.

The Thomistic fallacy notwithstanding, More's reminder of this metaphysical distinction indicates the failure of his entire endeavor. His intention is to present the argument in a more persuasive form so as to convince the atheist of the absurdity of infidelity. In order to achieve this end, he prefaces the final inference with an extended discussion of the idea of God, and in doing so he distinguishes the various steps in the argument more carefully than Descartes does. More thus obeys the ordinary laws of demonstration with admirable attentiveness. Like Descartes, he assents to the following maxim: "we are first to have a settled notion what God is, before we go about to demonstrate that he is."[26] The various subsidiary arguments to the minor premise (the proof of innateness, the deduction of necessary existence from the idea of God, etc.) serve this end, comprising a preliminary examination of the essence or notion of God. The inference to God's actual existence appears only at the end of this discussion. This last fact, however, represents the fatal consequence of the systematic presentation of the ontological argument: in order to clarify the various steps in the argument, it was necessary to distinguish the essence of God (i.e., "what God is") from his existence ("that he is"). The systematic presentation of the ontological argument thereby contradicts the basic presupposition of that same argument, viz., that the essence and existence of God are inseparable.

The Thomistic objector, then, is not as dull-witted as More would have us believe. That objector, like the empirical objector, indeed overlooks the fact that essence and existence are supposed to be inseparable in the case of God. In presenting the argument in its demonstrative form, however, Descartes and More make the exact same error. The distinction between hypothetical and absolute necessity is thus an appropriate response to *the syllogistic presentation* of the ontological argument; in presenting it the objector is merely insisting upon accepted norms of demonstration, norms that Descartes and More make a pretense of respecting. Although More is correct to indicate the fallacy underlying the distinction in question, his is, at that point in the argument, an unfair move; it is he who begins by distinguishing (in his proofs of the premises) the essence from the existence of God. It is nothing short of hypocrisy to subsequently blame an objector for so distinguishing.

The lesson to be learned from More's failure is an important one: the insight at the core of the ontological argument is at odds with the presentation of that same argument. In other words, although the crux of the argument is the claim that essence and existence are inseparable in the case of God, the need for demonstration requires that these nonetheless be distinguished. The tension between intuition and demonstration that we find in Descartes is thus a natural development of the argument itself. More's attempt to remove the intuition is unsuccessful, not because his argument remains intuitive, but rather because the demonstration is self-defeating. Any ontological syllogism is inherently misleading. Malebranche's attempt to eliminate the semblance of demonstration provides a more promising direction, although this leads ultimately to the cul-de-sac of rationalist metaphysics, not only in Malebranche but also in Spinoza. In these cases any hope of convincing the atheist with an ontological argument is abandoned.

CUDWORTH AND THE REFUTATION OF ATHEISM

Like More, Ralph Cudworth is concerned to prevent the rise of atheism in England. The influence of Hobbesian materialism in particular is an ever-present worry for both authors. In this context, the measure of any demonstration of God's existence is its usefulness in converting nonbelievers, or at least in dissuading young philosophers from succumbing to the extreme materialism of Hobbes. The employment of the Cartesian ontological argument to this end reaches its pinnacle in More's *Antidote*. No other philosopher in the modern period will share More's optimism in this regard.[27] Throughout the latter half of the seventeenth century, the philosophers at Cambridge and elsewhere become increasingly wary of the Cartesian argument, although no important objections accompany the argument's demise. By the turn of the eighteenth century the ontological argument plays virtually no role in the defense of theism in English philosophy.[28] The downfall of the argument occurs here on different grounds than it does in Germany a century afterward. There are no claims that it contains an irreparable formal flaw. Rather, it becomes the accepted opinion that the argument represents a piece of reasoning too subtle to sway the minds of the irreligious. Cudworth's *The True Intellectual System of the Universe* (1678) voices one of the earliest pronouncements of this judgment.

Only a few years younger than More, Ralph Cudworth (1617–1689) also spends his entire career in Cambridge. Although the two "Platonists" are friends and hold a number of philosophical positions in common, their public presentations of philosophy could not be more different. While More is an inimitable stylist who offers only the most concise and accessible arguments and expresses these with great clarity and wit, Cudworth disperses his arguments among tedious, loosely connected treatments of ancient sources. For that reason the *True System* is one of the most impenetrable works of the time period. In it Cudworth indeed provides arguments that are as thorough and precise as those found in Henry More. Since these arguments are buried within literally thousands of pages of reports, however, they are difficult even to find. This fact colors with irony the author's repeatedly stated concern for convincing the masses: the masses are indeed unlikely to dig so deeply for his arguments.[29] The *True System* is, however, not without its virtues, and among them is the fact that it represents something of a landmark in classical learning. For this reason, and surely for others, it remains an important source into the eighteenth century. In 1733, J. L. Mosheim translates it into Latin, after which time it enjoys some popularity also in Germany.[30]

In regards to the ontological argument Cudworth occupies a unique position with respect to the problem of demonstrability. Of all those who write extensively on the argument, he is the only one who refrains from taking a position concerning its validity. He presents the argument in an insightful fashion, and he moves carefully from one variation of it to another. His discussion of the several objections to the argument indicates his awareness of the difficulties that the Cartesian proof involves; this awareness is balanced by his judicious consideration of the defense of the argument.

The undeniable fact that the argument suffers considerable disrepute both before and after Descartes is alone cause for hesitation, as Cudworth sees it. If the goal is to convince people, then even a perfectly sound argument that only appears invalid is of little use. Descartes is no less aware of this than is Cudworth, and it is only More who is naïve in this respect. Of course, Descartes remains convinced of the soundness of his argument, and he makes concessions only of its pedagogical weakness. For Cudworth, however, the strength of any argument lies at least partly in its persuasiveness, and in this regard he is right to find every version of the ontological argument lacking. For that reason he refuses to lend his authority to what he calls the "Cartesian argument." His cautious position soon becomes the standard among English philosophers; for the remainder of the seventeenth century references to the proof of God's existence "from his idea" reflect Cudworth's caution.

Although Cudworth ultimately deems unpersuasive each of the arguments he summarizes, he also refrains from overtly attacking the ontological inference. In this regard he asserts that he has no interest in refuting an argument in favor of the noble cause. At the same time, however, he does not wish to endorse one that is unlikely to be successful:

> ... it is certain, that by one means or another, this (Cartesian) argument has not hitherto proved so fortunate and successful, there being many who cannot be made sensible of any efficacy therein, and not a few, who condemn it to be a mere sophism. As for ourselves, we neither have any mind to quarrel with other men's arguments *pro Deo*; nor yet would we be thought, in this cause, to lay stress upon anything which is not in every way solid and substantial.[31]

He then proceeds to summarize the case to be made both for and against the "Cartesian argument." We note here in passing that Cudworth omits the major premise of the argument, an omission that soon becomes commonplace in formulations of the supposedly Cartesian proof. On Cudworth's telling, Descartes had argued only that "God, or an absolutely perfect being, includeth necessary existence in his very idea; and therefore he is."[32] Cudworth's elaboration of the objections and the replies thereto, however, demonstrates a more thorough familiarity with the relevant debates. There is much evidence that he learned of the proof primarily from More's *Antidote*[33] (hence his failure to notice that the latter follows the format of the Cartesian syllogism), although he is aware that his friend is merely borrowing from their (now long deceased) French contemporary. His reliance upon More explains his emphasis on the modal objection, which he formulates as follows:

> Wherefore here lies a fallacy in this argumentation, when from the necessity of existence affirmed only hypothetically, or upon supposition of a perfect being, the conclusion is made concerning it absolutely.... From the idea of a perfect being including necessary existence in it, it follows undeniably, that if there be anything absolutely perfect, it must exist necessarily, and not contingently: but it doth not follow, that there must of necessity be such a perfect being existing; these two propositions carrying a very different sense from one another.[34]

In his statement of the defense of the ontological argument, Cudworth furnishes a reply to this objection that is slightly less precise than the one More proposes, but that nonetheless reveals a grasp of the underlying thesis of the ontological argument (viz., that essence and existence are inseparable in the case of God). His contention is similar to one that Descartes reiterates *ad nauseum*: from the fact that something is true of creatures it does not follow that the same is also true of God. We can imagine finite things to not exist precisely because necessary existence does not belong to their nature. Supposition of the existence of such finite things is always merely hypothetical, not necessary. It does not follow from this general truth, however, that the same is also true of the idea of God. The premise asserts God's existence absolutely, not hypothetically:

> True, indeed, we have the ideas of many things in our minds, that never were, nor will be; but these are only such as include no necessary, but contingent existence in their nature; and it does not therefore follow, that a perfect being, which includes necessity of existence in its idea, may, notwithstanding, not be. Wherefore this necessity of existence, or impossibility of non-existence, contained in the idea of a perfect being, must not be taken hypothetically or only consequentially ... but absolutely....[35]

With this Cudworth states both the principal objection to the argument as a demonstration of theism, viz. that arguments of this type assert existence only hypothetically, and the appropriate reply to that objection, viz., that this particular argument asserts something uniquely absolute. The ontological argument is indeed in this respect a very unusual argument. Both the objection and its reply appear valid, the former as concerns the norms of demonstration, the latter as concerns consistency with the assumptions of the proof. This perplexing appearance, of course, results precisely from the fact that the argument's underlying assumptions are at odds with those norms of demonstration. Cudworth's indecision is thus not inappropriate. He leaves it to "the impartial reader" to make his own judgment, noting that "it is not very probable that many atheists will be convinced thereby."[36]

LOCKE AND THE DISSOLUTION OF THE CONTEXT OF THE PROOF

Although it is not impossible that Cudworth achieves his state of indecision as a result merely of sustained contemplation of the form of the ontological argument, as he finds this in More's *Antidote* and (perhaps) the *Meditations*, it is more likely that some historical inefficacy of this argument motivates his position. In 1678 there is probably less reason to be optimistic about an a priori proof for theism than in 1652.[37] Cudworth's language in the *True System* suggests that his concern lies indeed with efficacy, and in the twenty-five years following the *Antidote* More seems to have persuaded very few, if any, to subscribe to the Cartesian proof. On the other hand, Cudworth's hesitation in criticizing the argument also becomes almost *de rigueur* for the remainder of the century: although no one seems to actually advocate the proof, philosophers of all sorts profess to lack any direct criticism of its form. Among these philosophers is, curiously enough, John Locke.

Although Locke (1632–1704) is certainly familiar with the writings of the Cambridge philosophers (Locke is associated with Cudworth's daughter),[38] his orientation to philosophy is dramatically different. From the earliest he appears to be an opponent of Cartesianism, and he famously develops a critique of the doctrine of innate ideas.[39] In the process he not only adopts the old maxim that "there is nothing in the intellect that was not previously in the senses," but also defends this principle with an extensive account of the human mind. Given the centrality to the available versions of the ontological argument (More's and Descartes') of the doctrine of innate ideas, then, it seems that Locke would have as much right as anyone to reject the proof out of hand. When he arrives at the argument in his *Essay Concerning Human Understanding* (1789), however, he assumes the same cautious stance we find in Cudworth:

> How far the idea of a most perfect Being, which a man may frame in his mind, does or does not prove the existence of a God, I will not here examine. For in the different make of men's tempers, and application of their thoughts, some arguments prevail more on one, and some on another, for the confirmation of the same truth. But yet, I think, this I may say, that it is an ill way of establishing this truth, and silencing atheists, to lay the whole stress of so important a point, as this, upon that sole foundation.[40]

Although Locke neglects to offer any direct objections to the ontological argument, his successes in the *Essay* indeed serve to contribute to the downfall of this proof in England. Due in no small part to his efforts, empiricism soon becomes prominent in philosophy throughout Britain.[41] Although there appears among them no objector to the ontological argument of the quality of Kant or Gassendi, the philosophers in Britain follow Locke's lead in dissolving the entire context in which the argument was able to flourish. With Locke the doctrine of innate ideas becomes unfashionable; among English philosophers after Henry More there seems to be little in the direction of a doctrine of clear and distinct ideas; the theological doctrines that maintain currency in France and Germany find few, if any, proponents north of the Channel.[42] Philosophers like Locke thereby succeed in defeating the ontological argument, at least historically if not philosophically, despite their refusal to examine its validity.

"SOMETHING VERY SINGULAR": CLARKE'S *DEMONSTRATION*

Both Cudworth and Locke limit their remarks on the "Cartesian" argument to summary of previously espoused views, together with the observation that the matter is both difficult to decide and inconsequential with regard to the vital task of persuading potential atheists. Cudworth's presentation of the argument is in some respects inferior to More's presentation of the same: his biggest innovation is an argument from possibility that he could have borrowed from Mersenne, and that he also proposes with Pyrrhonian equanimity.[43] Locke, on the other hand, writes in a way suggestive of familiarity with some context of the dispute, but casts the matter aside before adding any insight of his own.[44] The distinguishing characteristic of both discussions is a reservation concerning the ability of the argument to compel others to assume the faith. This worry accompanies references to the a priori argument into the eighteenth century. The most notable discussion of the ontological argument in the decades following the *Essay* appears in Samuel Clarke's 1705 treatise *A Demonstration of the Being and Attributes of God*.

The repute of Clarke (1675–1729) is due principally to his defense of Newton against Leibniz regarding the nature of space, and his correspondence with Leibniz belongs to the canon of early modern philosophy.[45] His contribution to philosophical theology, however, also warrants recognition. In the *Demonstration* he offers cosmological argument for the existence of a "necessary being," and he presents this type of reasoning in a powerful yet accessible manner. In the context of defending his argument he deals also with certain weaknesses in the ontological proof as he is aware of it.[46] A difficulty in assessing his view on the latter argument, however, lies in the fact that he changes the tenor of this discussion throughout the many editions of his *Demonstration*.[47]

Clarke's opinion of the ontological argument indeed appears to vary over the course of his career. The later editions of the *Demonstration* suggest that he considers the argument to be unsound, and this impression is strengthened by a passage from his correspondence in which he dismisses the "scholastic way" of demonstrating the divine existence.[48] In the first edition (1705) of the *Demonstration*, however, Clarke's position is nearly indiscernible from Cudworth's. In that text he professes his inability to refute the Cartesian proof. His subsequent impatience with the proof represents only a change in emphasis, rather than a substantive shift of positions. In the editions of the 1720s he simply omits the several passages indicative of his indecision regarding the ontological argument (now a safer move, with no Englishman alive who would defend this argument), but he nonetheless allows in his preface that most *pro Deo* arguments are at least capable of satisfactory form.[49] The first edition had applied this admission specifically to the ontological proof:

> I do not mean to say positively, that the argument drawn from our including self-existence in the idea of God, or from our comprehending it in the definition or notion we frame of him, is wholly inconclusive and ineffectual to

prove his actual existence. Possible by a very nice and accurate deduction, it may be found to be a satisfactory proof.[50]

Such open-mindedness is qualified by his conviction, which he shares with Cudworth and Locke, that the very controversy over the argument speaks against its utility.[51] Clarke's intention in discussing the ontological proof is only to show that this argument is inferior to his own cosmological proof of the deity, and this further reduces the urgency of passing judgment concerning the Cartesian argument. He nonetheless makes a few insightful comments regarding the shortcoming of the demonstration of the argument, and these reveal an even greater acuity than is to be found in Cudworth and More.

Clarke provides one concise objection to the ontological argument that indicates a fundamental problem with some presentations of that proof: the "nominal idea" asserted in the premise fails to proffer the connection to the "real idea" required for the conclusion.[52] It is not enough, Clarke repeats, to have the idea "in my mind," but I must also acquire the idea "of the thing." This rather awkwardly stated objection appears, on the surface, to be Thomistic. Thomistic objections, however, stem from merely logical considerations.[53] Clarke's objection is much deeper. He is not baldly asserting, like Thomas or Caterus, that as a rule there can be no inferences from thought to existence. Unlike the Thomist, Clarke recognizes that "there is something very singular in the idea of necessary existence."[54] He does not, then, simply remind us that there is a distinction between thought and existence, since he recognizes that the question is precisely whether this distinction holds in this one, unique case. He is rather noting that the brief presentation of the ontological argument does not explain why this instance is unique, and it thus fails to persuade anyone who is not predisposed to accepting it. The definition of God, he reminds us, as a necessarily existent being does not *alone* convey the insight that is required in order to accept the conclusion.

He concludes with the claim that "I must see wherein consists the absolute impossibility of removing that idea." What is required is some explanation of the relationship between the idea of God that is "in my mind" and God himself, one that would also explain why the idea is constitutive of the mind (and thus not removable from it). With this objection, Clarke demonstrates both remarkable discernment with respect to the argument and unawareness of its more complete formulations. Cartesian philosophers as early as the 1650s recognize this same need, and seek to explain the human mind and its idea of God accordingly.[55] The result is that the argument is gradually freed from its dependence upon the nominal definition of God, so that the relevance of a criticism like this one gradually diminishes. Eventually, both Spinoza and Malebranche present the argument in such a manner that it lacks even an apparent distinction between the idea of God and God himself (i.e., between the "nominal" and "real" ideas).

Although it is not impossible that Clarke read either Malebranche's *Search for the Truth*, this having been translated into English, or some Spinoza prior to 1705, it is also understandable that he fails to consider how their respective philosophies of mind address the criticism he raises. First, Clarke is likely to have sided with Henry More in the latter's polemic against Spinoza.[56] Second, even if Clarke read the chapter on "Descartes' proof" from Malebranche's *Search*, he does not seem to have that text in mind when he compiles the *Demonstration*. His brief reference to an argument like the "Cartesian" suggests he is thinking of presentations like that found in More's *Antidote*, against which his objection is entirely appropriate.[57]

NOTES

1. All citations will be from the *Philosophical Writings of Henry More*, ed. Flora Mackinnon, Oxford University Press, 1925. The text reprinted in that volume is based on the third edition of 1662. I frequently modernize the spelling and remove capitalization from More's text. All references are by book, chapter, and section number, so as to facilitate reference to other editions.

2. More also employs an argument similar to Descartes' *a posteriori* argument, as well as a number of teleological arguments.

3. See http://www.veg.ca/content/view/52/83/, and, e.g., Hartshorne, pp. 176–78.

4. Henrich was apparently impressed by passages like that from the *True Intellectual System of the Universe* (hereafter "*True System*"), v. 2, pp. 144–45. References to Cudworth's text are by page and volume number to the First American Edition by Andover (1839), which is based on the 1731 London edition.

5. Apart from the *Antidote*, his books include *The Immortality of the Soul* (1659), *Enchiridion Ethicum* (1666), and *Enchiridion Metaphysicum* (1671).

6. The correspondence begins late in 1648 and continues into 1649.

7. A passage from Cudworth (*True System*, v.2, p. 147) defines the atheism debate of the time in distinctly materialist terms: "... here is the state of controversy

betwixt the theists and atheists, whether that, which existed of itself from all eternity, and was the cause of all other things, were a perfect being and God, or the most imperfect of all things whatsoever, inanimate and senseless matter."

8. *Antidote*, bk. I, chap. II, sec. 1.

9. Ibid., sec. 3–5.

10. Ibid., sec. 5.

11. Ibid., sec. 2 (my emphasis). For an elaboration of More's doctrine of assent and his refutation of skepticism, see Francesco Tomasoni's "'Conjecture,' 'Conceivability,' 'Existence' between Henry More and Ralph Cudworth," in *The Return of Scepticism: from Hobbes and Descartes to Bayle*, Kluwer 2003.

12 Henri Gouhier is the classical proponent of this view. See his "La prevue ontologique de Descartes," in *Revue Internationale de Philosophie* 7, 1954, 295ff. Henrich (p. 20) sides with Gouhier and against Guerolt by claiming that the architectonic of the *Meditations* is irrelevant to the formulation of the ontological argument: "Whether or not the proof is dependent upon the wider context of Descartes' system is entirely without consequence for the history of ontotheology."

13. The argument in the *Fifth Meditation* thus has three premises, which the syllogistic presentation compacts into just two by referring to the nature of God, rather than the idea.

14. AT VII 45; CSM II 31.

15. In chapter 8, sec. 5 he is more thorough, supplying the missing premise: ". . . we must needs attribute to the idea of God either contingency, impossibility or necessity of actual existence (some one of these belonging to every idea imaginable). . . ."

16. *Second Replies*: AT VII 150–51; CSM II 107.

17. For a similar argument by Descartes, see AT VII 381–82; CSM II 262. The reading of Platonic texts seems to have been fairly common at Cambridge in seventeenth century. See W. R. Sorley's *A History of British Philosophy to 1900*, 2nd ed., Cambridge, 1965, pp. 75–103.

18. *Antidote*, bk. I, ch. 6, sec. 1.

19. More's account is more Platonic than Cartesian, although he provides some insight into the connection between these positions. He also proposes a perceptive criticism of those theories that take innate to mean "always present," anticipating Leibniz's criticism of Locke and echoing Descartes' reply to Hobbes (AT VII 189; CSM II 132).

20. *Antidote*, bk. I, chap. 7, sec. 2.

21. Ibid., chap. 8, sec. 1.

22. Ibid., sec. 3.

23. Ibid., sec. 2.

24. More obviously borrows from the *Fifth Meditation*, AT VII 66; CSM II 45–46. There Descartes writes, "Since I have been accustomed to distinguish between

existence and essence in everything else, I find it easy to persuade myself that existence can also be separated from the essence of God. . . ."

25. *Antidote*, bk. I, chapter 8, sec. 2.

26. Ibid., bk. I, chap. 3, section heading 1; cf. Descartes, *First Replies*.

27. Perhaps Leibniz, at certain points of his career, had a similar confidence.

28. More is the last important English philosopher of the modern period, to my knowledge, who is an unqualified proponent of the argument. Cudworth, Clarke, and others show degrees of indecision about the argument.

29. I owe thanks to an anonymous referee for emphasizing the irony in this.

30. *Cudworthi systema intellectuale*, Jena, 1733.

31. *True System*, v. 2, p. 141.

32. Ibid., v. 2, p. 140.

33. E.g., Cudworth (p. 143) repeats the modal arguments from More's *Antidote*, bk. I, chap. 8, sec. 4; Cudworth, however, attributes the main argument to Descartes, not to More. Perhaps he read the *Fifth Meditation* and considered his own formulation to be an abbreviation of the perfection argument. In any case, it is clear that he is not thinking of the improved and elaborated syllogisms of the *First* and *Second Replies*.

34. *True Systems*, v. 2, p. 142.

35. Ibid., v. 2, p. 143; Cudworth takes this idea from More's *Antidote*, bk. I, chapter 8, sec. 2.

36. Ibid., v. 2, p. 144.

37. For a brief discussion of the state of philosophy in England at this time, see Sorley, chaps. 5 and 6.

38. Locke lived with Cudworth's daughter, Lady Masham, and her husband after 1791. Any account of Locke's life and work will provide the details of this arrangement, as well as of Locke's longtime relation to Masham (see Richard Aaron, *John Locke*, 2nd ed., Oxford, 1965, pp. 36–50).

39. *An Essay Concerning Human Understanding*, bk. I, chaps. 1–4.

40. Ibid., bk. 4, chap. 10, #7. I have taken the quotes from this text from the edition by Peter H. Nidditch (Oxford, 1975). I have, however, taken the liberty of modifying the spelling. It is likely that Locke's formulates this position independently of Cudworth, since much of book 4 of the essay appears to have been written in the 1670s, or before the appearance of the *True System*. For details, consult Richard Aaron's "How the *Essay* was written," in his *John Locke*, 2nd ed., Oxford, 1965, pp. 50–55.

41. Although there are some defenses of innatism in England after Locke (e.g., John Norris, *An Essay towards the Theory of the Ideal or Intelligible World*, 1704), Locke seems to have been victorious regarding the most import matters of epistemology.

42. The post-Lockean period saw the predominance of deism in theology (see Sorley, chap. 7).

43. *True Systems*, v. 2, pp. 144–45.

44. Locke refers to an unnamed philosopher who uses the ontological as the sole proof of the divinity. Perhaps he is referring to Descartes, in which case Locke means to refer to the various Cartesian arguments when he writes of a proof "from the idea of a most perfect Being."

45. *G. W. Leibniz and Samuel Clarke: Correspondence*, edited by Roger Ariew, Hackett, 2000.

46. At this point in England the sources for the argument are more numerous. Apart from Descartes, More, and Cudworth, whose books are still in circulation, Malebranche's *Search for Truth* is available in English translation from 1694.

47. The *Demonstration* undergoes roughly eight editions, with some considerable changes, between 1705 and Clarke's death. The primary impetus for the changes are Clarke's evolving views on the trinity.

48. "The answer to a sixth letter being part of a letter written to another gentleman. . . ." (reprinted in the Cambridge edition of the *Demonstration* [*A Demonstration of the Being and Attributes of God and Other Writings*, ed. Ezio Vailati, Cambridge, 1998], p. 113). The Cambridge edition is based on the *The Works of Samuel Clarke* (New York, Garland, 1978) and thus on the 1738 edition. A reprint of the first edition is available through Frommann Verlag (Stuttgart, 1964, hereafter "1705").

49. The arguments simply need to be separated "from the false and uncertain reasoning which have sometimes been intermixed with them" (Cambridge edition, p. 7).

50. 1705, p. 38.

51. "But that it is not a clear and obvious demonstration fitted to convince and put the atheist to silence; appears from the endless disputes maintained by learned men concerning it, without being able to falsify each other on either side of the question" (ibid.). The similarity between this passage and the above-cited passage from the *True System* suggests that Clarke's view of the ontological argument in this period is strongly influenced by Cudworth.

52. This terminology, though not the gist of the criticism, also disappears from the later editions.

53. Hence Henrich labels the Thomistic objection "the logical objection."

54. 1705, p. 40. In the later editions Clarke replaces "it is not easy to disprove, because, it must be confessed, there is something very singular in the idea of necessary existence" with (Cambridge edition, p. 16) "their subtle arguments upon this head are sufficient to raise a cloud not very easy to be seen through."

55. Arnold Geulincx, Malebranche, and Spinoza are the best examples of this (see chapters 3 and 4 below).

56. The texts containing More's criticisms of Spinoza are reproduced in *Henry More's Refutation of Spinoza*, Hildesheim, New York, 1991.

57. The references to "the idea of God" or "the definition or notion we frame of him," as well as the emphasis on the impossibility of "removing" the idea, suggest that

Clarke is referring either to More's *Antidote* or a text very much like it. Cudworth indeed holds a view on the human mind in relation to God that is very similar to that found among French philosophers of the time (and Clarke had to be aware of Cudworth's view), but he does not relate this theory explicitly to the ontological argument (see *True Systems*, v. 2, pp. 160 ff.).

Chapter Three

BEING AND INTUITION

Malebranche's Appropriation of the Argument

Although the decline of the ontological argument within English philosophy suggests that the argument lacks any efficacy in converting the atheist, this result establishes nothing concerning the actual strength of the reasoning involved in the Cartesian proof. Soundness is to be distinguished from persuasiveness. If Descartes' ontological argument possesses any of the former, this fact is discoverable only in a very abstract speculative context. The second path pursued by the defenders of the Cartesian argument consists in the refinement of that context. In this case, the task is not to present the argument in a popular and accessible form, but rather to bring all aspects of philosophical knowledge into conformity with the central insight expressed in the argument. Of the numerous philosophers who contribute to this development, Malebranche is the first to make significant progress.

In stark contrast to Henry More, Malebranche makes no pretenses concerning the pedagogical value of the ontological argument. The very placement of the argument within his *Search after the Truth* already provides an apologia for the inaccessibility of the proof.[1] Book four of that work is titled "The Inclinations: Or, The Mind's Natural Impulses." The eleventh chapter of this book deals with "The Love of Pleasure in Relation to the Speculative Sciences." The third and final section of that chapter provides an "Elucidation of Descartes' Proof of the Existence of God." Why does Malebranche discuss one of the most abstruse arguments from the metaphysicians' book in a chapter on pleasure? His intention is to explain how lively sensations inhibit our ability to comprehend abstract truths. In general, men are too engrossed in the pleasures of the senses to grasp even the most evident truths, if these latter are not such as appeal to sensation. It should only be expected, then, that very few are capable of grasping a subtle metaphysical argument like the Cartesian one; his subsequent elucidation of that argument ends with the proclamation: "but it is rather useless to propose these demonstrations to ordinary men."[2]

THE CARTESIAN ARGUMENT AND THE THOMISTIC OBJECTIONS

Since the inaccessibility of the argument derives partly from its dependence upon epistemological dogma, Malebranche approaches his explanation of Descartes' argument via a discussion of the importance of the major premise. The second section of the chapter in question provides examples of simple truths that are not commonly known due to the fact that they make no impression on the senses. The most important such example is the first principle of science, the Cartesian "rule for truth."[3] Although fewer men assent to this rule ("that everything one clearly conceives is precisely such as one conceives it") than to some other maxims, such as that "the whole is greater than its parts,"[4] the popularity of these maxims is no indication of either their importance or their degree of evidence. Universality of assent does not determine logical priority. In this particular case, according to Malebranche, the second, more common rule concerning wholes and parts is dependent on the first, more abstract principle. The Cartesian rule is an axiom from which we can infer the other principle, and not vice versa.

The purpose of demonstrating the dependence of logical maxims upon the Cartesian rule is to illustrate the indispensability of that principle for any knowledge claim whatsoever. In this context the ontological argument appears only as a controversial employment of a rule, rather than as a singular argument; the syllogistic presentation of that argument is a piece of reasoning analogous, at least in its dependence on the rule for truth, to any other knowledge claim. All knowledge claims, including our knowledge that the whole is greater than its parts, consist of inferences from the same major premise:

> Here is the first principle: one should attribute to a thing what one clearly conceives to be included in the idea that represents it; we clearly conceive that

there is more magnitude in our idea of a whole than in our idea of its part; that possible existence is contained in the idea of a mountain of marble; that impossible existence is part of the idea of a mountain without a valley, and that necessary existence is contained in the idea we have of God, i.e., in our idea of an infinitely perfect being: therefore, the whole is greater than its parts; . . . therefore, God or the infinitely perfect being necessarily exists.[5]

The conclusions are all at an equal remove from the same first premise, and thus are equally evident: "it is therefore as evident that God exists as that the whole is greater than its part."[6] In light of this analogy between the Cartesian argument and all other knowledge claims, the Thomistic objector appears to be a universal skeptic. To demonstrate this point Malebranche reapplies his analogy in response to the second formulation of that objection (i.e., the claim "that the argument results in this conclusion only if we assume it to be true that God exists").[7] Granting the analogy, even basic geometrical claims conceal inferences from the rule for truth. Thomas's objection is thus as applicable to those claims as it is to the ontological argument. The objectors, then, must conclude that "a square has four sides only assuming that it has them." In other words, if the ontological argument is question-begging, then so is every other knowledge claim.[8]

The discussion to this point demonstrates only Malebranche's awareness of the context of the Cartesian argument. Descartes had already successfully defended his argument against the Thomistic objections, and in the passage in question Malebranche is merely explaining this defense; his clarification of his predecessor's view does not, in this instance, imply his own assent.[9] The analogy he draws serves as a reminder that the Cartesian argument appears in a philosophical context in which the proof of the existence of God stands on the same terrain as every other truth; the ontological syllogism is merely a way of condensing that context.

This initial defense of Descartes is somewhat trivial. Only those who overlook the fact that the rule for truth serves as a premise in the argument (i.e., those who attack the perfection argument instead of the complete syllogism) are capable of being misled about the Thomistic objection. The thoroughness with which philosophers in the seventeenth century studied the Cartesian texts, however, makes this prefatory discussion superfluous, except retrospectively. It is not until the eighteenth century that ignorance of the full Cartesian argument prevails, and only then does the Thomistic objection also regain prevalence. In the middle and late seventeenth century it is rather other aspects of the argument, such as the idea of God and the relation of this to the finitude of our minds, that require elaboration.

BEING AND BEINGS: A SOLUTION TO THE EMPIRICISTS' DILEMMA

It is in response to Gassendi's empirical objection that Malebranche takes his first strides beyond Descartes. The latter had indeed succeeded only in revealing a certain shortsightedness in the empirical objection.[10] The claim in the minor premise of the ontological argument, Descartes had reminded his opponents, is not simply that existence is a property, but rather that necessary existence is a property uniquely ascribable to God. While real existence does not belong to the idea of any thing, modality of existence does belong to ideas. In respect to modality of existence the idea of God is to be distinguished from every other idea. Objections like Gassendi's arise only as a result of a failure to attend to (or a refusal to accept) this distinction. Malebranche heeds this warning, but manages to discourage misunderstandings like Gassendi's by securing a more consistent position on the nature of God.

One can hardly deny that Descartes' reply to Gassendi appears *ad hoc*. It is an entirely natural response to the ontological argument of the *Meditations* to imagine a similitude between the idea of God and other ideas, especially in light of both the analogy with the triangle and the universal applicability of the major premise. Descartes' psychological manner of procedure provides further encouragement to the empirical objector. In his *Third Meditation*, for instance, he discovers the idea of God in the "storehouse" of his own mind alongside so many other ideas.[11] Even Cartesian philosophers like Clauberg, who are sensitive to other shortcomings of Descartes' approach, emphasize that we have an idea of God "among our other ideas."[12] It is only understandable, then, if objectors tend to attribute some of the general characteristics of ideas to the idea of God; for the Cartesians to *subsequently* reply that this one idea is dramatically different seems a bit unfair. At the very least it must be admitted that, even if the empirical objection is a terrible misunderstanding, the Cartesian formulation of the argument lends itself to this misunderstanding.

Malebranche's solution to this dilemma is ingenious. On his account we possess no "idea" of God. This is not to say that we possess no knowledge of God, but rather that we know God immediately or "through himself." He adapts his understanding of what it means to have an "idea" accordingly: we perceive things through ideas only to the extent that their existence is separable from their essence. Since these are not separable in the case of God, the latter is not perceivable through any idea distinct from him, but only directly. The intention here is to remove the misleading analogy between the idea of God and other ideas, an analogy that leads almost inevitably to the empirical objection, by emphasizing the immediate, non-ideational character of our knowledge of God.[13]

It is unfortunate that Malebranche is not entirely unequivocal in this regard. Despite any inconsistencies in his terminology, however, his writings show a noticeable tendency toward the avoidance of discussing any "idea of God." While a number of passages in the *Search* employ that misleading locution, the later *Dialogues on Metaphysics* are more consistent. In that text he more explicitly restricts the term "idea" to finite entities; hence we find Theodore (who represents Malebranche) repeatedly remarking that no idea can be representative of God or the infinite.[14]

In any case, the univocal use of the term "idea" signals a dramatic departure from philosophical convention, especially in the wake of Descartes. The latter defines an idea as the immediate object of the mind,[15] but at the same time he discusses ideas as things "within the mind" or modalities of the mind,[16] an equivocation that causes him difficulties with materialists like Hobbes.[17] Malebranche resolves this confusion by using "idea" to refer only to the object of the mind, and not to the modality of the mind itself, and this clarification is central to his extended encounter with Arnauld.[18] This allows him to specify that the ideas we perceive are not inside the mind. The removal of the other equivocation is a mere addendum to this point: only those things that we perceive through some archetype (viz., creatures), and not through themselves, are represented by ideas.

If the restricted application of the term "idea" is one way of emphasizing the difference between God and creatures, Malebranche does not limit himself to this. More important is his equation of (the idea of) God with (the idea of) being simpliciter. The difference between God and creatures, he explains, is the difference between "being without limit" (*l'etre sans restriction*) and particular or "such" beings (*un tel etre*). The fallacy in which the empirical objector finds himself trapped, then, is the fallacy of thinking of God as a particular being, or as an individual subsumable under the species "thing" or "entity." "For those who do not see that God exists," he concludes, "usually do not consider being, but a *such being* and consequently a being that can be or not be."[19]

This metaphysical distinction signals another advance in clarity from the Cartesian presentation. Although it is not uncommon in philosophical theology to equate God with being in general,[20] most presentations of the proofs of his existence proceed as if God were a particular being or entity. Descartes in particular engages in blatant equivocation in this regard. Not only does he encourage misunderstanding by comparing the idea of God to other ideas, he also misleads his critics by defining God as an *ens perfectissimum* (i.e., as a particular entity that differs from other entities only by degree). Just as it is natural for critics to imagine the idea of God to be like other ideas, so are they prone to considering even a perfect entity to be like other entities (i.e., to share the basic properties of a "thing" in general). Malebranche defines God, however, as "*l'etre sans restriction*," specifying that this is not any particular entity, and he thereby discourages misunderstandings like the empirical objection.[21]

In light of this clarification, the conclusion of the ontological argument appears such that it no longer contradicts either common parlance or the rules of demonstration, and in this respect it is less susceptible to both empirical and Thomistic objections. The argument no longer claims that existence follows from the idea of a certain entity, since we are dealing neither with an idea nor with an entity. The conclusion is rather that "being necessarily is." Malebranche's argument is thus also more thoroughly ontological than the Cartesian argument.[22] It is a claim regarding being, rather than any particular being. A contradiction lies in the claim, not that a particular entity does not exist, but rather that "being is not." Even if there were nothing in particular, Malebranche writes, there would still be being.[23]

Malebranche finds a final concession to the empirical objector in Descartes' ambivalence about attributing possibility to God, and it is worth mentioning how he corrects this problem. In many passages Descartes allows that it makes sense to discuss whether God is possible. Although he rejects Mersenne's possibility argument, the argument Leibniz later adopts, he nonetheless fails to consistently avoid appearing vulnerable to the possibility objection. The latter objection does not purport to be fatal to the argument,[24] but the arguments based on the objection make the ontological argument susceptible to the empirical objection. The reason for this is that the possibility arguments require a separation, at least as far as our thought is concerned, of the idea of God from the existence of the same. Malebranche, like Spinoza and Hegel after him, is more consistent on this point. Just as it is a mistake to speak of an idea that represents God, or being, so is it erroneous to speak of being as possible: "one cannot conceive (of God) simply as a possible being."[25] Possibility is a characteristic of ideas, and these are separable from the things they represent. Since there can be no idea or representation of being or God, it is wrong to attribute possibility to them.

THE CONCEIVABILITY PROBLEM AND THE RELATION OF THE HUMAN MIND TO GOD

Another unfortunate ambivalence that pervades the Cartesian presentation of the ontological argument becomes the subject of Malebranche's revision. On the one hand, Descartes admits of an infinite gulf between our mind and God. On the other hand, he insists that we possess a clear and distinct idea of the essence of (certain attributes of) God. In the first instance, Descartes advocates a radical subjectivism in which our finite human minds are separate from God; at the same time, however, he asserts that there is something divine about the human mind, and this assertion is necessary in order to justify his theological claims.[26] With respect to the proofs for the existence of God, Descartes resolves this conflict only by distinguishing between clear and adequate knowledge. Our finite minds are incapable of adequately conceiving of God, but God has placed in us a clear idea of at least part of his nature. Unfortunately, he offers no elaboration of how the idea of God in our finite minds relates to God himself, although he insists that we can infer from the former to the latter.[27]

In his immediate context Descartes already draws significant attention for his claim that he possessed a clear idea of God. For one, this doctrine seems to display a lack of reverence for the inconceivability of the deity.[28] Further, many (such as Revius) object that an image within a finite intellect could not represent an infinite being.[29] Subsequent proponents of the argument address these problems by progressively eliminating the subjectivism of Descartes' position. The gulf between our minds and God is not unbridgeable, it is claimed, not because God is conceivable, but because our mind is already a part of God. However insufficient our idea of God is, then, this insufficiency is qualified by the fact that our idea of God is an actual, albeit incomplete, part of God's own mind. If our idea of God is already present in God's mind, there is no infinite gap to bridge in the first place. Arnold Geulincx provides a quaint metaphor in explanation of this point:

In a field that is divided into numerous lots, each of which is separated from the others by a wall, the individual lots are nonetheless parts of the field. In this same way we are both divided from God and in him. And although we are limited, this is no ground for saying that God himself is limited — just as it is not said that the field itself is bound by walls, but rather that the lots are so bound.[30]

Much of post-Cartesian rationalist metaphysics consists largely in an elaboration of this metaphor, and it is only in such a context that an adequate response to the various epistemological objections to the ontological argument is possible. As in so many other instances, Malebranche makes a substantial advance in this regard. Like Geulincx, he employs a spatial allegory to explain the relation of the mind to God: "God is the intelligible world or the place of minds, as the material world is the place of bodies."[31] He goes beyond this, however, by removing the objects of our thought from our own minds, thereby completing the move away from the solipsism of Cartesian philosophy. Among his most well-known doctrines is the claim that "we see all things in God."[32] Our idea of any object, such as a geometrical figure, a body, etc., is not "in" our minds, as Descartes suggests it is. Rather, our mind and our ideas are separate from one another, although both are in God. In addition to the fact that this doctrine describes the human mind as more intimately dependent upon God, it is also a doctrine more amenable to realism than is Cartesian subjectivism: no longer is there any apparent contradiction between our fleeting mental states and the mind-independence of the objects of thought.[33] The ideas we perceive are not modifications of our own mind, but rather real entities in the intelligible world (i.e., in God).

The paradox implied by the presence of a representation of the infinite being within finite minds finds its solution in this same doctrine of "vision in God" (i.e., in the doctrine that our ideas are not internal to our minds). The ingenuity of this position lies in that it takes what appears to be an objection to ontotheology, viz. that "nothing finite can represent the infinite," and it converts it into a premise of the ontological argument. Indeed, from our very incapacity to represent the infinite Malebranche infers the existence of the same. We are incapable of representing God; if we think of him, then, it must be because he exists, in which case our thought of him is the immediate perception of his actuality.[34]

Although these reflections signal a distinct advance from the Cartesian position, a disproportion between the mind and its perception of God remains to be explained. In this context Malebranche resorts to a repetition of the distinction between clarity and adequacy: "we have of (the infinite), I do not say an *understanding* or a perception that describes and embraces it, but some perception of it, i.e., an infinitely limited perception, by contrast to a perfect understanding."[35] His only meager elaboration of this point involves an appeal to algebraic concepts: the product of our infinitely small perception and God's infinite nature is the "finite and constant magnitude" of the "soul's thinking capacity."[36] This unfortunate passage hints at the flaw in Malebranche's revision of the Cartesian argument: although his metaphysics resolves some of the paradoxes inherent to Descartes' ontological argument, Malebranche does not succeed in providing a suitable epistemological background for his theological claims.

THE ARISTES PARADOX AND THE INTUITION GOD

Malebranche indeed falls short of a complete removal of the tension between assertions about our (finite) perception of God and those about the (infinite) existent reality of God. Although his doctrine of the immediate intuition of God addresses, in one move, both the theological complaint that God's reality is inconceivable and the logical complaint that the finite cannot represent the infinite, he nonetheless fails to reconcile that intuition of God with the limitations of our faculties. To that extent his insistence that our perception of God is a direct perception of his reality only apparently eliminates the Cartesian confusion. In conceding that we do not comprehend God's nature, Malebranche places the alleged identity of essence and existence, and with that the entire efficacy of the ontological argument, beyond our intellective grasp. In the *Dialogues on Metaphysics* Theodore concedes this problem by distinguishing between our knowledge *what* God is and our knowledge *that* God is:

> In a sense, then, it is the divine substance of God that we see. But in this life we only see it in a way so confused and distant, that we see rather *that* it is than *what* it is; we see rather that it is the source and archetype of all being than its own nature or its perfections in themselves.[37]

The disciple Aristes astutely detects the contradiction in Theodore's position.[38] The entire purpose of distinguishing between being and beings, God and creatures, had been to show that God or being is not subject to representation and that the thought of God is therefore an immediate perception of his reality. At the end of the day, however, Malebranche concedes that we do not see the reality of God in itself, and that, *at least with respect to our perception*, there is a difference between what God is (i.e., the essence) and that God is (i.e., the existence). This division does not destroy the internal consistency of the ontological argument, but it does place the central insight of that argument (viz., the identity of God's essence and existence) beyond the realm of human knowledge. Theodore does not adequately reply to Aristes, but only takes solace in distinguishing two senses of our perception of God: "we see it in itself in the sense that we do not see it through any finite thing representing it, but we do not see it in itself in the sense that we can reach its simplicity or discover its perfections."[39]

Theodore follows this proclamation by posing the same psychological observation that we find both in the *Fifth Meditation* and More's *Antidote*: we are accustomed to distinguishing between essence and existence in all other things, and are therefore prone to do the same in the case of God. All three philosophers (Malebranche, More, and Descartes) agree that the distinction is inappropriate in the case of God, and that this very point lies at the heart of the ontological argument. For that reason they chastise the objectors who persistently overlook this point. The tendency to distinguish the essence of God from his existence, however, does not belong only to the objectors who fail to comprehend the argument. More and Descartes distinguish essence and existence to the extent that they subject the existence of God to logical demonstration; Malebranche does the same by removing the ontological insight from our finite understanding. The latter insists, at one moment, that God's essence and existence are the same, but at the next moment he concedes that it characterizes our finitude to distinguish these.

Malebranche understands this problem (Aristes is a character of his invention), yet he fails to overcome it. For him our perception of God is immediate.[40] In this respect he dispenses with the Cartesian syllogism: our knowledge of the existence of God is not analogous to other knowledge claims, since our knowledge of the former is direct and intuitive, whereas all other items of knowledge are mediated by representations and inferences. By distinguishing God as "being" from all creatures or "such beings," and by emphasizing the non-ideational character of our knowledge of the former, Malebranche eliminates both the analogy between the ontological proof and other knowledge claims as well as the syllogistic reasoning that this analogy supports. This is indeed what was required in order to make the ontological argument consistent. Where Malebranche fails is that he does not bring this intuition into harmony with the finitude of our minds. He understands that the ontological argument, if it is to be consistent, must reduce to an intuition. At the same time, however, he allows that we do not really have the required intuition. For all his successful elucidation and improvement of the ontological argument, then, Malebranche does not succeed in reconciling the relevant insight with human knowledge. Both Spinoza and Hegel supersede him in their efforts to complete this part of the proof.

BEYOND "THE SHADOWS OF AMBIGUITY": HUET'S CRITIQUE OF MALEBRANCHE

Opponents of Cartesian philosophy do not fail to address Malebranche's several revisions of the ontological argument. One of the chief anti-Cartesians of the end of the seventeenth century attacks a distinctly Malebranchean version of the argument, although he does so under the guise of refuting Descartes himself. The skeptic and scholar Pierre-Daniel Huet (1630–1721) publishes his treatise *Against Cartesian Philosophy* (hereafter *Censura*) in 1689. The work is significant not only for Huet's skeptical arguments against Cartesian philosophy, but also for the insight Huet provides into the classical sources of Descartes' ideas. The fourth chapter of the *Censura* offers both an accurate summary and a penetrating critique of the ontological argument as it had developed among French philosophers of the previous half-century.[41] The distinction of Huet's chapter is that it marks the only occurrence prior to the *Critique of Pure Reason* on which nearly all the objections to the ontological argument appear in a single, brief exposition.

Although Huet's position rests on a strong, skeptical interpretation of the Thomistic objections, and he wastes much effort distinguishing "mental existence" from "real existence," he does succeed in formulating three rather original objections to Malebranche's arguments.[42] These objections reveal both the consistency of Malebranche's reasoning as well as two principal shortcomings of his approach. The first of the objections concerns Descartes' analogy, and Huet appropriately attacks this in response to Malebranche's "elucidation" of the Cartesian argument. As explained above, Malebranche defends Descartes against the Thomistic objections by emphasizing the analogy between the Cartesian argument and all other knowledge claims, showing how even the simplest claims consist of inferences from the Cartesian rule for truth. The Thomistic objector, then, if he is consistent, must hesitate as much before the conclusion "a square has four sides" as he does before the claim "a perfect being necessarily exists." Huet, echoing Gassendi, attacks the analogy here by reminding that, while we do clearly perceive that a square has four sides, the same cannot be said so uncontroversially concerning the necessary existence of God. In other words, even if we concede that both analogs draw from the same major premise, a dissimilitude in the minor premises destroys the analogy:

> Yet they would deceive us here also; for there is a big difference between the minor premises of each of the syllogisms. In the first minor premise, viz., "I clearly and distinctly know three angles to be contained in a triangle," what is attributed to the triangle is that without which it cannot be and which constitutes its nature; for it entirely belongs to the nature of a triangle to have three angles. But in the other minor premise, viz., "I clearly and distinctly know that existence is contained in the idea of an infinite and supremely perfect thing," it is not known what kind of thing is attributed to an infinite and supremely perfect thing, or whether the former belongs to the nature of the latter.[43]

Huet obscures his own objection by immediately relapsing into a purely skeptical discourse, again distinguishing "mental" from "real" existence. The critique of the analogy, however, highlights an important shortcoming in the Cartesian argument and Malebranche's initial defense of that argument. The relation between three angles and a triangle or between four sides and a square is at least apparently different from the relation between "a perfect being" and "necessary existence." If there is a connection between the latter two, some explanation of that fact is necessary, as Gassendi had previously noted by requesting a demonstration of their relation.[44] This objection, overlooked for the most part in the seventeenth century, motivates much of the eighteenth-century controversy over the ontological argument.

Malebranche's revision of the argument succeeds in eluding this critical trap, a fact that is not lost on Huet. Although he neglects the explicit demonstration that Gassendi once requested of Descartes, Malebranche attempts to avoid the problem altogether by explicitly identifying "God" and "being." In other words, his response to the objection under discussion is simply that the

Cartesian analogy is indeed misleading; Malebranche's own "argument" is intuitive and so proceeds without reference to that analogy. "Necessary existence," for Malebranche, is not a property that comprises the essence of a particular entity, an *ens perfectissimum*. Rather, God is not any *ens*, but *esse* in general. There is no longer need for a demonstration (such as the ignominious perfection argument) that a certain entity possesses a certain property. Our knowledge of God as *esse* is knowledge *par simple vue*. That "being necessarily is," Malebranche believes, is an identical proposition that contains no synthesis.

Aware of this, Huet puts forth a second objection that criticizes the doctrine that God is "being." That doctrine, he claims, does not decisively overcome even the first Thomistic objection. In other words, by identifying "God" and "being," Malebranche is still faced with the difficulty of proving that "being" is no mere notion but rather "real being," and the Cartesian major premise is not available to rescue him from this problem:

> The Cartesians go even further and say that an infinite and supremely perfect thing is being itself par excellence, general being or infinite being ... they thus continue to seek the shadows of ambiguity; for this general being is a kind of notion of the mind, put together from the notions of singular beings. . . .[45]

For all his consistency, then, Malebranche fails to defeat the nominalist. Of course, his own doctrine is that being permits of no representation, so that our, admittedly vague, "thought" of being is supposed to be an immediate perception of being itself. It is nonetheless fair to object that this claim is less than evident (i.e., that it seems there should be a difference between "being" and the idea of the same). In his exposition of the doctrine in question, Malebranche notes that the observation that God is not known through any idea "must be added" to the Cartesian argument. In this he anticipates Huet's objection and provides the additional doctrine needed to make the entire argument consistent. His defense amounts, nevertheless, to a bald assertion (i.e., he does not support with any proof the claim that being permits of no representation).

By no means, however, does Huet get the better of Malebranche. Although he reveals an incompleteness in the latter's argument, Huet is a mere dogmatic nominalist, and it is not even clear that he fully appreciates the subtlety and consistency of Malebranche's position. Like in so many other instances, this stage of the dispute over the ontological argument remains at an impasse. Neither Huet's crude nominalism nor Malebranche's claim that we have immediate knowledge of being could sway an impartial observer. An awareness of just this problem that encourages the neutrality of both Clarke and Cudworth, and their position appears, at this point, to have been a rather reasonable one.

For his part, Huet also displays an awareness of the spurious nature of the dispute between the proponents of the Cartesian argument and the objectors, and this awareness informs his third important objection. His final complaint concerns the *ad hominem* defense of the ontological argument that is ubiquitous among its seventeenth-century proponents. Huet astutely notices that an escape from any objection is built into both Malebranche's and Descartes' presentations of the argument, one that allows the proponent always to rescue consistency at the expense of credibility: whoever does not immediately perceive the necessary existence of God fails to do so only because they are immersed in the pleasures of the senses (Malebranche) or because they have not freed themselves from preconceived notions (Descartes). Huet appropriately asserts that the objectors have every right to perceive this elitism as empty vanity. In an amusing passage he likens the proponent of the ontological argument to a madman who, in a manner similar to Descartes and Malebranche, claims to see what others cannot. To this comparison he adds that the objectors possess more credibility than the proponents of the Cartesian argument:

> Should Descartes say that the rest of men are stupid and that only he is sensible, we shall laugh; for which madman or fanatic will not justify his delusions with a similar response? . . . It should have been further asked of him why serious and intelligent men, although advised of (this idea of God) and having sought it in their souls, were unaware of so wonderful and illustrious an idea, and why only he was conscious of it. For what reasonable and more likely response might he have made to this? How much more credible is it that deluded by a vain imagination, he thought he saw what he did not see, than that everyone else did not see what is right before their eyes?[46]

THREE SHORTCOMINGS OF THE INTUITIVE ARGUMENT

Although Malebranche's metaphysical system provides a more appropriate context for the ontological argument, this has not sufficed to eliminate the efficacy of all objections to that argument. The strength of his revisions consists chiefly in the fact that the intuitive approach to the argument discourages both the empirical and epistemological objections. In regard to the first of these, the identification of "God" with "being as such" removes the misleading appearance that the ontological argument treats "existence" as a property of a certain "entity." The restriction of the term "idea" along with the doctrine of "vision in God" limits the effectiveness of the epistemological objections. In Malebranche's argument, there is no "idea" of God to justify, as well as no paradox concerning the representation of the infinite. This apparent concession to the objectors (that we have no idea of God), although it brings him disrepute among more orthodox Cartesians like Arnauld, allows Malebranche to defend an extremely simple argument that renders unnecessary much of the dispute surrounding the Cartesian formulation.

Gassendi's request for a deduction of "necessary existence" from the concept of a perfect being also appears superfluous in light of Malebranche's argument. The appearance that there are two concepts here, the connection of which would require some justification, dominates the entire eighteenth- and nineteenth-century history of the argument. The philosophers involved in that controversy can indeed revert to Descartes for an attempted solution to the problem. They will find several (perhaps incompatible) answers, such as the perfection argument, the omnipotence argument, and most importantly, a reference to a unique but clear and distinct perception. None of these are to be found in Malebranche, however. He does not begin with the concept of an *ens perfectissimum*, but relies instead on the simple assertion that "being is." Malebranche's is an ontological "argument" that concerns *neither* the concept of perfection *nor* the concept of necessity, since it concerns no concept at all, but only an alleged awareness of what is meant by *l'etre sans restriction*.

Three glaring shortcomings nonetheless arise in the course of the Malebranchean defense of his ontological argument. First, Malebranche fails to reconcile the intuition of God or being with his account of human knowledge, and he (in the voice of Aristes) even concedes that he contradicts himself in this regard. The result of this is that the ontological argument now consists in an assertion the insight into which lies beyond the capacity even of a trained philosopher. Malebranche is ambivalent about whether even he, wise Cartesian philosopher that he is, has insight into the immediacy of God's existence.[47]

Second, the revised form of the argument is indefensible against the nominalist's objection that "being" is a mere concept. The Cartesian defenses against nominalism, viz., the infamous "rule for truth" together with the doctrine of innate ideas, are unavailable to Malebranche. Since Malebranche's "being" is neither clear nor an idea, the rule concerning the validation of clear and distinct ideas provides no assistance here. Moreover, Malebranche rejects the doctrine of innate ideas.[48] Finally, the claim that we know God's existence immediately makes any deductive argument both superfluous and misleading, so that even a revised major premise is an impossibility for him.

The third and final problem with Malebranche's argument finds expression in Huet's sarcastic animadversion. There is simply no reason why anyone should believe Malebranche (or Descartes, for that matter) when they claim (if they claim) awareness of God's necessary existence through means (viz., an intuition or perception) that are at least apparently unavailable to the rest of us. Some kind of assertion of a privileged standpoint is essential to the seventeenth-century argument, and Malebranche exemplifies this to a greater degree than anyone else. Of course, Malebranche does not intend to be persuasive, and his exposition of the argument precludes any effort at making it widely accessible. Huet's objection to this cannot reveal an internal flaw in Malebranche's reasoning, but it does indicate the fate of that argument; the Malebranchean argument is condemned to be a mere passing episode about which we can make no final judgment.

Notes

1. Citations from this text (hereafter "*Search*") will be, with only occasional and slight alterations, from the translation by Thomas Lennon and Paul Olscamp, Ohio State University Press, 1980. Reference to the French text will be to *Oeuvres Completes de Malebranche*, J Vrin, Paris, 1958, ed. Henri Gouhier (hereafter "*Oeuvres*").

2. *Search*, p. 323; *Oeuvres* II 103.

3. Although he often calls this the first principle, a few pages later he explains that even the Cartesian rule is derivative from another axiom, that "nothingness or the false is not perceptible or intelligible" (*Search*, p. 320; *Oeuvres* II 99).

4. *Search*, p. 316; *Oeuvres*, II 92.

5. *Search*, p. 317; *Oeuvres* II 93.

6. *Oeuvres* II 94.

7. Ibid.

8. Ibid., 94–95:"Here is a similar argument (to the second Thomistic objection): one should attribute to a thing what one clearly conceives to be included in the idea that represents it; this is the principle. We clearly conceive that four angles are included

in the idea that represents a square, or, we clearly conceive that possible existence is included in the idea of a marble tower; therefore, a square has four angles; therefore, a marble tower is possible. I say that these conclusions are true, assuming that the square has four angles, and that the marble tower is possible, just as they say that God exists, assuming that He exists, i.e., in a word that the conclusions of these demonstrations are true, assuming that they are true."

9. In introducing the second Thomistic objection Malebranche gives a parenthetical reminder that the argument in question is Descartes': "this proof of the existence of God (which is Descartes')" (my emphasis). Only in the subsequent section does he make his own alterations to the argument.

10. See, among other texts, AT VII 115–17; CSM II 83.

11. *Meditation Three*, AT VII 51; Cf. AT VII 67 (*Fifth Meditation*).

12. *Opera omnia philosophica*, II, pp. 602ff. (Georg Olms, Hildesheim, 1968).

13. This is one of the main conclusions of part three of the *Search*.

14. References to *Dialogues on Metaphysics and on Religion* (hereafter *Dialogues*) are to the translation by Morris Ginsberg, George Allen and Unwin, 1923, p. 90 (*Oeuvres* XII 53).

15. *Third Replies*, AT VII 181; CSM II 127.

16. *Principles* I, p. 61, for instance, suggests that an idea is a mode of the mind.

17. AT VII 179–81; CSM II 126–28.

18. *Search* II, pt. 2; this is one issue on which there is a considerable literature. See Richard Watson's "Malebranche and Arnauld on Ideas," in *Modern Schoolman* 71(4), 1994, pp. 259–70 and Russell Wahl's "The Arnauld-Malebranche Controversy and Descartes' Ideas," *Monist* 71, 1988, pp. 560–72 (also cite Lennon).

19. *Search*, p. 318; *Oeuvres* II 96.

20. E.g., Aquinas; among proponents of the ontological argument, it is Bonaventure whom Malebranche is following here (see Bonansea, p. 147).

21. A related instance of Cartesian equivocation occurs in the definition of "substance" (Principles I, 51), which Descartes defines such that the term is properly attributable only to God. In the very next line, however, he writes of the "other substances," and of how there is no univocal meaning of the term applicable to both God and creatures. It is only natural for critics to overlook even a supposedly absolute distinction when terminology does not reflect that distinction. Malebranche simply removes these equivocations by distinguishing systematically between being and beings and by restricting his use of "idea." Spinoza's solution is perhaps superior. He restricts the term "substance" to God and considers all other entities to be mere modifications of God. In this case, there is almost no threat of conceiving of God as a creature, since one would then have to think of God as a mode of something else. On this, see chapter four below.

22 Cf. Jean-Luc Marion's essay "Is the Ontological Argument Ontological?" in *Journal of the History of Philosophy* 30 (2), April 1992.

23. *Search*, p. 318; *Oeuvres* II 95.

24. Mersenne, Leibniz, Cudworth, and others concede the objection, but think it can be shown independently that God is possible. On this point the proponents of the ontological argument are split. Leibniz, Mersenne, and Cudworth affirm the possibility of God, whereas Malebranche, Spinoza, and Hegel reject the possibility arguments, recognizing that to distinguish the essence or idea of God from his existence is already to make too great a concession to the objectors (see chapter five).

25. *Search,* p. 318; *Oeuvres* II 96.

26. Descartes addresses this in the *Regulae* (AT X 373; CSM I 17) and the *Meditations* (AT VII 51; CSM II 35).

27. The objection that Clarke raises (see above, chap. 2) is thus a serious charge against Descartes, although not against any of his successors.

28. E.g., J. Revius' *Methodi cartesianae consideratio theologica* (Leiden, 1648) and C. Lentulus' *Nova sapientia*. For a discussion of their criticisms and of Clauberg's reply on Descartes' behalf, see Aza Goudriaan's "Die Erkennbarkeit Gottes in der Philosophie Claubergs," in *Johannes Clauberg and Cartesian Philosophy in the Seventeenth Century*, ed. Theo Verbeek, Dordrecht, 1999. For an English-language introduction to Revius' criticisms, see Goudriaan's edition of that author (Jacobus Revius, *A Theological Examination of Cartesian Philosophy*, Brill, Leiden, 2002).

29. Among others, Caterus (AT VII 96; CSM II 60–70) raises this objection.

30. Geulincx, *Opera philosophica*, ed. J. P. N. Land, Martinus Nijhoff, 1892, vol. 2, p. 293. The original text dates from 1691. I owe this reference to Rohls, who produces a German translation of a longer passage from Geulincx on p. 230 of his book.

31. *Search*, p. 235.

32. See *Search*, bk. 3, part 2, chap. 6 (pp. 230–205), and *Dialogues*, chap. 1.

33. Malebranche even compares Descartes' doctrine of ideas with nominalism. See *Search*, bk. 3, part 2, chaps. 2–5 (pp. 220–30).

34. *Search*, p. 318 (*Oeuvres* II 96): ". . . nothing limits it; nothing can represent it. Therefore, if one thinks of it, it must exist." Cf. *Dialogues on Metaphysics* (p. 90); *Oeuvres* XII 53: "The infinite, on the other hand, can only be seen in itself, for nothing finite can represent the infinite. If we think of God, it follows that he exists."

35. Ibid., p. 321 (*Oeuvres* II 101).

36. Ibid., p. 322 (*Oeuvres* II 101–102).

37. *Dialogues*, p. 92; *Oeuvres* XII 55.

38. "Is there not a contradiction in what you are saying? If nothing finite can have enough reality to represent the infinite (and this appears evident), does it not necessarily follow that we see the divine substance in itself?" *Dialogues*, p. 92; *Oeuvres* XII 55.

39. *Dialogues*, p. 92; *Oeuvres* XII 56.

40. On this point see Beatrice K. Rome's *The Philosophy of Malebranche* (Henry

Regnery Company, Chicago, 1963), pp. 150–52. See also Jean-Marie Ladic's "Malebranche et l'argument ontologique," in *Revue Philosophique de la France et de l'Etranger*, 1996, pp. 513–19 and Michael J. Buckley's *At the Origins of Modern Atheism*, Yale University Press, 1987, pp. 145–66.

41. References to this text (hereafter "*Censura*") will be to the new translation by Thomas M. Lennon, JHP Book Series, Humanity Books, 2003.

42. It is very unfortunate that the few historians of the ontological argument who treat Huet do not recognize that he offers objections other than the Thomistic (see Rohls, p. 258 and Henrich, pp. 83–87).

43. *Censura*, p. 168.

44. A page earlier (p. 167), Huet briefly states the same point, but in that instance he also subsequently recedes in to mere Thomism: "With these ambiguities sorted out, the very knot of the difficulty is revealed, which lies entirely in the connection between the two parts of the (minor) premise, the first being "what is supremely perfect" and the other 'necessarily exists.'"

45. *Censura*, p. 169.

46. *Censura*, p. 171.

47. On the one hand, the elitism described earlier in this chapter suggests that a privileged understanding belongs to trained metaphysicians. At the same time, however, in moments of Christian humility Malebranche emphasizes the unavailability of the intuition to us in our separation from God.

48. See book three of the *Search* or the "First Dialogue" in *Dialogues*.

Chapter Four

AN ADEQUATE CONCEPTION

The Argument in Spinoza's Philosophy

Contemporaneously with Malebranche, Spinoza brings the ontological argument into a different philosophical context that nevertheless effects similar modifications in the Cartesian reasoning.
Spinoza likewise begins with the syllogism of Descartes' *First Set of Replies*,
eventually changing the argument by reducing the importance of the major
premise. He defends the argument against the Thomistic and empirical objections in a manner analogous to that of his French contemporary: he emphasizes the difference between God and creatures, and his monism offers a novel
interpretation of the relationship between these. Like so many other seventeenth-century philosophers, he elaborates the relationship between the finite
human intellect and God's infinite intellect by placing the former within the
latter. Spinoza's version of this last doctrine brings about the final step in the
move away from the subjective form of the Cartesian argument.

Two important innovations characterize the Spinozistic defense of the
argument. First, he contradicts both Malebranche and Descartes by asserting
that the human mind possesses an adequate concept of the essence of God.
Spinoza thereby provides the first suitable epistemological background for
the assertion of God's existence, and in this respect his is the most complete
ontological argument in seventeenth-century philosophy. Second, his epistemology emphasizes the primacy of the intuitive argument without denying
the utility of the demonstrative argument. Spinoza's argument is one that, like
Malebranche's, aims at an immediate intuition of God's existence. In

Spinoza's case, however, that intuition is no longer in conflict with the argumentative form.

Spinoza's approach addresses the several shortcomings that befall Malebranche's intuitive approach. To begin with, his system is the first in which the ontological insight does not stand in conflict with other instances of human knowledge. The claim that we have an adequate conception of God instead serves as the basis of his entire epistemology; for Spinoza, all forms of knowledge (ethical, physical, and metaphysical) derive ultimately from our idea of God.[1] Second, the nominalistic objections with which Huet and others attack Malebranche pose no threat to Spinoza, since the latter even shares the nominalist's view on general concepts. Lastly, the axiomatic form in which Spinoza expounds his metaphysics provides the argument with greater accessibility than is the case with Malebranche.

SPINOZA THE CARTESIAN

However important Descartes is or is not for Spinoza's development as a philosopher,[2] as a proponent of the ontological argument Spinoza begins as an orthodox Cartesian. Not only does his *Descartes' Principles of Philosophy* provide a precise version of the Cartesian syllogism from the Geometrical Demonstration,[3] his other early works likewise include fully Cartesian versions of the proof for God's existence. Chief among these is his early textbook *Short Treatise on God, Man, and His Well-Being*. The opening passage of that text offers an argument based on the Cartesian major premise: "Whatever we clearly and distinctly understand to belong to the nature of a thing, we can truly affirm of that thing."[4] The earliest exposition of Spinoza's philosophy thus begins with the Cartesian ontological syllogism; the centrality of this proof will not change for Spinoza, although later his *Ethics* brings significant revision to the form of the argument.[5]

A number of early texts suggest that Spinoza possesses a clear awareness of the entire dispute over this argument. His familiarity with the traditional objections to the Cartesian argument is evident from the *Short Treatise* text, from the Scholium to proposition 5 in the *Principia*, and from his correspondence with Henry Oldenburg in the autumn of 1661. To the *Short Treatise* argument he adds a note that considers a version of the Thomistic objection, although his reply to this is rather awkward.[6] It is probably to a later, but undoubtedly similar version of the argument to which Oldenburg poses, in one concise though incomplete statement, the Thomistic, empirical, and transition objections.[7] This exchange with Oldenburg verifies Spinoza's agreement with the entire Cartesian defense of the ontological argument. Oldenburg condenses the objections of Caterus, Gassendi, and Mersenne by juxtaposing the three objections; the result is that they appear to have a cumulatively detrimental effect:

> When I reflect that definitions contain only our mind's concepts, that our minds conceive many things that do not exist, and that it is most fruitful in multiplying and increasing things once they have been conceived, I do not yet see how I can infer God's existence from the concept I have from him.[8]

In response Spinoza provides the standard defense against the first two objections. With respect to Oldenburg's worry that the claim that "necessary existence" belongs to God by definition, Spinoza alludes to Cartesian reply to Caterus. His formulation of the reply, however, anticipates his own variation of the predication rule: he identifies "clear and distinct idea" with "definition."[9] For Spinoza a definition is a true idea of a real essence and not a mere nominal stipulation.[10] In stating his view on definitions, he also draws the connection between the responses to the empirical and Thomistic objections by reminding Oldenburg that only in the unique case of God can a definition provide the basis for an existential claim.[11] This exchange foreshadows Spinoza's later geometric appropriation of the ontological argument: in the *Ethics* he will rely mainly on a list of definitions, but these are to be understood as having the same metaphysical import as the Cartesian clear and distinct ideas.

To this last remark Spinoza adds a reference to a lost scholium that purportedly "stated clearly enough the ground of this difference (between the definitions of God and of everything else)."[12] In all likelihood Spinoza's justification for this distinction is modal: modality of existence belongs to all definienda; necessary existence belongs only to the definition of God; actual existence thus follows exclusively from that definition.[13] In any case, he must have given some detailed account of the difference between God's existence and the existence of everything else, whether this should concern modality or other characteristics such as eternity.[14]

In the *Principia* Spinoza adds a scholium to the proposition devoted to the proof of God's existence, and the similarity between this text and Letter 4 provides the strongest evidence that Spinoza's defense of the ontological argument is consciously Cartesian. Here he also points to the importance of the difference between God and creatures, and he adds that this difference applies "with respect both to his essence and to his existence."[15] He directs the reader to the *First Set of Replies*, and writes that upon consulting that text anyone "will see that the idea of God is very different from the idea of other things." In the same passage he refers to the chapter of his *Cogitata metaphysica* that provides an account of this difference. The conclusion to be drawn, then, is that Spinoza's lifelong resolve in explicating the difference between God and other things (a number of passages from that appendix anticipate the positions of the *Ethics*[16]) represents a conscious observance of the caveat that Descartes issues in the *First Replies*.

Descartes is clearly not the principal philosopher from whom Spinoza learns the doctrine of equivocal attribution, although the latter is aware that Descartes takes the idea of God to be entirely different from any other idea. It is more likely that Spinoza first discovers this doctrine in Maimonides' *Guide for the Perplexed*, or some other Hebrew writer to whom he had access in his youth.[17] His Maimonidean background, however, only explains Spinoza's special sensitivity to passages like the one from the *First Set of Replies* to which he refers in his *Principia*, and his acute awareness that this doctrine is essential to the defense of the Cartesian ontological argument. Spinoza recognizes that Descartes' argument requires that the meaning of the term "existence" in "God exists" not be analogous to the use of this term in any other instance. His acquaintance with Maimonides aided him in developing this doctrine, a more consistent version of which is to be found in his *Ethics*.[18]

Spinoza's reply to Oldenburg's transition argument demonstrates not only his further adherence to Cartesian philosophical dogma, but also a tendency toward the *ad hominem* argumentation that characterizes the Cartesian defense of the argument. To the standard epistemological reply to the transition objection (viz., that there is a discernible "difference between a fiction and a clear and distinct concept") Spinoza adds the observation that "a philosopher" is supposed to be acquainted with this difference as well as with the major premise/Cartesian rule (viz., "the axiom that every definition, *or* clear and distinct idea, is true").[19] As is the case with both Descartes and Malebranche, Spinoza here provides the *ad hominem* as an apology for the argument's lack of persuasiveness. The requisite perception is available only to a philosopher (of a distinctly Cartesian sort), since a philosopher will be attentive to the difference between God and creatures, the difference between fiction and intellection, and will have overcome skepticism by the Cartesian rule for truth or some analog to it. Indeed, Spinoza even surpasses Descartes' vigilance in designating the objections to the ontological argument as *unphilosophical*. Whoever poses the traditional objections, in Spinoza's view, simply has not made progress in the pursuit of truth.

There is further evidence that indicates Spinoza's relative lack of concern with objections like those that begin from our capacity to invent fictions. In his *Principles of Philosophy*, Descartes devotes an entire section (I, 16) to an explanation of why not everyone is capable of attaining to the perception to which the minor premise refers[20]; Malebranche offers a similar explanation in his chapter on "the pursuit of pleasure in relation to the speculative sciences."[21] While these explanations are consistent with Spinoza's philosophy,[22] they play a reduced role in his presentation of it. In his exposition of Descartes' *Principles*, for example, he omits the relevant Cartesian text.[23] His more hesitant admission that not everyone understands the ontological argument precedes a relatively optimistic assertion that "anyone moved by a good intention . . . will doubtless understand it as clearly as possible."[24] In Spinoza's mind, then, the objectors are not merely metaphysical novices, but are arguing in bad faith. Refuting them would thus be an extraneous concern.

This indifferent attitude toward his opponents is indicative of an important philosophical tendency that ultimately influences the version of the argument that we find in the *Ethics*: in Spinoza's presentations of the ontological argument, the replies to the objections suffer from diminishing importance. Although he is in agreement on each point with the Cartesian defense of the argument, he does not, like Descartes does, engage in open and public dispute with objectors. The tendentiousness necessary to provide a full elucidation of the context of the argument is altogether foreign to Spinoza, and in most cases he sacrifices persuasiveness for the sake of efficiency of expression and consistency. His oft-stated distaste for dispute[25] facilitates, but is not the reason for, his eventual suppression of the major premise from his presentation of the ontological argument in the *Ethics*.

SPINOZA OR MALEBRANCHE?
A SECOND SOLUTION TO THE DILEMMA

Although both Spinoza and Malebranche make similar revisions to the presentation of the Cartesian proof, the specifics of these changes vary significantly. The similitude of their approaches is limited mainly to the fact that both take their departure from the *First Replies* syllogism, as well as the fact that both attempt to provide a more consistent context for the claim asserted in the minor premise of the argument. Like Malebranche, Spinoza recognizes that the analogy with geometry had exposed the argument to the Thomistic and empirical objections. He thus eliminates this analogy from the proof and instead emphasizes the difference between God and finite entities.[26] Spinoza's monism provides a different avenue upon which to circumvent those objections. His epistemology also provides a novel approach both to the problem of God's conceivability and to the finite-infinite paradox.

Malebranche's distinction between being simpliciter and particular beings is a move that is unavailable to Spinoza. The notion of being simpliciter, as Huet shows, remains vulnerable to nominalistic objections, and Spinoza is among those philosophers who would assent to these objections. For Spinoza general concepts like "being" are indeed fictions.[27] His opposition to the empirical objection accordingly comes in a different form. If the latter objection depends on an analogy between God and all other entities, then a second rather obvious option is open to the proponent of the ontological argument. In either case, the misleading appearance that "God" and "creatures/finite things" are all individuals of the same species "entity" requires correction. Whereas Malebranche denies that God is an entity, Spinoza instead denies that creatures are properly understood as entities.

Spinoza's solution to the empiricists' dilemma is to explain God as the only existent "thing."[28] He accomplishes this by employing the term "substance" univocally and he thereby avoids any apparent analogy between God and creatures. If "substance" means primarily "independent existent," then God is the only substance.[29] Instead of using the same term equivocally to describe creatures, which equivocation encourages the empirical objection, Spinoza describes particular entities as modifications of the one substance.[30] In this context it is less natural to understand "God" by analogy with creatures; this is only done to the extent that we mistakenly imagine creatures also to be independent, and to avoid just that error, especially with respect to ourselves, is the principal aim of Spinozistic philosophizing. In further emphasis of the distinction in question Spinoza describes the characteristics of a mode in dia-metrical opposition to the characteristics of a substance.[31]

In the context of Spinoza's philosophy, then, the empirical and Thomistic objections appear less appropriate. It is not a natural response to his presenta-tion of the argument, as it is to Descartes' formulation of it, to imagine that the proof of God's existence should proceed in the same manner as the proof of the existence of any other object. Any analogy between God and particulars is destroyed in advance by his concept of an infinite and unique substance. Spinoza is thus more justified than Descartes or More are in excluding the replies to the empirical and Thomistic objections from his actual demonstra-tion of the assertion of God's existence. His metaphysics provides the context in which a relatively brief ontological argument can appear without the threat of these standard objections.

Spinoza is also in basic agreement with the remaining revisions that we find in Malebranche. Like his French contemporary he circumvents the possi-bility argument and provides a detailed reply to the epistemological objec-tions. In regards to the first point, he is even more emphatic than the other sev-enteenth-century proponents of the proof in his exclusion of the notion of possibility from God's nature. Not only does he follow Descartes in distin-guishing contingent from necessary existence, but he also more closely and more precisely associates possibility with contingency. For Spinoza, both pos-sibility and contingency stem solely from a defect in our understanding.[32] Moreover, both concepts refer to our knowledge of the external causes of a thing, a situation that is entirely irrelevant to the demonstration of the exis-tence of something that has no external cause. To preface the ontological infer-ence with a demonstration of God's possibility, then, would constitute an attri-bution to God's nature of a property foreign to him in these two important respects. Mersenne's argument is mistaken, not because God's possibility is inferred from our knowledge of his existence, but rather because possibility is not a relevant consideration in the case of God.[33]

Echoing Malebranche and Geulincx, Spinoza also places the individual, finite mind within God's nature. Like all particular things, man is merely a modification of God's infinite nature.[34] The human mind is thus a modifica-tion or part of the divine mind.[35] Spinoza's consistency on this point is remarkable. He emphasizes the dependence of man on God to the extent that he treats statements about individual men as translatable into statements about God "insofar as" he undergoes a certain modification: ". . . when we say that the human mind perceives this or that, we are saying nothing but that God, not insofar as he is infinite, but . . . insofar as he constitutes the essence of the human mind, has this or that idea."[36] This doctrine aids him in overcoming the epistemological objections to the ontological argument. There is no longer difficulty in conceiving of how a finite mind can perceive the infinite; Spinoza needs to explain only how a finite mode of the infinite thinks of the infinite as such. In this context the objection that Clarke later proposes finds a reply in advance; there is no difficulty in understanding how an idea can serve as the basis for an existential claim, and no difference between my subjective idea and the "real idea" of God: if my idea of God is a modification of God, it is indeed evidence of his existence.

In respect to the idea of the infinite Spinoza manages to elude Malebranche's Aristes paradox, so that the *Ethics* marks the first occasion on which the *argumentum cartesianum* finds support in a suitable epistemology. Like Descartes, Malebranche remains ambivalent about the extent to which we possess knowledge of God. On the one hand, we have an immediate perception of God as *l'etre sans restriction*. At the same time, however, we do not really (in this life, anyway) perceive what God is. While the first point provides consistency with the claim of the ontological argument, the second places that claim beyond the limits of human knowledge. Unencumbered by any comparable commitment to the inconceivability of the deity, Spinoza simply eliminates the stipulation that we do not have a genuine perception of God's nature, and he develops his epistemology on the basis of the claim that we possess an adequate concept of God.[37]

THE INVERSION OF THE PREMISES

Spinoza deals with the individual, finite mind and the relationship of this to the divine intellect in the middle of book two of his *Ethics*. The significance of his account lies in the fact that he inverts the position of Cartesian epistemology: we clearly conceive of God's nature, but not of our own. The clear and distinct concept of God that the ontological argument requires does not, on Spinoza's view, exceed our limited capacities; rather, that concept belongs essentially to our minds even as finite, and it serves as the basis for the most adequate form of human knowledge. That we have a more adequate knowledge of God than of ourselves provides the primary reason for reducing the role of the major premise of the ontological argument. There can be no appeal to the veracity of our faculties in establishing the existence of God, since our knowledge even of our own faculties derives from our prior knowledge of God.

The account of the human mind in book two begins with an apparently pessimistic assessment of human knowledge.[38] As is well-known, Spinoza considers the human mind to be the "idea of the body."[39] By this he means that the mind and the body are the same modification of God's nature, but expressed under different attributes.[40] The fact that the mind is a mere modification of God's mind indicates the principal shortcoming of human knowledge: our individual mind, considered as an individual, does not consist of a clear and distinct idea. In the Scholium to proposition 28 Spinoza writes that "... the idea that constitutes the nature of the human mind is not, *considered in itself alone*, clear and distinct" (my italics).[41] In the demonstration of the same proposition Spinoza adds that particular ideas within the human mind "insofar as they are related only to the human mind" are likewise confused, not clear and distinct. This doctrine is an indirect consequence of his monism; if the independence of finite entities is illusory, then individual thoughts should be conceived with respect to the attribute of thought as this expresses the whole of nature, and should not be considered merely in isolation or with respect only to a single modification like the human mind.

In the subsequent propositions Spinoza elaborates the distinction between the mind of God as such and the mind of man as a particular modification of God, especially as this concerns the adequacy of knowledge. Adequate knowledge of ourselves or of other particular entities is in God, not to the extent that he undergoes a single modification (i.e., the true knowledge is not in an individual mind considered independently), but rather to the extent that God's intellect expresses the whole of nature: "adequate knowledge of how things are constituted is in God, insofar as he has the ideas of all of them, and not insofar as he has only the idea of the human body."[42] All ideas, including the one that constitutes a given individual human mind, are true, but only to the extent that they are related to the whole of the attribute of thought or to God.[43] In other words, to the extent that we in fact participate in God's nature, we do possess adequate knowledge. An idea can be inadequate or confused only to the extent that it is considered in relation to a particular mind, rather than to the infinite intellect.[44]

What Spinoza claims here is that, *pace* Descartes, we as individuals do not have a clear and distinct conception of either our minds or our bodies. This doctrine explains the starting point of Spinoza's philosophy and by extension both the exclusion of the major premise and the revision of the minor premise of the ontological argument. For Descartes, the starting point of philosophy is the immediate awareness of the existence of the self. The ontological argument derives from this awareness and from the subsequently deduced doctrine that all other clearly and distinctly perceived ideas are true (i.e., the major premise of the ontological argument). The minor premise of the ontological argument is also subjective; it states that "I" perceive among my other ideas a clear concept of God as necessarily existing. For Spinoza, by contrast, the certainty of the existence of the self is derived from the certainty of the existence of God, and not vice versa.[45] Knowledge of God is accordingly the beginning, not the end, of philosophical inquiry. The consequence of this view for the ontological argument is predictable: that argument now rests at the beginning of philosophy. The ontological argument, for Spinoza, does not presuppose other doctrines, but rather all other doctrines presuppose it. It is also, in Spinoza's hands, a briefer argument; it requires only a definition of substance (in place of the minor premise) and an objective interpretation of definitions (in lieu of the major premise).

Having established that only God possesses adequate knowledge of the self, it remains for Spinoza to explain what and how human minds do adequately know. This represents the theme of a portion of book two that begins with the second Scholium to proposition 40. That text delineates three kinds of knowledge, two of which are necessarily true knowledge.[46] Knowledge of the first kind, including experiential knowledge, faith, hearsay, etc., is at least potentially fallacious. The second kind, roughly speaking, is demonstrative knowledge, or knowledge derived from the so-called "common notions."[47] The third kind of knowledge of which Spinoza speaks is called "*scientia intuitiva*," which occurs when we perceive the truth of a proposition "in one glance."

Although Spinoza distinguishes at least three ways in which we can know something, he does not determine unequivocally which type of knowledge we primarily have of God. He does state unambiguously, however, *that* we have adequate knowledge of God's nature; proposition 47 asserts this doctrine, which represents the decisive break from views like those of the Cartesians or of Malebranche: "the human mind has an adequate knowledge of God's eternal and infinite essence." The proof of this proposition refers to the preceding two propositions, viz. 45 and 46. In the former of these Spinoza claims that each singular idea, whether considered as a whole or as a part, "involves" an eternal and infinite essence of God. Knowledge of God is thus in each individual mind, not only considered in relation to the infinite intellect, but even in each singular mind considered as such.[48]

In the Scholium to proposition 47 Spinoza claims that this knowledge of God is the basis for the third kind of knowledge, but not yet that such knowledge is an instance of *scientia intuitiva*: ". . . it follows that we can deduce from this knowledge a great many things which we know adequately, and so can form that third kind of knowledge of which we spoke in P40S2 . . ." The intuitive knowledge of which Spinoza speaks here is indeed derived from the idea of God, to the extent that this adequate knowledge consists largely in conceiving of finite things as modifications of God's nature, i.e., in immediately recognizing the dependence of each "thing" or mode on the whole of nature. The formation of such knowledge is part of the ultimate aim of the *Ethics*.[49] This suggests that Spinoza does endorse something like the intuitive version of the ontological argument that we find in Malebranche (i.e., our knowledge of God's existence is immediate, and to that extent it is not an inference from antecedently established premises). The intuitive nature of such knowledge, however, is balanced by Spinoza's claim that the third kind of knowledge (intuition) develops from the second kind (demonstration).[50] For Spinoza, then, the demonstrative and intuitive versions of the argument are compatible. We become aware of the existence of God by means of the proof from premises, but these premises are ultimately dispensable.[51]

THE DEMONSTRATION OF EIP11 IN LIGHT OF THE *FIRST REPLIES* SYLLOGISM

Although Spinoza was an advocate of the Cartesian argument early in his career, that argument does not explicitly appear anywhere in the *Ethics*. Nonetheless he offers at least three a priori proofs of God's existence, and these are included among four arguments in the demonstration to proposition 11 of book one. The question remains, then, concerning what relation these arguments bear, not only to one another, but to the Cartesian syllogism of which Spinoza was for a long time a proponent. Although this fact is less than obvious, the first demonstration of P11 is a version of the Cartesian argument.[52] Like Malebranche's argument, Spinoza's demonstration eliminates the major premise. Two reasons for Spinoza's endorsement of this move have already been given. First, he makes assumptions about what anyone studying a philosophical text should already know, such as what constitutes a true definition. Second, and more importantly, since knowledge of God's existence is the starting point of human knowledge and thus also of philosophy, to begin with epistemological considerations like the one expressed in Descartes' major premise would represent a reversal of the proper procedure of inquiry.

In his now classic book on Spinoza's philosophy, Harry Wolfson provided a very intricate discussion of IP11 that suggests the derivation of this argument from the *First Replies* syllogism. He is among the very few scholars who have recognized both that the latter is the primary Cartesian ontological argument and that in the *Ethics* Spinoza is concerned with developing this argument. He even goes as far as to say that the first demonstration of IP11 is reducible to the *First Replies* syllogism.[53] In another passage, however, he admits that the Spinoza of the *Ethics* endorses the Cartesian syllogism only "with some modification."[54] He explains Spinoza's modified syllogism to be the following:

P1: Everything whose essence involves existence exists
P2: God's essence involves existence
Conclusion: God exists

This reconstruction of Spinoza's reasoning is actually quite accurate, although it assumes an axiom that Spinoza does not include in the *Ethics*. The complicity between Spinoza's demonstration and Descartes' syllogism lies most evidently in the conclusion. Descartes writes that God or an *ens perfectissimum* necessarily exists, whereas Spinoza reinterprets the concept of a supremely perfect being in terms of substance and attributes.[55] Spinoza's conclusion is thus that "God, or a substance consisting of infinite attributes, each of which expresses eternal and infinite essence, necessarily exists."[56]

The demonstration of this conclusion proceeds in accordance with Spinoza's preferred method of *reductio*,[57] and it is primarily the negative aspect of the demonstration that disguises the relation to the Cartesian syllogism. The first line of the *reductio* requests that the objector try to conceive that such a being does not exist.[58] It would follow that God's essence does not include existence, since (according to axiom seven) the essence of anything whose nonexistence is conceivable does not include existence. In proposition seven Spinoza had already shown that "it pertains to the nature of a substance to exist," which contradicts what we derive from the hypothesis (viz., that the nature of one particular substance, God, does not include existence), so that that hypothesis ("God does not exist") is thereby shown to be "absurd." Spinoza concludes that "therefore God necessarily exists."

Although he omits the banal details that would explain this point, Wolfson's syllogism is nothing but an affirmative version of Spinoza's demonstration, with the addition of one suppressed premise.[59] He apparently recognizes that axiom seven is the contrapositive of the otherwise unstated premise "anything whose essence involves existence cannot be conceived as not existing." Spinoza's definition of God as an infinite substance (definition 6) together with P7 yields "the essence of God involves existence," so that the conclusion "God cannot be conceived as not existing" follows (from that claim together with A7). As is now obvious, Spinoza makes one further assumption: whatever cannot be conceived as not existing (necessarily) exists. Wolfson merely couples this assumption with (the contrapositive of) axiom seven to derive the major premise of his syllogism "everything whose essence involves existence (necessarily) exists."

It is fair to ask why Spinoza omits an important assumption (viz., if we cannot conceive of a thing to not exist, it necessarily exists) from his demonstration of P11. This last axiom, which is a negative version of the major premise of the Cartesian ontological argument, is indeed an assumption that underlies, not only the demonstration of P11, but the entire geometric presentation of metaphysical concepts.[60] Wolfson was thus right to maintain that Spinoza proposes a revised version of the Cartesian syllogism. He defends a version of this that begins with cognition of God, and only later deduces certain facts about the human mind. At the same time, however, the account presupposes that the readers (who are "philosophers") have eliminated certain common prejudices, have contemplated God, etc., so that his omission of the major premise does not expose the argument to Thomistic objections. These are admissions made by Spinoza in his letter to Oldenburg and in other passages.[61]

POSTSCRIPT: THE ONTOLOGICAL ARGUMENT IN SEVENTEENTH-CENTURY PHILOSOPHY

The philosophical systems of Spinoza and Malebranche are in large part developments of the doctrines underlying the intuitive version of the Cartesian ontological argument. These philosophers develop the central insight that "necessary existence belongs to the nature of God" by adhering to the Cartesian premises, but at the same time altering the form of the *First Replies* syllogism. They do not advocate versions of the perfection argument, but instead view God's "existence" to be *synonymous* with his "essence," and thus not merely one perfection among others. In God there is simply no difference between essence and existence, so that any inference from the former to the latter would be entirely superfluous. Existence is not a characteristic of God that is deduced from his essence, but is instead that essence itself.

While the Cartesian defense of this claim takes the form of the elaboration of a single syllogistic argument (with its many caveats like the rule for truth, the doctrine of equivocal attribution, the theory of innate ideas, etc.), Spinoza and Malebranche transform that defense into the complete context of their philosophies. They provide more consistent versions of the relevant doctrines so that, viewed from the standpoint of their systems, the necessary existence of God becomes an immediate truth. In other words, anyone who accepts, for example, Malebranche's theory of ideas, his distinction between "being" simpliciter and finite entities or "such beings," etc., cannot avoid also accepting his ontological argument. The concern is no longer merely with the premises of a single, formal argument, but rather with an entire philosophical context.

The problem of defending the premises of an argument thus becomes the problem of convincing others to entertain that philosophy. Huet's last objection is appropriate here. His claim is that potential objectors have no reason to believe that the proponents of the ontological argument indeed perceive God's necessary existence. In the context of Spinoza's system in particular, this perception is a prerequisite for the entire philosophy; his ontological argument derives from definitions and axioms, and the former are considered real definitions, not nominal definitions. The presupposition of (at least the communication of) his philosophy is that the reader comprehend these definitions and axioms. Huet's objection is no longer an objection to an argument, but rather to an entire system: the objectors have no reason to entertain these definitions, or to believe that they are in fact genuine definitions (i.e., no one not already committed to philosophy in the manner of a Spinoza, and who does not acknowledge the metaphysically valid truth of his definitions, could be convinced by his geometric proofs).[62]

Disregarding his entire philosophical endeavor is the only means of objecting to an ontological argument like Spinoza's. An empirical objection is impossible for anyone who accepts his monism. A Thomistic objection is impossible for anyone who accepts his theory of definitions. No one who accepts his epistemology can distinguish the idea of God from the existence of God; likewise, a transition objection is possible only on very un-Spinozistic grounds. Conversely, no one can accept his argument without accepting his other doctrines *in toto*, or at least without offering alternative versions of them. Acceptance or rejection of the ontological argument involves the acceptance or rejection of an entire philosophy.

NOTES

1. The *Treatise on the Emendation of the Intellect* makes this point perhaps most clearly, since it alleges that all ideas should be derived from the "standard of truth," which is the idea of a "unique and infinite being" (see #76ff.). All translations of Spinoza's works, unless otherwise indicated, will be from *The Collected Works of Spinoza*, ed. Edwin Curley, Princeton, 1985 (hereafter "Curley"), p. 34; Latin references will be to *Spinoza Opera*, ed. Gebhart, Heidelberg 1925 (hereafter "*Opera*"), II 29ff.

2. The extent of Spinoza's influence on Descartes is a matter of disagreement. See Curley's *Behind the Geometrical Method*, Princeton, 1988, for a Cartesian reading of Spinoza. For a dissenting view, see Yirmiyahu Yovel's "Spinoza, the First Anti-Cartesian," in *Idealistic Studies* 33(2–3), 2003, pp. 121–40. My intention here is to demonstrate Spinoza's defense of the ontological argument in Cartesian terms, which does not necessarily require a Cartesian reading of Spinoza's entire philosophy.

3. Curley, p. 246; *Opera* I 158–59. Cf. AT VII 166–67; CSM II 117.

4. Curley, p. 61; *Opera* I 15.

5. The ontological argument is essential to nearly every work Spinoza wrote, including, in addition to the *Short Treatise* and the *Principles*, also the *TdIE* and the *Ethics*.

6. See note b in Curley, pp. 61–62 (*Opera* I 15). Curley suggests that the text is defective. See note 4 on his page 62.

7. See Letter 3 (Curley, p. 168, *Opera* IV 10). See also Curley's note on the "lost geometric enclosure" to Spinoza's Letter 2; presumably, the enclosure provided a version of the Cartesian argument as well as a scholium listing some of the qualifications mentioned in Letter 4. Curley attempts a reconstruction of its contents, but his version does not mention the all-important scholium. It is likely that this scholium is similar to the one that Spinoza adds to proposition 5 of the *Principia*.

8. The first clause states the key premise to the Thomistic objection; the second clause does not explicitly formulate the empirical objection, but it does state the psycho-

logical motivation for assenting to that objection; consider Kant's exposition of the empirical objection in *KrV* and the *Critique of Judgment*, as well as Descartes' *Principles of Philosophy* I 16. The third clause formulates only part of the transition objection, but the following sentence makes it unmistakable that Oldenburg has that objection in mind.

9. Letter 4 (*Opera* IV 13): "... every definition *or* clear and distinct idea is true (... omnis definitio *sive* clara et distincta idea sit vera)."

10. See *Treatise on the Emendation of the Intellect* #95ff. On Spinoza's concept of definition, see Curley's essay "Spinoza's Geometric Method," in *Studia Spinozana* 2 (1986), pp. 151–68. For an alternative reading, see Guerolt's *Spinoza I: Dieu (Ethique, I)*, Hildesheim, 1968.

11. Letter 4: "To the first, then, I say that it is not from the definition of anything whatever that the existence of the thing defined follows, ... (but only) from the definition ... of a thing that is conceived through itself and in itself."

12. I have followed Shirley (Spinoza, *Letters*, ed. Samuel Shirley, Hackett, 1995, p. 67) in the translation of this passage. Curley translates it as "the reason for this difference." Concerning this scholium, see note 7 above.

13. At least he argues this way in the *Principia*. See axiom 6 of that work (Curley p. 243; *Opera* I 155).

14. The claim that "existence" is equivocal is central to Spinoza's philosophy. The primary text devoted to the point is part 2 of the *Cogitata metaphysica* (Curley, pp. 315ff.; *Opera* I, 249ff.): "In this chapter we shall attempt to show as clearly as we can that God's existence differs entirely from the existence of created things." For Spinoza's view on theological equivocation in another context, see *Ethics* IP17.

15. Curley, p. 247; *Opera* I 159.

16. E.g., Spinoza's comments about duration at *Opera* I 250 (Curley, p. 316) are similar to those in the *Ethics*. In any case, Spinoza's devotion to the doctrine of equivocal attribution is undeniable, and the scholium provides evidence of his awareness of the importance of this doctrine for the Cartesian ontological argument.

17. See, for instance, *Guide*, chapter 56: "Those who believe in the presence of essential attributes in God, viz., existence, life, power, wisdom and will, should know that these attributes, when applied to God, have not the same meaning as when applied to us, and that the difference does not only consist in magnitude...." (Moses Maimonides, *Guide for the Perplexed*, trans. M. Friedlander, Pardes Publishing House, 1904, p. 79.)

18. See the comparison of his notion of "substance" with Malebranche's notion of God, below.

19. Letter 4 (Curley, p. 170, *Opera* IV 13); I have followed Curley in emphasizing "or" when it translates "sive."

20. AT VIIIa 10; CSM I 198.

21. *Search*, chap. 3.

22. Passages are not uncommon in which Spinoza offers psychological accounts of how views contradictory to his are arrived at; consider, among other examples, IIP10CS.

23. The reader is advised (*Opera* I 159; Curley, 246) to consult the relevant paragraph in Descartes' *Principles*.

24. "I confess, of course, that certain prejudices stand in the way of everyone's understanding this so easily. . . ."

25. See, among many such passages, Letter 6 (*Opera* IV 36; Curley, p. 188).

26. Spinoza actually bases a second a priori proof on this analogy, but he does so in such a way that avoids confusing the idea of God with other ideas. See *Short Treatise* I (Curley, p. 61; *Opera* I 15). Although Wolfson (I 181–82) is right to compare this to the Cartesian analogy, Spinoza does not employ that analogy here in the same misleading way in which Descartes employs it, but rather he emphasizes the fact that God's essence is different from every other essence.

27. EIIP40S2 is the standard text for Spinoza's view on general concepts.

28. EPI14: "Except for God, no substance can be or be conceived."

29. Spinoza, *Ethics* ID3; Descartes, *PP* I 51.

30. EIP15: "Whatever is, is in God, and nothing else can be or be conceived without God." Cf. EIP25C: "Particular things are nothing but affections of God's attributes, or modes by which God's attributes are expressed in a certain and determinate way."

31. For example, substance is "in itself" while modes are "in another," essence and existence are distinct for modes, inseparable for substance, etc.

32. *Cogitata metaphysica*, pt. 3, chap. 3 (Curley, p. 308; *Opera* I, p. 242): "(contingency and possibility) are nothing but a defect in our perception and nothing real." Cf. *Ethics* IP33S1 (Curley p. 436; *Opera* II, p. 74). Spinoza also allows that the terms "possibility" and "contingency" are interchangeable, and that his employment of a distinction between them is a mere stipulation.

33. Little is to be made of the fact that Leibniz claims to have received Spinoza's approval of the argument from *Quod ens perfectissimum existit* (see below, chapter 5). The only evidence that Spinoza is perhaps not fully opposed to Leibniz's argument lies in his inclusion of non-contradictoriness among the criteria of a true definition.

34. EIIP10: "The being of substance does not pertain to the essence of man." Cf. The corollary to the same proposition: ". . . the essence of man is constituted by certain of God's attributes."

35. EIIP11C: ". . . the human mind is a part of the divine intellect."

36. On the employment of "insofar as" in Spinoza, see Jean-Paul Brodeur, "Quatenus: de la contradiction en philosophie," *Dialogue* 16 (1977); pp. 22–67.

37. Spinoza voices his opposition to the notion of divine inconceivability in the appendix to *Ethics*, bk. I.

38. There is, of course, a considerable literature on Spinoza's epistemology. In the following I summarize only a few points that I take to be relatively uncontroversial, and I do so only with reference to Spinoza's text. See Margaret Wilson's "Spinoza's Theory of Knowledge," in *The Cambridge Companion to Spinoza*, ed. Don Garrett, Cambridge, 1996.

39. IIP13.

40. See IIP7.

41. IIP47S.

42. IIP30Dem.

43. IIP32: "All ideas, insofar as they are related to God, are true."

44. IIP36Dem: "And so there are no inadequate or confused ideas except insofar as they are related to the singular mind of someone."

45. Spinoza does not discuss the existence of the self (considered as mind or body) until propositions 10–12 of book 2. He discusses the importance of beginning philosophy with the contemplation of God in the Scholium to the Corollary to IIP10.

46. P41: "Knowledge of the first kind is the only cause of falsity, whereas knowledge of the second and of the third kind is necessarily true."

47. Wolfson (II pp. 138–40) equates the common notions with axioms or first principles. The example in Scholium II supports this, if we assume that the clause "from the force of the demonstration of P7 in Bk. VII of Euclid, viz. from the common property of proportionals" refers to this kind of knowledge.

48. IIP46Dem: ". . . what gives knowledge of an eternal and infinite essence of God is common to all, and is equally in the part and in the whole."

49. Book V, propositions 31–33; intellectual love of God (the goal of ethical philosophy) derives from the third kind of knowledge.

50. EVP28; that the second and third kinds of knowledge are compatible is actually a controversial issue. A number of commentators (see G. H. R. Parkinson's *Spinoza's Theory of Knowledge*, London, 1954, and Curley's "Experience in Spinoza's Theory of Knowledge" in Grene, pp. 25–59) have tried to distinguish the kinds of knowledge in terms of subject matter (based on EVP36CS), which interpretation would prohibit our reading of the demonstrative and intuitive ontological arguments as compatible with one another. Spencer Carr, however, has very convincingly dismissed that view. See his "Spinoza's Distinction between Rational and Intuitive Knowledge," in *The Philosophical Review* 87, 1978, pp. 241–52. Among other problems with the Curley/Parkinson view, the example of the "fourth proportional" from EIIP48S2 becomes incomprehensible on that reading. For a similar view, see Roed (p. 86) and also his "Spinoza's Idee der scientia intuitiva und die Spinozanische Wissenschaftskonzeption," in *Zeitschrift fuer philosophische Forschung* 31, 1977, pp. 497–510.

51. Wolfson (I, 171) attributes a view like this to Descartes, in which case problems like the apparent incompatibility of the perfection argument with the intuitive minor premise would be resolvable.

52. See Wolfson I, 179–84. The same view is defended by William Earle in "The Ontological Argument in Spinoza" (Earle 1) and "The Ontological Argument in Spinoza: Twenty Years Later" (Earle 2) in Marjorie Grene, ed., *Spinoza: A Collection of Critical Essays*, Anchor Books, Doubleday, 1973, pp. 213–19, 220–26 respectively. An alternative interpretation is offered by Don Garret ("Spinoza's Ontological Argument," *Philosophical Review* 88, 1979, pp. 198–223 (reprinted in Genevieve Lloyd, ed., *Spinoza: Critical Assessments*. Routledge, 2001) and Willis Doney ("Spinoza's Ontological Proof," in *The Philosophy of Baruch Spinoza*, ed. Richard Kennington, Catholic University of America Press, 1980, pp. 35–52).

53. Wolfson I, 184.

54. Wolfson I, 183.

55. In Letter 60 Spinoza criticizes the definition of God as *ens perfectissimum* on the grounds that God's attributes are not deducible from this formula. His conception of an infinite substance with an infinite number of attributes, each of which is infinite in its own kind, however, is clearly a reinterpretation of that concept. I take Spinoza's point to be that "perfection" is not a sufficiently well-defined concept. His claim is that God is the unity of every attribute, rather than of every perfection. In any case, Spinoza cannot be said to advocate the perfection argument of the *Fifth Meditation*, since (among numerous other reasons) he does not claim that existence is an attribute. Existence is synonymous with God (EIP22), rather than one among his attributes.

56. EIP11 (Curley, p. 417; *Opera* II 53); Leibniz recognizes the affinity between the Cartesian and Spinozistic conceptions.

57. See Letter 64 (Shirley, p. 299)

58. "If you deny this, conceive, if you can, that God does not exist." Richard Mason (*The God of Spinoza: A Philosophical Study*, Cambridge, 1997, p. 22) offers a reminder that in this instance the hypothesis is inconceivable, since God cannot be conceived except as existing. Cf. *Treatise on the Emendation of the Intellect* #54, note t (Curley, p. 24; *Opera* II 20).

59. Garrett is thus mistaken in "Spinoza's Ontological Argument" (in *Spinoza: Critical Assessments*, ed. Genevieve Lloyd, Routledge, 200, p. 4) when he writes that "not a single premise or conclusion of Wolfson's "analytical syllogisms" about our experience occurs anywhere among" the arguments in P11Dem.

60. Roed (p. 81) makes a slightly stronger but related claim: "It could be said that for Spinoza the geometric method and the ontological argument are connected from the beginning."

61. The text from the *Treatise on the Emendation of the Intellect* provides the appropriate background, since it trains the reader in the elimination of prejudice and the formation of definitions, both of which seem requisite for successful study of the *Ethics*. Spinoza clearly held at the time he composed the earlier text that this prelude is necessary; whether he abandoned that view is another story. A passage in IIP40S (*Opera* II 120, 24; Curley, p. 476) suggests that he did not.

62. Hence, Spinoza interpreters like Richard Mason (*The God of Spinoza*, Cambridge, 1997) as well as Wolfson and Earle, emphasize that Spinoza's ontological arguments are not intended to convince potential atheists.

Chapter Five

ONTOLOGICAL ARGUMENTS IN LEIBNIZ AND THE GERMAN ENLIGHTENMENT

I n the systems of Spinoza and Malebranche the intuitive version of the Cartesian ontological argument runs its course to completion. In those two cases the syllogism of the *First Replies* receives extended revision and defense in light of the many objections brought forth over the latter half of the seventeenth century. Both philosophers begin from an orthodoxly Cartesian position, and both reply to the objections with arguments that they first discovered by reading texts like the *First*, *Second*, and *Fifth Replies*. The significant departures that these authors take from Descartes stem from their concerted efforts at providing the central claim of the Cartesian argument with a consistent context; the defense of the Cartesian argument leads ultimately to positions that Descartes himself did not hold. The noticeable discrepancy between their respective defenses of the argument results from the fact that there is more than one way of rendering it consistent. These are the last noteworthy attempts, however, at developing the context of the intuitive argument into a philosophical system. Subsequent defenders of the seventeenth-century argument, and they are few, operate primarily in response to the eighteenth-century critique of the argument.

As a result of the attempt to justify the intuitive nature of the ontological argument, the idea of God as a necessarily existing being had become the starting point of a systematic philosophy, rather than the conclusion of extended argumentation. The position of the argument as the foundation of a philosophy has two significant consequences. First, the argument possesses virtually no strength whatsover in relation to convincing atheists, an admission made by even the chief proponents of the proof. Second, the central insight involved in the argument is unavailable to anyone who refuses to think from the standpoint of a very particular philosophy. These consequences, of course, are entirely consistent with the argument's reference to a private intuition. Moreover, any objections of this sort meet with the additional *ad hominem* argumentation that is almost ubiquitous among the argument's seventeenth-century proponents.

In the eighteenth century these aspects of the defense of the argument begin to dissolve, and the philosophies of Malebranche and Spinoza are of relatively little consequence for the "natural theology" of the early part of that century. It is instead Leibniz whose interpretation of the argument influences its fate among the subsequent generations of philosophers. Leibniz's numerous writings on the ontological argument represent the beginning of a long process of providing the a priori proof with a thorough logical and metaphysical grounding. In his philosophy and in the writings of his German successors the ontological argument again becomes the subject of detailed demonstration, although this occurs in a very different manner than it had previously in the works of Descartes and More.

Although in some places Leibniz emphasizes his complicity with Descartes,[1] at no point does he actually defend the *First Replies* argument against the standard objections. Unlike Spinoza, Leibniz rejects the Cartesian argument even in his earliest writings on it.[2] His defense and revision of the argument is one that begins by conceding the main points to the objectors (i.e., in most of the debates outlined in the preceding chapters Leibniz sides with the objectors to the argument rather than with its proponents). We find him assenting to, for instance, both versions of the Thomistic objection, as well as to the modal objection that we find discussed by More, Huet, and Cudworth.[3] He also rejects many of the theological doctrines, such as the doctrine of equivocal attribution and the equation of God with "being," that are essential to the seventeenth-century argument.[4] For these reasons his eventual endorsement of an ontological proof represents a fundamental change in the context of the a priori demonstration of the existence of God, rather than a mere development of the Cartesian context.

Some of the changes that Leibniz makes to the argument are fairly well-known, while other, equally important revisions have elicited comparatively little notice. His first move is to side with Scotus and Mersenne in insisting that the proof requires a preliminary demonstration of the possibility or non-contradictoriness of the idea of God. This point dominates his attention from approximately 1675 through the turn of the eighteenth century. Although Leibniz never abandons this idea, other difficulties with the argument preoccupy his later writings. Most important among these is the distinction of two lines of ontological proof, which he accomplishes by separating the concept of a perfect being from the concept of a necessary being. The distinction itself is nothing new to Leibniz, and he likely discovered it by reading Gassendi or other critics of the argument.[5] He is among the first, however, who acknowledges this distinction and still ultimately endorses an a priori demonstration of God's existence. On his view, these distinct concepts serve as the basis for two different ontological arguments, so that the moniker "ontologcial argument" later appears in the plural.[6] Finally, Leibniz is the first to subject the constituent concepts of the ontological argument to a derivation from other divisions of philosophy, and this is the theme of his final treatments of the proof. In his and in subsequent systems, the ontological argument becomes partially dependent upon cosmology and psychology.

LEIBNIZ AND THE POSSIBILITY PREMISE

The supplementary proof

As suggested above, even Leibniz's earliest writings on the ontological argument express his assent to at least some of the objections to the proof. At no point does he appear to have endorsed the Cartesian argument as he found it. Nonetheless, whether he emphasizes the fact that he is criticizing the Cartesian argument or the fact that he is revising it depends upon the context. In his notebooks and correspondence he assumes the character of a relentless critic of both Descartes and Spinoza; in some of his published works, however, he plays the role of defender of what he takes to be the core of the Cartesian argument. It is the latter role that he assumes in the *New Essays*, a passage from which is the *locus classicus* for the possibility objection in Leibniz's corpus. The text has the following characteristics: first, Leibniz considers only the perfection argument, although he is aware of the fact that Descartes considers the *First Replies* syllogism to be the more vital proof[7]; second, he claims (unlike Descartes and unlike himself in other writings) that Aquinas in particular was mistaken in his opposition to Anselm's argument.[8] Part of the passage runs:

God is the greatest or the most perfect of beings; which is to say that he is a being whose greatness or perfection is supreme, containing within himself every degree of it. That is the notion of God. Now here is how existence follows from that notion. Existing is something more than not existing, i.e., existence adds a degree to the greatness or to the perfection—as Descartes puts it, existence is itself a perfection.... (This argument) is not fallacious, but it is an incomplete demonstration, which assumes something which should also be proved in order to make the argument mathematically evident. The point is that it is tacitly assumed that this idea of a wholly great or wholly perfect being is possible and does not imply a contradiction.[9]

This is only one of many instances in which Leibniz, quite knowingly, reiterates Mersenne's contention that the *Fifth Meditation* argument suffices only to prove that "if God is possible, he exists."[10] What distinguishes Leibniz's position with respect to this objection is that he actually provides the required supplementary proof, whereas Mersenne had merely (and unsuccessfully) requested such a demonstration from Descartes. Although in the *New Essays* and other popular texts he only alludes to such a proof,[11] in several private sketches he follows through with his auxiliary argument. The most celebrated form of the possibility proof appears in *Quod ens perfectissimum existit*,[12] a text famous for its allegedly having received approval from Spinoza during Leibniz's 1676 interview with that philosopher.[13] The proof is as follows: a supremely perfect being is defined as the union of all perfections, and this concept is possible only if all perfections are compatible. Leibniz defines a "perfection" as essentially simple and "purely positive," so that no perfection contains anything with which it could contradict another perfection (i.e., no perfection implies the negation of any other). All perfections are thus compatible, so that a single subject or union of all perfections is possible.[14]

With this proof complete, Leibniz has now put forward the following revised ontological argument: if an *ens perfectissimum* is possible, it exists; an *ens perfectissimum* is possible; therefore it exists. As suggested, Leibniz is fully aware that he is not posing a novel argument, but is only lending "mathematical certainty" to the argument that Mersenne borrows from Duns Scotus.[15] He is also aware that the most esteemed among his immediate philosophical predecessors rejected the possibility premise and thus his revised ontological proof, although extended argumentation with those philosophers is not an overriding concern of his.

Three Objections to the Possibility Premise

Among the proponents of the ontological argument in the two generations prior to Leibniz, three replies to the possibility objection are predominant. First, Descartes replies to Mersenne that the possibility (i.e., non-contradictoriness)[16] of God is inferred from the existence of God, not vice versa. Second, the philosophers in question consider possibility to be a modality that is ascribable to finite entities, but not to God. This view is shared by Malebranche, Spinoza, and sometimes by Descartes.[17] The third response is that God's nature is simple, so that any equiry into the non-contradictoriness of that nature would be superfluous. This is Malebranche's main contribution to the debate, which Spinoza shares in some works and at which Descartes occasionally also hints.[18] Although only the last objection was directly presented to Leibniz, his replies to each of the objections are discernible from various positions he takes.

It is probable that Leibniz read the *Second Replies* and therefore knew that Descartes rejected a version of the possibility argument by claiming that knowledge of God's possibility or non-contradictoriness is consequent to knowledge of his existence. There is also evidence, moreover, that Leibniz endorses and sometimes utilizes inferences from actuality to possibility.[19] What Leibniz disputes, then, is not Descartes' contention that, given an adequate proof for God's existence, we would need no further proof for his possibility. Instead, he disputes only that God's existence can be known a priori without prior recourse to modal logic. This result indicates an important difference between Leibniz and his predecessors: Descartes could infer possibility from actuality only on the basis of prior awareness of God's actuality, an awareness which is in essence immediate. For Descartes, that God exists is apparent immediately upon consideration of the idea of him. Leibniz, by contrast, does not take the ontological argument to express this direct awareness of God's existence, a fact evidenced further by his axiomatization of even the modal principle that "if God is possible, he exists."[20] The possibility objection is in the first place an objection to the immediacy of the ontological argument.

The second objection to the Leibnizian premise is that possibility is ascribable only to finite entities. This objection also occurs in Descartes' writings, although it appears more prominently in Spinoza and Malebranche. The dispute between Leibniz and those philosophers on this point is largely a matter of definition, but not one without important consequences. All parties agree that God's essence and existence are inseparable. The disagreement lies only in the consequences of this doctrine for the analysis of the ontological argument. In Leibniz's terminology, "possibility" (regarded as possible existence) is nearly equivalent with "essence": "the essence of a thing is but the specific reason for its possibility."[21] This premise is key to the proof that in the case of God (in which essence and existence are inseparable), an immediate inference from possibility to actuality is valid. Leibniz's inference is from God's essence qua possibility to his existence. This evidently presupposes that God's essence is known prior to his existence.

Malebranche and Spinoza deny just this last point, and this denial determines their understanding of what is meant by "possible existence." For them, "possible existence" refers to the essence of a thing only if that essence is distinct from its existence, which is why that property is incompatible with "necessary existence." In other words, finite entities possess possible existence precisely to the extent that their essence is distinguishable from their existence; God, by contrast, possesses necessary existence to the extent that his essence and existence are inseparable. No inference from the essence to the existence is needed, since the point is precisely that the essence is not distinct from the existence. Since God's essence and existence are inseparable, they should be perceived simultaneously, which is to say that proper knowledge of God's existence is immediate.

The discrepancy between Leibniz's interpretation of possibility and the seventeenth-century reading stems partly from their divergent views on definitions. Leibniz insists that all definitions, including the definition of God, are merely hypothetical.[22] In this he appears to overlook the caveat from Descartes' *First Replies*, which is the same point that Spinoza discusses in his correspondence with Oldenburg. For Descartes and Spinoza, all definitions *except* the definition of God are merely hypothetical; this is another reason why possible existence belongs only to the definition of finite entities. As Spinoza suggests in his *Treatise on the Intellect*, the requirements and status of a definition differ with respect to the finitude or infinity of the definiendum.[23] Although Leibniz likewise recognizes the difference between God and finite entities, he interprets this in a different manner. He considers all definitions, *without exception*, to be hypothetical (which is why he attributes "possible existence" even to God), and he subordinates the distinction between God and finite entities by asserting that only in the case of God can we infer his actuality from his possibility or his necessity from mere hypothesis. We have here

simply two ways of understanding the difference between God and finite entities as this pertains to definitions (and thus also to the requirements of
demonstration); one view (Spinoza's) reflects the doctrine of equivocal attribution, the other (Leibniz's) reflects the doctrine of theological analogy.[24]

Malebranche's theory of ideas represents an elaboration of and improvement upon the Cartesian/Spinozistic version of the difference between the
definition of God and other definitions, and in light of his view Leibniz's
move appears to be an error, rather than a mere discrepancy in definitions.
Instead of emphasizing an alleged infinite difference between the idea of God
and other ideas, Malebranche simply stipulates that we have no idea of God.
He appropriately understands "idea" to refer to the paradigm of an entity in
separation from the existence of that entity; our idea of something refers to its
essence, *to the extent that this is distinct from its existence.* In the case of God,
where no essence is distinguishable from existence, there is no "idea." It would
be similar to say that God has no "essence" (Descartes and Spinoza are consciously equivocating when they speak of the essence of God), at least as this
word is otherwise understood, since our thought of God is a direct perception
of his existence, rather than being mediated by a paradigm or idea.

On this view, what Leibniz is doing in treating the "possibility" of God
prior to the proof of his existence is overlooking the central claim that God's
"essence" or "possibility" is not something distinct from his existence. Again,
Leibniz is not ignorant of this identity (otherwise he would not be a proponent of the a priori proof), but his procedure of proof is incommensurate with
the view. He treats the idea of God first as if this were distinct from God's existence, only to remind us in the next premise that it is not.[25] As Kant later
notices, Leibniz's two premises contradict one another.[26] It is amusing enough
that Kant thereby unknowingly sides with Malebranche, Spinoza, and
Descartes. Leibniz's move essentially inserts a contradiction at the point where
the seventeenth-century theory appears merely arbitrary.[27]

The third objection to the possibility premise raises a point similar to the
previous. On Malebranche's view, God's nature is simple or non-analyzable. In
the *Cogitata Metaphysica* Spinoza expresses the same idea by defining God as
an *ens simplicissimum.*[28] Leibniz was made aware of this view by his correspon-
dent Arnold Eckhard, who appropriately defends the Cartesian argument
against the possibility objection by insisting on the simplicity of God's
nature.[29] In that case it is entirely unnecessary to worry about whether the idea
of God could contain a contradiction, since a simple idea cannot be contradic-

tory. As Eckhard points out, contradiction is possible only where two distinct concepts are conjoined.[30]

By contrast, Leibniz, at least in his early writings, understands God as a perfect entity to be an *unio perfectorum*, a unity of distinct perfections. The perfections are indeed simple, but their relation is not, which is why a proof of their compatibility is required. Leibniz emphasizes this interpretation when he refers to God as an "aggregate" of perfections.[31] God is a subject of numerous and distinct predicates or perfections. On this point Leibniz goes against the grain of traditional philosophical theology (at least of the theology common to proponents of the a priori proof), according to which the qualities of God are indistinguishable within his nature.[32] He rejects the related Malebranchean notion (with which Eckhard acquaints him) that God is "being" simpliciter, since he holds that being is always the being of something, the existence of some particular essence, and that it is senseless to speak of being "as such."[33]

This also contributes to the explanation of Leibniz's emphasis on the perfection argument; for him, what requires proof is that existence is among the perfections contained within God's nature. This auxiliary argument from the *Fifth Meditation* became superfluous in Malebranche's system and subordinate in Spinoza's, since those philosophers view God's existence to be the same as his essence, rather than a property or relation of that essence that would follow by mere implication. The perfection argument is merely one way of mediating the relationship between the concept of God and the concept of his existence.[34] If that relationship, however, is immediate (i.e. if there is no difference between God and his existence), and thus no relationship at all, as is the case if God is defined as "being" simpliciter, then no mediating argument is necessary. All that is required is that God be conceived/perceived as "being" or, as Spinoza would prefer to say, "eternal existence."

Leibniz, on the other hand, at no point idenitifes "existence" with "God," as is the case with Malebranche and Spinoza, or with anyone who views God's attributes as indistinct.[35] Such an identification inevitably would have led him to the intuitive explanation of the connection between God's essence and existence. Instead Leibniz views God's existence as a charachteristic that follows from God's nature, but never as itself equivalent to that nature.[36] For him the perfection argument is thus indispensable, and he devotes much effort to the revision of it. In this regard he is both aware of and sympathetic to the empirical objection. In his later writings he recognizes that existence is not a characteristic like many other predicates, but rather a relational predicate. He never-theless takes existence to follow demonstrably from the definition of God's nature, since he holds that it is better to exist than not to exist.

The Possibility Premise as a Defense of the Cartesian Argument

Although the Leibnizian possibility syllogism seems to reflect either an oversight or disagreement concerning the idea of God, the argument is not merely a result of that dissent. It derives instead from a critique of the epis-temological foundation of the Cartesian argument. The latter argument hinges upon the veracity of clear and distinct ideas, or more specifically upon the reality of clearly conceived predicates: from the fact that I clearly perceive that existence belongs to God's nature, I infer that God in fact exists, since what I perceive to belong to a thing really belongs to the thing. Leibniz takes issue with the subjective nature of the Cartesian major premise, in that it reflects only what a given individual (albeit a philosopher who reasons from a privileged standpoint) perceives to belong to some-thing, rather than what demonstrably belongs to that thing. For Leibniz, the subjectivity of the doctrine of clear and distinct ideas is evidence of its arbitrariness: "what appears clear to one does not appear clear to another."[37] This indeed points to a shortcoming of the Cartesian approach, and in fact very few (even among trained philosophers, contrary to the Cartesian *ad hominem* stipulation) were able to clearly perceive that existence belongs to God's nature.

Another method is thus requisite for establishing the veracity of ideas, and Leibniz purports to have discovered this method in the analysis of possi-bility. He equates "the possibility of a thing" with "the truth of its idea."[38] Without a demonstration of possibility, there is no good reason to believe that the perception cited in the Cartesian minor premise is not a *merely* subjective perception, as well as that it contains no contradiction. Leibniz accordingly associates the possibility objection with both versions of the Thomistic objec-tion:[39] without a logical demonstration of possibility, the connection between God's essence and existence could at least seem to occur only in thought. In proving the possibility of God, then, Leibniz understands himself to be forti-fying the argument against the Thomistic objections.

Leibniz's theory of possibility in effect condenses nearly all of the objections to the ontological argument. Without a proof of possibility, Leibniz believes, the argument falls victim not only to the two Thomistic objections, but also to the modal objection. This is evident from the fact that Leibniz, contra Descartes, Spinoza, More, and Cudworth, considers even the definition of God to express merely hypothetical necessity. He is also in agreement with Huet's last objection, viz., the claim that an objector has no reason to lend credence to any of the at least apparently arbitrary claims of the intuitive argument. Finally, Leibniz views possibility as the primary indicator that an idea is not fictitious, so that without a possibility premise the argument would be vulnerable also to the epistemological objections. In his view, then, the single premise concerning possibility overcomes each of these objections to the argument. The proof of possibility at once eliminates the subjective nature of the argument (thus disarming Huet's objection in addition to the Thomistic quibbles) while it establishes the link between hypothetical and absolute necessity (thus meeting the modal objection) and secures the non-contradictory and nonfictional nature of the idea of God (responding to the possibility and transition objections).

The contradiction that Kant uncovers in the possibility argument, then, would appear fatal to the ontological argument if it were not the case that Kant stands in aggreement on that very point with Descartes, Spinoza, Malebranche, and Hegel. The fact that the possibility premise contradicts the central claim in the ontological argument is rather a mere instance of a more general problem with that argument, one about which the key proponents were well aware. If the problem with the possibility premise is that it treats the essence of God as if this were distinct from his existence, in direct contradiction to what the minor premise asserts, this is also the case with *any* preliminary discussion of the idea or essence of God. Exactly this problem appears first in More's *Antidote*, and similar considerations led Malebranche and Spinoza to eliminate the major premise of the argument and to emphasize the immediacy of our knowledge of God. The failure of Leibniz's possibility argument is thus exemplary of the failure of all demonstrative versions of the argument. Among the arguments proposed in the seventeenth and eighteenth centuries, only the intuitive arguments are consistent, although these suffer from a lack of persuasiveness.

THE TWO-CONCEPT THESIS: FROM THE JAQUELOT LETTERS (1702) TO THE WORKS OF 1714

Since Leibniz rejects both the identification of "God" with "being" and the intuitive version of the Cartesian minor premise, the relation of the concept of "necessary existence" to the concept of an "*ens perfectissimum*" becomes problematic for him. As with all other aspects of the ontological argument, Leibniz is here developing a theme that he could have easily discovered in various texts from the seventeenth century. Gassendi seems to have been the first to suggest that the connection between the two concepts in question requires demonstration.[40] Huet also claims that the minor premise of the Cartesian argument asserts an unjustified connection between necessary existence and supreme perfection,[41] and his *Censura* appeared prior to the period in which Leibniz begins to emphasize the plurality of ontological arguments.[42] Of course, the efficacy of these objections against the most consistent versions of the Cartesian argument is minimal, since they do not apply to the intuitive version of the minor premise, and they overlook the conception of God as simple.

In any case, Leibniz's initial distinction between two arguments appears to have arisen in the interest of lending greater efficiency to the possibility argument, rather than as a defense against objectors like Gassendi or Huet. By the time he wrote his 1700 criticism of the Cartesian argument "Against Descartes on the Existence of God," his possibility syllogism had become rather involved. He had conducted a number of supplementary proofs for the possibility of an *ens perfectissimum*; he had also developed an intricate proof for the remaining premise that "if such a being is possible, it exists." Various difficulties in presenting this elaborate argument led him to the realization that an ontological argument is possible "even omitting all reference to perfection."[43] This context is perhaps of great siginificance, since it is mainly in his later, popular expositions of his philosophy that he begins with the concept of necessity rather than with the notion of perfection. In other words, it is possible that Leibniz's concern here was more pedagogical than philosophical.

An argument from necessity is indeed noticeably simpler. Whereas the premise "if a perfect being is possible, it exists" requires proof (such as the controversial perfection argument), the premise "if a necessary being is possible, it exists" appears to be tautological. All that remains, then, is to demonstrate the possibility of a necessary being. Leibniz offers a number of arguments to this end, some of which contain a posteriori premises.[44] These are among his most influential theological arguments. He argues, for instance, that no beings at all are possible if a necessary being is not possible, since only a necessary being could provide a sufficient reason for the possibility of contingent beings.[45] It is an argument similar to this that Kant proposes in his 1763 text *The Only Possible Ground for Proof of the Existence of God*.[46] That Kant follows Leibniz in this argument is significant, and his subsequent rejection of the ontological argument in the *First Critique* concerns a distinctly Leibnizian version of the proof.

Any proof of the possibility of a necessary being leads quickly to the assertion of the existence of a necessary being; the question still remains, however, of whether the necessary being corresponds to the idea of a God or perfect being. Leibniz accordingly sees the need to provide a proof that a necessary being is also a perfect being. This last point (whether the existence of a supremely perfect being follows from the existence of a necessary being) represents the heart of the entire eighteenth-century dispute over the ontological proof, and it is noteworthy that we find some variation concerning it among Leibnizian texts. In several instances between 1702 and 1705 Leibniz appears doubtful about the possibility of such a proof. He later offers a rough outline for the argument, and it is these arguments that influence German rationalists like Christian Wolff and Alexander Baumgarten.

Shortly after the turn of the eighteenth century Leibniz begins a correspondence with the exiled French philosopher Isaac Jaquelot, at which point the ontological argument became the subject of his renewed attention. Jaquelot had been a noteworthy figure in the philosophical landscape, the author of several contributions to the debate over both the proofs for the existence of God in general and the a priori proof in particular.[47] Perhaps the most important of his writings, however, is a letter he writes to Leibniz some time near the end of 1702.[48] It is Jaquelot who first provides Leibniz with a version of the Cartesian argument that hinges on a clear distinction of the two constituent concepts of the minor premise. This argument subsequently receives attention from Leibniz, and it seems to influence much of his thought over the next decade. Jaquelot poses the following argument as an addendum to a very faithful reproduction of the *First Replies* syllogism:

> When two concepts are necessarily conjoined, a conclusion from the existence of one (corresponding entity) to the existence of the other is legitimate. The idea of necessary existence is necessarily conjoined to the idea of a supremely perfect being. Therefore a conclusion from the existence of one (being) to the other is legitimate.[49]

Leibniz makes the following observation concerning this conclusion:

> There is an ambiguity in this conclusion ... it can be said that the existence of a necessary being follows from the existence of a supremely perfect being (supposing that both are possible) *sed non vice versa*, but not the reverse, since it has not been proven that the existence of a supremely perfect being follows from the existence of a necessary being.[50]

According to Leibniz, we can reason from the existence of an *ens perfectissimum* to the existence of a necessary being (via a revised perfection argument), but not vice versa.[51] A few years later Leibniz makes a similar observation in a letter to Christian Wolff, although this time he claims only that the desired proof is not easy.[52] It is of particular interest that Leibniz alerts Wolff to this point from his discussion with Jaquelot, since the proof in question comes to occupy the thought of both Leibniz and Wolff. In this instance Leibniz defines the notion of a necessary being, echoing Spinoza, as an *ens a se*, or a "being from itself." Although a proof of the existence of such a being is possible, Leibniz notices that the concept of it seems to bear little relation to the concept of God as a perfect entity. The concept of a necessary being or *ens a se*, he suggests, could as well be instantiated by physical atoms: "Lucretius could have claimed that his atoms exist *a se*."[53]

A decade later, however, he indeed infers the existence of God as a supremely perfect being from the existence of a necessary being. This line of reasoning appears in the popular works "The Principles of Nature and of Grace Based on Reason" and *The Monadology*.[54] In both cases he arrives at the notion of a necessary being on the basis of a consideration of the "universe" or the "series of contingent beings."[55] This series requires a sufficient reason outside the series, or in a necessary being. That necessary being, which Leibniz immediately identifies by (the term) "God," cannot likewise be dependent upon anything outside it, since otherwise it would not be the final ground of the universe. Leibniz infers other attributes of the necessary being from the characteristics of the series (e.g., from the fact that there is only one series, he concludes that there must be only one God). This unique, independent, and necessary being, finally, "must be incapable of limits and must contain as much reality as possible."[56]

From the fact that God possesses the highest degree of reality, together with the definition of perfection as "the quantity of positive reality taken strictly," it follows that God is "absolutely perfect." So Leibniz clearly thinks that he can deduce the concept of a perfect being from the concept of a necessary one. In this case he has made the proof of the existence of God as a perfect being contingent upon a posteriori premises. Subsequent to this, however, he claims that God is the sufficient ground, not only of existences, but also of essences. Without God, then, there would be "not only nothing existent but also nothing possible."[57] In this case the existence of the necessary being, and by extension the perfect being,[58] derives from "essences" or the reality of possibility, and these are known a priori.

The proof structure of these works thus runs as follows. The existence of a necessary entity follows from the existence of contingent entities and/or from the reality of possibility. Contingent entities are known to exist; the reality of possibility, on the other hand, is demonstrable in two ways. First, since contingent things exist, at least these are possible. Second, since there are eternal truths, there are possible (non-contradictory) essences. The existence of contingent beings requires a necessary being; the eternal truths and the essences of contingent things require a necessary subject in which they inhere. The existence of a necessary being follows either (a posteriori) from a cosmological argument or (a priori) from "the argument from eternal truths" or (an admixture of a priori and a posteriori) from an argument from the essences of contingent things. Lastly, certain characteristics of contingent beings and/or eternal truths suggest characteristics of the being on which they depend, and these correspond to the known attributes of God (eternity, omniscience, omnipotence, perfection, etc.). The necessary being, whose existence is proven first, is also a perfect being.

It is only *after* Leibniz succeeds in proving that the necessary entity is also a perfect entity (*Monadology* numbers 36–44) that he proceeds to discuss the ontological argument (number 45). In other words, it is only because we know that God is *both* a perfect being *and* the absolute ground of the realms of creation and eternal truth that we know that his existence follows from his possibility. Leibniz has made the ontological argument dependent upon ideas from cosmology, even where he manages to conduct the proof without axioms from experience. He does not discover, as Descartes alleges to have done, the idea of "necessary existence" in the idea of God (nor does he consider them identical concepts, as Spinoza seems to do), but instead borrows this idea from other arguments before applying it to God.[59] The textbooks of the German "school philosophy" follow this procedure, and it is those textbooks that influence the structure of Kant's "Transcendental Dialectic" and with it the apparent downfall of rationalist metaphysics.

THE TWO-ARGUMENT THESIS IN WOLFF'S *THEOLOGIA NATURALIS*

Leibniz's popular works of 1714 provide the rough outline that forms the basis for German philosophical theology throughout the middle part of the eighteenth century. The most influential figure in German philosophy from that period is Christian Wolff (1679–1754), whose *Theologia naturalis* of 1736 offers the detailed arguments not found in works like the *Monadology*. Wolff apparently had taken very seriously the warning Leibniz gave him in 1705: the ontological proof requires a difficult deduction of the concept of a perfect being from the concept of a necessary one. His own natural theology seeks to complete the argument. Like Leibniz, he arrives at the concept of a necessary being via a posteriori arguments, and only subsequently shows this necessary being to correspond to the notion of God as a perfect being.

Wolff is the first name in German philosophy from the early decades of the eighteenth century to the time of Kant's later philosophy. His long, deductive treatises cover nearly every conceivable branch of philosophy, and in many cases they develop the principles of Leibniz's philosophy into more complete and systematic arguments. The *Theologia naturalis* is a preeminent example of his style; this massive text divides into two parts and covers three large volumes, including detailed statements of each proposition of theology. The first part is entitled "Natural Theology Part I, in which the divine existence and attributes are demonstrated a posteriori." The first chapter of that part deals with the existence of a necessary being, as well as with the deduction of a number of divine attributes, such as independence and immateriality. It is the second part of the work that proceeds with an a priori demonstration of the existence of God; that part accordingly begins instead with the definition of an *ens perfectissimum*.

Although Wolff shares with Leibniz the general outline of beginning with a proof of a necessary being and only subsequently arguing that a necessary being is perfect, he arrives at the notion of a necessary being on the basis of a different premise. Instead of referring to cosmology, Wolff begins his natural theology with a reference to his empirical psychology.[60] The demonstration of the first proposition (number 24: "an *ens necessarium* exists")[61] of the first chapter departs from the assertion that "the human soul exists, or we exist." From this assertion, together with axioms from his *Ontologia*, such as the principle of sufficient reason, he argues that only the existence of a necessary being could provide a sufficent reason for the existence of the human soul.

It is indicative of Wolff's argumentative tendency that he does not immediately deduce other attributes from the notion of a necessary being, but (at least in some cases) first proves that an entity corresponding to those other attributes exists, after which he proves that it is one and the same entity in question. Proposition number 29, for instance, asserts that "there is an *ens a se*," and only in proposition number 33 do we discover that "the *ens necessarium* is the *ens a se*." This leads to an enormous proliferation of propositions and accounts for the fact that Wolff devotes hundreds of pages to arguments that Leibniz had glossed in only a few lines.

The remainder of the first chapter deduces a number of attributes for the "*en a se*," which we now know to exist necessarily. Wolff explains, for example, that this entity has no beginning (number 35), no end (number 36), and is not complex (number 47) but rather simple (number 49). Addressing Leibniz's earlier worry, he demonstrates (number 53) that "material atoms are not *entia a se*." All of this demonstration, however, is a mere prelude to the claims put forth in proposition numbers 67–69, in which he finally shows that the *ens a se* is indeed the God of whom sacred scripture speaks, and who is the sufficient ground of the world and of the human soul. When he finally writes (number 69) that "God exists," he has completed a lengthy a posteriori proof of the theological propositions that God exists necessarily and by virtue of his own essence.[62]

In chapter one of part two of the *Theologia naturalis*, Wolff begins with the notion of an *ens perfectissimum* as "that in which every compossible reality inheres to the absolutely highest degree." He then proceeds with an ontological argument of the type advocated by Leibniz some fifty years prior. In other words, after demonstrating (number 13) that this "supremely perfect being is possible," he proves that existence is a reality and that necessary existence is the absolute highest degree of existence (number 20). The subsequent proposition (number 21) then concludes: "God necessarily exists." His ontological argument is thus the Leibnizian syllogism (possibility premise/perfection argument/conclusion) that throughout and after the eighteenth century became synonymous with *the* ontological argument, as if this had always constituted the form of the a priori proof.

It is important to note that Wolff does *not* follow Leibniz in inferring the existence of a perfect being directly and explicitly from the argument for a necessary being. Instead he proves the necessary existence of an *ens perfectissimum* by virtue of a perfection argument (together with a possibility premise), and thus offers a version of the ontological argument reminiscent more of the Leibniz of 1684 than of 1714. Wolff does not derive the ontological argument from the cosmological, but instead tries to demonstrate the existence of an *ens perfectissimum* independently of the other argument. Only after the proof that a perfect being exists does he try to prove that the perfect being is the same being as the necessary being.

That this is Wolff's intention is clear from the fact that the title of this chapter promises a purely a priori proof of the existence of a supremely perfect being. He fails, however, to keep his promise, since his perfection argument imports a proposition from the a posteriori part of his work. This occurs in the demonstration of proposition number 20, in which Wolff appeals to the existence of a necessary being in order to prove that necessary existence is a reality or perfection.[63] Wolff's procedure seems to represent a confusion of two doctrines. On the one hand, his intention is to advocate an ontological argument for the existence of an *ens perfectissimum* without any assistance from cosmology (i.e., to conduct the proof a priori). He nevertheless inadvertantly confirms the dependence of this proof on the antecedent demonstration of the existence of a necessary being.

After reaching the conclusion of his pseudo-ontological argument, Wolff proceeds with his explicit proof that the *ens perfectissimum*, whose necessary existence has at least allegedly been proven a priori, is in fact one and the same *ens necessarium* whose existence was demonstrated a posteriori in part one. Once this identification is established, he deduces the remainder of the divine attributes only with explicit reference to part one of the work. In other words, the remaining demonstrations are of the form: the perfect being is the necessary being; the necessary being is independent; therefore the perfect being is independent. The remainder of Wolff's a priori natural theology makes constant and explicit appeal to a posteriori premises.

BAUMGARTEN'S ONTOLOGICAL ARGUMENT

Most of the important eighteenth-century German textbooks on metaphysics follow this procedure that Wolff adopts from Leibniz. Among these is

Alexander Baumgarten's *Metaphysica* of 1739.[64] The historical significance of this work is not small: Kant employed that text in his lectures for most of his "pre-Critical" period, and it is mainly Baumgarten's definitions, terminology, and proofs that influence the "Transcendental Dialectic" of the *Critique of Pure Reason*.[65] Kant's critique of the ontological argument is essentially a critique of the proof structure of the *Metaphysica*. That proof structure derives, with some notable revisions, both from the textbooks of Baumgarten's teacher, Wolff, as well as from the popular works of Leibniz's Vienna period.

In the organization of his philosophy Baumgarten (1714–1762) appears to make only minor changes from that of his mentor. His "metaphysics" embodies the disciplines to which Wolff had devoted separate treatises. "Natural theology" follows ontology, cosmology, and psychology. (It is worth noting here how far we have come from Spinoza's *Ethics*, in which the ontological argument serves as the *beginning*, rather than the end, of philosophy). One significant departure from Wolff's organization, however, is important to the development of the ontological argument: Baumgarten's a posteriori arguments do not appear within the discipline of "natural theology," but rather within his "cosmology." In other words, his proof of the existence of a necessary being *does not* serve as the basis for a deduction of the divine attributes; instead he asserts only that cosmological precepts require the existence of a necessary being, although these same precepts do not alone indicate which being is necessary. Whereas Wolff's cosmology is already a theology, Baumgarten concludes from his cosmology only that *some being* exists whose nonexistence would be contradictory (number 361).

That the necessary being is also God is the result of, not a precondition for, Baumgarten's ontological proof, and this point determines Kant's understanding of that argument. As Leibniz had instructed Jaquelot more than three decades prior, from the fact that we can prove the existence of a necessary being it does not follow that we know which being is necessary. This last is the subject of an altogether different inquiry. In paragraph numbers 803–23 Baumgarten conducts just this inquiry by arguing from the nominal definition of an *ens perfectissimum* to the inclusion of "necessary existence" within the concept of that entity.[66] His procedure can be summarized as follows. A perfect being is an *ens realissimum* or most real being (number 806), and thus contains every reality (number 807).[67] Existence is included among the realities (number 810) and therefore the *ens perfecissimum* (or God, number 811) exists. In the subsequent propositions Baumgarten reinterprets the inclusion of "existence" within God's nature in order to show that the nonexistence of God is contradictory (number 823); his existence is therefore logically necessary.[68] From the fact that the inclusion of existence within God's nature is necessary, Baumgarten concludes that God is the necessary being whose existence had been demonstrated in the "cosmology."

Although Baumgarten thereby reduces the degree to which the ontological argument depends upon the cosmological, he exposes the a priori proof to a more obvious objection. In determining the attributes of the *ens necessarium* only by an ontological proof (rather than by an a posteriori theology) he leaves himself with no explanation of why the logical necessity of the inclusion of existence within the nature of an *ens perfectissimum* is also the metaphysical necessity required by a cosmology. The duality of Wolff's theology, by contrast, allows him to avoid inferring directly (at least explicitly) from logical to metaphysical necessity. Since Baumgarten offers no justification for this inference analogous to the Cartesian rule for truth or to a Spinozistic epistemology, even the oldest and easiest of objections suffices to refute his argument. In the coming decades both Crusius and Kant successfully raise the Thomistic objections against this argument of Baumgarten's.[69]

It is also Baumgarten's interpretation of the relationship between cosmology and the ontological argument that becomes the subject of criticism in Kant's "Transcendental Dialectic." Kant adopts the idea that cosmology instructs us only that some being is necessary, and that this discipline cannot serve as the basis for a deduction of the divine attributes. An ontological argument is thus needed in order to determine which properties belong to the *ens necessarium*. This thesis would seem peculiar if we were to jump directly from the *Fifth Meditation* to the *Critique of Pure Reason*. It is instead Baumgarten's *Metaphysica* that sets the table for the latter text, and the criticisms that Kant raises in it are only effective to the extent that Baumgarten's argument is the definitive one.[70]

ANTI-WOLFFIANA: CRUSIUS AND THE THOMISTIC OBJECTION

The shortcomings of Baumgarten's ontological argument were not lost on his contemporaries. One of the leading Anti-Wolffians of the mid-century, Christian August Crusius, objects precisely to the conflation of logical and ontological necessity with which Baumgarten burdens the proof. Crusius (1715–1775) is widely recognized as an important influence on Kant's development, particularly in the middle decades of the eighteenth century, and his critique of the ontological argument is among those points on which he and Kant agree.[71] His opposition to the Wolffians, which covers a range of points later widely assumed in the critique of that school, aids Kant in many other areas as well. In his chief metaphysical work, *Sketch of the Necessary Truths of Reason* (1745),[72] he achieves a number of breaks with the German rationalist tradition that Kant will soon make more familiar: he distinguishes formal from real possibility; he rejects determinism; he defines existence with reference to space-time; he argues for a theology based largely on morality; most importantly, he rejects the derivation of the principle of sufficient reason from the principle of contradiction. These accomplishments appear in a metaphysics textbook organized largely in the manner of his rationalist contemporaries.[73]

Although Crusius opposes the hyperrationalism of Wolff, Baumgarten, and the other figures of the mid-eighteenth century, he accepts their view of the relationship between the concepts of necessary and perfect existence. He even places a version of the perfection argument within his "Ontologie," arguing that the notion of a perfect being includes the concept of necessary existence.[74] It was probably Crusius's inclusion of this argument in his ontology, rather than in his natural theology, that encouraged Kant's later application of the title "ontological" to the a priori proof. In any case, assent to a version of the perfection argument, of course, does not constitute an unqualified approval of any "ontological" argument. As even Descartes had admitted to Caterus, the perfection argument alone does not suffice to prove the real existence of the deity.[75] Rather, that argument remains vulnerable to the objections outlined in Thomas's *Summa*. When Crusius returns to these concepts in his natural theology, then, he raises the Thomistic objection that the perfection argument, if taken to imply real existence, commits the fallacy of four terms (equivocation). With appeal to his careful distinction between real and ideal propositions, Crusius appropriately applies this Thomistic objection to the ontological arguments of the Wolffian school, which he recognizes as revisions of "the Cartesian argument":

> The argument should read: any entity that possesses every possible perfection, possesses also existence. God is an entity that possesses every possible perfection. According to this, then, God possesses existence, and thus there

is a God. This inference is indeed deceptive, since the first premise is an axiom, while the second is a definition. The argument is formally fallacious, because it is a syllogism with four terms. Specifically term "existence" has a different meaning in the conclusion than it does in the premise. In the premise the concern is with existence in the intellect alone (*im Verstande*), since a concept in the mind is said to contain existence within it, so that when this concept is thought or posited, existence is also thought or posited as a part of that concept. In the conclusion, however, the concern is with existence outside the intellect (*ausserhalb der Gedanke*). The premises are both ideal propositions (*Ideal-Saetze*), and yet the conclusion is supposed to be a real proposition (*Real-Satz*).[76]

It should be allowed that, in the context of this debate in Germany in the 1740s, Crusius gains the upper hand in the dispute. Baumgarten had indeed failed to justify the relationship between the logical necessity of the perfection argument and the ontological necessity required for the proof of the existence of God. One can thus hardly blame Crusius's younger colleague in Koenigsberg for assimilating this passage into his own Habilitationschrift one decade later. The epistemological and theological underpinnings that made ontological arguments possible in the seventeenth century have long been forgotten. The theories of clear and distinct ideas, real definitions, vision in God, etc. have faded from the pages of the philosophers' book, and with their demise comes the return of the Thomistic objections as legitimate problems for proponents of contemporary ontological arguments.

NOTES

1. The *New Essays* text (see below), for instance, expresses his argument as a revision, not a critique, of the Cartesian proof.

2. Leibniz appears as a critic of the ontological argument as early as 1675. See his letter to Oldenburg in *Die mathematischen Schriften von Gottfried Wilhelm Leibniz* (ed. Carl Immanuel Gerhardt, Berlin, Weidmann, 1849–55, 7 volumes; hereafter "GM" by volume and page numbers), I 385; a translation of the letter is in *Philosophical Papers and Letters* (ed. Leroy Loemker, 2nd ed., Riedel, 1969, hereafter "Loemker").

3. The modal objection is found in *Saemtliche Schriften und Briefe* (Berlin Academy, 1923; hereafter "A"), series 2, vol. I, p. 393; the Thomistic objection is equated with the possibility premise in *Die philosophischen Schriften von Gottfried Wilhelm Leibniz* (ed. Carl Immanuel Gerhardt. Berlin, Weidmann, 1849–55, 7 volumes;

hereafter "G" by volume and page numbers), III 444; See also G IV 424 (Loemker, p. 293).

4. For Leibniz's view on divine attribution, see, for instance, his essay "Reflections on the Common Concept of Justice," in Loemker, pp. 561–73.

5. Cudworth (*True System* II, pp. 145–46) and Huet (*Censura*, p. 167) likewise point to a distinction here.

6. Henrich (p. 45): "Leibniz was the first to distinguish two ontological arguments...."

7. See G I 212–15; G II 344; G IV 423 (Loemker, p. 292).

8. Leibniz typically makes no distinction between the scholastic and modern arguments. See, for example, G III 443. In other places (Loemker, p. 292) Leibniz claims that Thomas had refuted the argument.

9. *New Essays on Human Understanding*, trans. Remnant and Bennet, Cambridge 1981, p. 438.

10. Cf. G IV 423–24 (Loemker, pp. 292–93); G IV 294; G I 213; G V 18; G IV 401.

11. Cf. *Discourse on Metaphysics* #1.

12. G VII, 261 (Loemker, pp. 167–68). See also G I 224.

13. For details see *Leibniz et Spinoza*, Georges Friedman, Gallimard, 1962, chap. 3.

14. For analysis of this argument, see David Werther's "Leibniz and the Possibility of God's Existence" (in *Religious Studies* 32(1), 1996, pp. 37–48) and Adriano Bausola's "Die Moeglichkeit des volkommensten Wesens und der ontologische Gottesbeweis: die Position von Leibniz" (in *Studia Leibnitiana* 13, 1981, 1–24).

15. Mersenne is merely playing devil's advocate when he claims that the minor premise of this argument is uncertain; his point is that Descartes does not have the means of proving that God's essence is non-contradictory.

16. See the *Second Replies* (AT VII 150; CSM II 107).

17. AT VII 166.

18. See Spinoza's *Cogitata Metaphysica*, part 2, chap. 5 (*Opera* I 257ff., Curley, p. 323).

19. See Henrich, pp. 52ff.

20. A 2 I 390; on this text see Robert Merrihew Adams, *Leibniz: Determinist, Theist, Idealist*, Oxford University Press, 1994, pp. 136–37.

21. Ibid.

22. A 2 I 393.

23. *Treatise on the Emendation of the Intellect*, #95ff.

24. The proponent of Leibniz's view of definition has subjected God to epistemic or logical norms that the equivocist wants to reserve for created things.

25. Of course, the claim that the "idea" of God is not distinct from his existence

is the subject of Clarke's criticism, which Kant also discusses (KrV B 625). Spinoza and Malebranche remove the illusion of fallacy here through their anti-subjectivism; i.e., when I think of God this is not "my" idea, not a moment of my consciousness. Spinoza's monism is of assistance here, but ultimately it is only Hegel who confronts the problem directly with the bold claim that my idea of God is his idea of himself. As for Leibniz, he does not seem sensitive to this issue, which is perhaps why he favors the possibility argument.

26. KrV B625.

27. For an analysis of this point see Jose R. Silva's "A Criticism of Leibniz's Views on the Ontological Argument" (in *Dialogos* 68, 1996, pp. 133–92).

28. Curley, p. 324; *Opera* I 258.

29. G I 217ff. On the Eckhard correspondence, see Bausola, as well as Wolfgang Janke's "Das ontologische Argument in der Fruehzeit des leibnizschen Denkens [1676–78]" (in *Kant Studien* 54, 1963, pp. 259–87).

30. Ibid.: "A contradiction is always between two distinct concepts, when the nature of the things in question does not permit of conjunction."

31. A 6 III 574.

32. See Anselm's *Monologion*, chapter 17, as well as Descartes' *Mediation III* (AT VII 50; CSM II 34) and *Second Replies* (AT VII 137; CSM II 98).

33. See Bausola, p. 16. Leibniz discusses this issue in his correspondence with Wolff, circa 1705. As Bausola notes, however, his concern for this problem stems from his discussions with Eckhard twenty-five years prior.

34. Leibniz rejects the omnipotence argument that also explains this relationship, since that argument makes the fact of God's existence (like other necessary truths) dependent upon God's will and power. This, of course, represents one of his chief points of disagreement with Cartesian philosophy.

35. Spinoza, *EIP22*; Leibniz's successors like Baumgarten and Wolff consider God to be simple, but offer no account of our knowledge of God that is consistent with this claim.

36. On this and the following two points, consult the texts that Adams translates on pp. 164ff. of his book.

37. G III 449; also in "Meditations on Knowledge, Truth and Ideas" (G IV 422ff.; Loemker, pp. 292–93).

38. Ibid. See also G IV 424 (Loemker, p. 293).

39. G III 444–46

40. Gassendi's role as empirical objector assisted him here: if the perfection argument is fallacious, then some replacement for it is necessary, since a mere reference to intuition destroys the analogy with geometry.

41. *Censura*, p. 167

42. Janke traces Leibniz's use of the distinction to the Eckhard correspondence

(1676–78). Even if he is right, the problem does not come to the forefront until after the turn of the eighteenth century.

43. G IV 401; Nicholas Rescher (*Monadology*, Pittsburgh, 1991) translates part of this text, p. 154.

44. See David Blumenfield's "Leibniz's Ontological and Cosmological Arguments" (in *The Cambridge Companion to Leibniz*, ed. Nicholas Jolley, Cambridge 1995), pp. 363–64, on these premises and whether they are dispensable.

45. G IV 406.

46. In a footnote Henrich (p. 46) offers the following account of the difference between Leibniz's and Kant's respective arguments: "Leibniz claims that all a priori truths presuppose an actual subject through which they are validated. Kant wants to prove that all propositions (whether a priori or a posteriori) would have no object if there were no first ground of the actual things about which (things) we make utterances. Whereas Leibniz seeks the sufficient ground of formal possibility, Kant seeks the ground of material possibility. . . ." Henrich is probably thinking of passages in Kant like Reflection 5482 (AA 18 195).

47. Perhaps his most well-known work at the time was a teleologically oriented *Dissertation sur l'existence de Dieu* (Hague, 1697). His contributions to the ontological argument appeared in the journal *Histoire et Ouvrages des Savans* in 1700. His arguments were attacked by an anonymous contributor in *Nouvelles de la Republique des Lettres* in 1702 and 1703. Henrich (pp. 97–105) provides a detailed review of these publications.

48. Leibniz appended his own comments to each premise of Jaquelot's arguments and entitled the result *Arguments sent to me by Mr. Jaquelot in defense of Descartes' controversial proof of the existence of God, together with my replies.* The text appears in G III 442–48.

49. G III 445–46

50. G III 446 (I have left Leibniz's Latin standing and translated only his French)

51. He apparently does not notice that Spinoza employs a version of the perfection argument in this regard in *Prinicpia* I, Lemma I, Corollary (*Opera* I 165; Curley, p. 252).

52. *Briefwechsel zwischen Leibniz und Christian Wolff* (ed. Gebhardt, Hildesheim 1963, originally Halle, 1860), p. 50: "It is true that an *ens a se* exists, and that without it no dependent beings (*entia ab alio*) would exist, but it is not easy to demonstrate with accuracy that the *ens a se* is God, which is to say omniscient, omnipotent and unique."

53. Ibid. This as well as parts of the two previous quotes appear also in Bausola, pp. 15–16, and I am indebted to him for these and several other references.

54. Citations from both texts will be from Loemker.

55. Loemker, p. 639; G VI 602; Loemker, pp. 646–47; G VI 613.

56. *Monadology* #40 (Loemker p. 646; G VI 613). As is typical of his method in these works, Leibniz omits the many premises required for a complete proof of the proposition in question.

57. *Monadology* #43.

58. It is perhaps worth noting that Leibniz infers God's perfection only from the a posteriori argument, although he argues for the existence of a necessary being a priori.

59. Recall that in the *Principles* (AT VIIIa 10; CSM I 197) Descartes cites as proof of the veracity of the idea of a "necessarily existing perfect God" the fact that "necessary existence" is not an attribute that could have been borrowed from any other idea.

60. At least this is how he begins the first chapter (proposition 24).

61. The first twenty-three propositions comprise a "Prolegomena," the purpose of which is to justify natural theology as a science (in relation to the importance of scripture). Kant's exposition of the cosmological argument in KrV (B 632–33) apparently derives from this passage in Wolff.

62. Wolff actually continues (in propositions 70–72) to infer these points with reference to the antecedently demonstrated propositions (31–32) that the existence of the *ens a se* is necessary and follows from its essence alone.

63. The only other reference to the first, a posteriori part of the *Theologia naturalis* among the first twenty-one propositions of the second, a priori part is a merely tangential note appended to proposition 14 ("God is an *ens perfectissimum*") that claims that one and the same entity permits of multiple nominal definitions.

64. Citations from this text are to the seventh edition (Halle, 1779).

65. Henrich writes (p. 63) of Baumgarten's influence on Kant: "For nearly forty years the *Metaphysica* served as the basis of Kant's lectures. Its influence on the development of the Critical philosophy should therefore not be overlooked. When Kant speaks of "dogmatic philosophy," he is thinking primarily of Baumgarten. The latter's definitions and demonstrations were always present to Kant's consciousness, and Kant owes a great part of his terminology to Baumgarten."

66. Both Baumgarten and Wolff, in contrast to Spinoza, assert only a nominal status to the definition of an *ens perfectissimum*. For that reason their arguments are vulnerable to Thomistic objections, since they have no other replacement for the Cartesian major premise. Kant's pre-Critical Thomistic arguments are thus entirely appropriate, in the context of mid-eighteenth-century philosophical debate. See below, chapter 6.

67. Kant borrows the term "*omnitudo realitatis*" (KrV B 604ff.) from these passages.

68. Metaphysica #823: "God would not be an actual being enjoying all realities (*ens omnibus realitatibus*), if a given reality were missing from him. He would be determined in respect to all realities contained within him, insofar as a being can be determined with respect to what is contained within it, and yet in respect to some of his per-

fection he would not be so determined. Therefore the opposite of the divine existence is intrinsically impossible. The existence of God is absolutely necessary." (I owe thanks to Professor Terence Tunberg for his clarification of several philological difficulties presented by this passage.)

69. Kant does this in his 1755 dissertation *Nova Dilucidatio*, see below (chapter 6).

70. This is the conclusion that Henrich also reaches. He accepts the fact that Kant's criticisms of the ontological argument are directed at Baumgarten, but he tries to save Kant by showing that the proof underwent a consistent development from the *Meditations* to the *Metaphysica*. Like Kant himself, Henrich seems to think that Baumgarten was the greatest pre-Kantian philosopher, an opinion that should be shared by anyone who holds the conventional view that Kant's *First Critique* eliminated "dogmatic metaphysics." I have tried to show that the early modern history of the ontological argument does not consist of the kind of progressive story that Henrich depicts. The conclusion to be drawn is thus that Kant's criticisms apply only very locally.

71. For an introduction to Crusius's influence on Kant, see Lewis White Beck's *Early German Philosophy*, Harvard, 1969 and Max Wundt's *Die duetsche Schulphilosophie im Zeitalter der Aufklaerung*, Hildesheim, Olms, 1964.

72. *Entwurf der nohwendigen Vernuft-Wahrheiten*, Leipzig, 1745, reprinted by Georg Olms, Hildesheim, 1964. All translations from this text are my own.

73. Crusius preserves the fourfold division of metaphysics that he finds in Baumgarten and Wolff, and changes only their order. He places natural theology immediately after ontology.

74. *Sketch* #137: "... what is said to have so much perfection that nothing greater than it could be conceived, that thing must possess every perfection, and possess it in the highest conceivable degree. Since existence indeed belongs among the perfections, if we attribute to a thing the concept of an infinite perfection, we must also attribute to it the concept of a constant and necessary existence."

75. AT VII 115–16; CSM II 83.

76. *Sketch* #235.

Chapter Six

KANT'S SYSTEMATIC CRITIQUE OF THE ONTOLOGICAL ARGUMENT

K ant enters the debate over the a priori proofs in the time following the arguments of Baumgarten and Crusius. By roughly ten years the junior of these philosophers, Kant (1724–1804) appeals mainly to their works for his formulations of metaphysical questions. In regards to the ontological argument he sides with Crusius entirely and from the beginning, and his sympathies with the rationalists never extend as far as that argument. His initial position on the proof, in his 1755 dissertation, consists only in the Thomistic objection that he discovers in the *Sketch*, and it is not until the 1760s that Kant advances to a more interesting line of criticism. Throughout the subsequent two decades Kant refines his objection to the argument he later names "ontological," and he even attempts to replace this argument with his own quasi-ontological proof.[1] In the *Critique of Pure Reason*, however, he rejects in principle all "speculative" attempts to prove the existence of God, designating these as an extension of reason beyond its rightful limits. His brief application of this point to the "ontological argument" represents the most thorough criticism of that argument in the modern period.

Although his criticisms of "speculative theology" turn on his alleged demonstration of the limits of reason, Kant's explicit treatment of the ontological proof deals primarily with the traditional objections to that argument. Due in part to the heavy rhetoric of his magnum opus, Kant succeeds in presenting these objections, especially the empirical, in a very persuasive light. As a result he has often been believed to have raised only the empirical objection, this in his notorious formula "being is obviously not a real predicate." If this were the case, however, Kant would deserve little more than a footnote in this history, since that objection, considered in isolation, is entirely specious, and in any case Kant can say nothing in this regard that was not already clearly expressed by Gassendi. Kant's accomplishment, however, was to provide a framework within which the empirical objection appears inevitable. He does not blindly assert the rule that existence cannot belong to the nature of any entity, for this would beg the question of whether the case of God marks an exception to this rule, but instead he derives the rule from a complete theory of human cognition. Kant thus plays a role in the criticism of the ontological argument similar to the role Spinoza plays in its defense. Just as Spinoza provides the full metaphysical context for an earlier version of the argument, so does Kant supply the epistemological context for certain of the objections. His entire philosophical program amounts to an attack on the proof in question, and he does not rely as strongly as it seems on the misleading examples he gives in the chapter from the *Critique* devoted to the topic.

THOMISTIC AND EMPIRICAL OBJECTIONS IN THE PRE-CRITICAL PERIOD

In the decades prior to the *Critique of Pure Reason* Kant assumes a number of mutually incompatible positions with respect to the a priori proof, and it is only later that he achieves clarity about how these positions relate to one another. His earliest discussions of the ontological argument emphasize the Thomistic objections, and we find him siding with Crusius against the prevalent version of the argument. In the 1760s he switches to the stance of empirical objector as he begins to develop his own theory of existence and objectivity. In the *Critique*, however, he offers a sophisticated thesis concerning the conditions under which these two lines of objection are possible. Although he raises, in that work, both the Thomistic and empirical objections, his advocacy of these represents a significant advance from the positions of Crusius, Hume, Gassendi, etc.

From Crusius's Sketch *to*
Kant's Nova Dilucidatio

When Kant writes his Habilitationschrift of 1755, *Principiorum primorum cognitionis metaphysicae nova dilucidatio*, he appeals to Crusius for support in respect to many of his basic positions, and this includes his opposition to the "Cartesian argument." Even the title *"argumentum cartesianum"* rings of Crusius's influence, since it is that philosopher alone among Kant's German contemporaries who employs the moniker. Kant's formulation of the so-called Cartesian argument and the Thomistic objections, however, surpasses what we find in the *Sketch*. He succeeds specifically in relating these objections to the traditional definitions of God, so that his attack on the a priori proof is already incorporated into a larger attack on the philosophy of Wolff and Baumgarten. In proposition six he takes issue with the idea, common among the rationalists, that God contains the reason for his own existence: "It is inconsistent (*absonum*) that something should be said to contain the reason for its own existence within itself."[2]

Kant's objection to this concept anticipates his later criticisms of the equivocations that are so common in philosophical theology. His point is simply that the term "ratio" is not given its usual meaning in the definition of God. In this regard he appeals to the principle of sufficient reason, to which he had devoted propositions four and five. That principle implies, for Kant, that to the existence of everything belongs a reason or ground *distinct* from the thing itself. The definition of God according to which he is the reason for his own existence, on this view, represents a blatant violation of the notion of reason or ground. At this point Kant's argument is nothing more than a commonplace objection to the concept of a *causa sui*, although he no doubt imagines his point to be more novel than it is.[3] His related assumption that it belongs to the concept of "cause" that this is distinct from its "effect" is in fact one with a long tradition, and it was a hotly debated issue among Descartes' interlocutors. In the *First Set of Objections* Caterus raises this same point, and Arnauld later recommences the debate on Caterus's behalf. Most of what Kant writes on this topic in the *Nova dilucidatio* is nearly indistinguishable from what Arnauld writes in reply to Descartes.[4] It suffices here to say only that the matter is more complicated than Kant likely realizes in 1755, and that Descartes indeed provides a plausible justification for his use of the term "cause" in respect to God's existence.[5] Kant's position in this early text, then, is a coherent one and is consistent with the history of critique of the Cartesian argument, but also one to which an adequate reply had been offered by a consensus of the argument's proponents.

In explanation of his definition of "ratio" Kant borrows Crusius's concept of "determining cause" in order to distinguish the cause of existence from the cause of thought.[6] His purpose is to apply the latter distinction to Baumgarten's claim that the nonexistence of God implies a contradiction.[7] The corollary to the proposition asserts that this logical difficulty pertains only to the cause of the thought[8] (i.e., to say that the nonexistence of God is impossible is to give a reason for why we must think God exists, but not for why God actually exists). Impossibility, he claims, is a merely logical characteristic that does not suffice to establish a (positive) existential fact. The Cartesian concept of God (that Kant had discovered in both Wolff and Baumgarten)[9] provides only a *ratio cognoscendi*, not "an antecedent determining cause" (i.e., it indicates the reason for our knowledge of the divine existence, without at the same time asserting a cause of this existence).

With this qualification of the notion of a self-causing or self-grounding entity, Kant introduces the first version of the Thomistic objection against the *argumentum cartesianum*. The concept of *causa sui* pertains only to our idea of God; it indicates only that we must think of God as existing, but it does not itself ensure God's actuality:

> I am of course aware that this same concept of God is appealed to, from which the determinate existence of the same is postulated. It is, however, easy to see that this occurs only in thought (*idealiter*), not in reality (*non realiter*). The concept of such a being is constructed in which the sum of all realities is contained. Granted, one must assent to the existence of such a being. The proof thus proceeds: if all realities are to be united without limitation in one being, that being exists. *But if these are only conceived as unified, then the existence is also only conceived.* The following opinion ought therefore to have been expressed: if we form the concept of such a being, and name this "God," we have determined this concept in such a way that it includes being. *If this concept, therefore, is a true one, then that being exists.* This much is said for those who assent to the Cartesian argument. (My emphasis.)[10]

While the first italicized sentence presents the Thomistic objection in its first formulation, Kant closes the passage with a hypothetical that resembles the second formulation of that objection: if the concept is a true one, then God exists. By a "true idea" Kant means one for which a corresponding object is given.[11] The intention is to accuse the ontological argument of assuming the conclusion in the premises. Phrased tautologically, the objection asserts that "if our idea that God exists is true, then God exists."

It should be remembered here that the "Cartesian argument" that Kant considers is nothing but the perfection argument as this appears in Baumgarten and other German writers of the time.[12] Kant abstracts the argument specifically from *Metaphysica* number 823. The latter argument begins with the concept of a being that possesses all realities or perfections (*omnitudo realitatis*). Among these is "existence" or "necessary existence," so that the entity in question should be said to exist. Baumgarten's argument indeed possesses an analog in the *Fifth Meditation*, so that the title "Cartesian argument" is not entirely inaccurate. Descartes' perfection argument, however, appears there in support of the claim that serves as the minor premise of the complete argument.[13] In other words, Kant attacks only a premise of the Cartesian argument under the misunderstanding (conditioned by the argument's history) that this premise constitutes the entire proof.

As was shown above, Descartes accepts these Thomistic objections in the case of Anselm's argument, the perfection argument, and his own minor premise (considered alone), but he addresses the objections with his major premise (viz., the doctrine of clear and distinct ideas). Since Descartes himself makes this admission in the case of a perfection argument absent of the major premise, Kant's position in this text is actually closer to Descartes' than are the positions of the eighteenth-century proponents of the ontological argument. Kant is correct to pose these objections to Baumgarten, which is to say to the ontological argument as it is common at the time he writes the *Nova dilucidatio*. The objections, however, are without any more broadly applicable critical import.

There is one further point of note regarding the above-cited passage: Kant equates the concept of "a being that possesses the reason for his own existence" (*causa sui, ens necessarium*) with the concept of "a being in which all realities inhere" (*ens in quo est omnitudo realitatis*), an equation that shows him to be unaware of a significant aspect of the history of the argument. On this point also he follows Baumgarten and Crusius, both of whom move directly from the notion of a perfect being to the notion of necessary existence. All three philosophers (Baumgarten, Crusius, and Kant) overlook both Wolff's proof procedure and Leibniz's later works. Kant's earliest attack on the ontological argument involves the acceptance that the concept of necessary existence is unique to the concept of God as a supremely perfect being; it is precisely this problem that will become the focal point of his critique.

Kant's Discovery of the Empirical Objection

Roughly seven years after the appearance of the *Nova dilucidatio* Kant adopts simultaneously a criticism of the Thomistic objection and a version of the empirical objection. Like many of his arguments, these could have been easily discovered through even a quick survey of the history of the ontological argument, although it seems that Kant arrived at them without such help.[14] His rejection of the Thomistic objection echoes Malebranche's defense of Descartes in *The Search after Truth*, although it is unlikely that Kant consulted this text. His empirical objection is a standard version of the argument from Gassendi's *Fifth Set of Objections*. Despite the glaring similarities in their positions, however, it does not seem that Kant read Gassendi. Crusius could not have provided much assistance in regards to the empirical objection.[15] It is most likely that only his own lasting preoccupation with the notion of "existence" permitted Kant to rediscover Gassendi's idea. He explains his discovery in a note from his *Nachlass*:

> If existence could be ascribed to a thing on the basis of the inclusion of this among the many predicates of the thing, then no proof could be required to demonstrate existence of God that would be more conclusive and at the same time more comprehensible than the Cartesian argument. One objects only in vain that the possibility of such a thing would include existence only in thought. One could not object, that is, that the thing exists only in thought, and not outside the mind, because by the same reasoning it would follow for all predicates that they belonged to things only in thought and not in fact.[16]

This passage asserts Gassendi's objection only by implication. The counterfactuals suggest that Kant's argument is that "if the empirical objection were not valid, the Cartesian argument would be valid." He clearly does not think that the Cartesian argument is valid, so that his point must be that "existence" cannot be included among the predicates of a given thing. A number of notes from this period show the predominance of the empirical objection in his thinking.[17] In one case he explains the objection in conjunction with Hume's famous stipulation concerning existential claims, which Kant had discovered both in Hume and Crusius.[18] Although Kant's notes do not provide evidence that he arrives at the empirical objection upon reflecting on this problem, he clearly does understand it as a justification for the universality of Hume's rule: "the opposite of an existence (claim) is never self-contradictory; a contradiction is always between a subject and a predicate, and "existence" is not a predicate."[19]

Kant's Malebranchean rejection of the Thomistic objections ("by the same reasoning it would follow for all predicates . . ."), however, reveals a surprising point of agreement between him and the rationalists. He recognizes that acceptance of Thomas's quibbles leads to universal skepticism. If we accept the objections, we are not entitled to claim that *any* perceived attribute belongs to a thing "in reality." Descartes had indeed engaged in such skepticism, and this is overcome with the help of the same dogma that supports the major premise in the *First Replies* argument. Malebranche and Henry More likewise explain how the Thomistic objection would be fatal to all instances of human knowledge. This prospect leads the proponents of the ontological argument to propose either a major premise addressing the objection (Descartes, More) or a similar epistemological context (Malebranche, Spinoza).

In the long note number 3706 Kant proposes an alternative to the Cartesian major premise: the rationalist axiom is discarded in favor of a kind of naïve realism. The Thomistic objection is thus refuted indirectly: *if* we accept this objection, *then* we also accept a universal skepticism. Kant's point seems to be that such skepticism is evidently and obviously unacceptable; therefore the objection is just as unacceptable. The hesitation concerning the Thomistic objection, in this stage of Kant's thinking, results not from epistemological axioms but from a more general philosophical orientation that rejects "external world" skepticism less directly than does the rationalism of the previous century. The objection, at least here, is discarded due to its affinity with skepticism, and during this period Kant is engaged in discovering alternatives to the Cartesian solution to the skeptical problem.[20]

THE PLACE OF THE TRADITIONAL OBJECTIONS IN THE *FIRST CRITIQUE*

An analogy revisited: Thomistic and modal objections

It would be a mistake to conclude from Reflection 3706 and similar remarks from the 1760s that Kant altogether rejects the Thomistic objections.[21] The note, and the orientation toward realism that it expresses, is only one among so many Kantian discussions of those objections. We have still to account for the fact that Thomas's arguments receive a very detailed treatment in the "Transcendental Dialectic." Kant, it seems, does not completely abandon the Thomistic position. Instead he provides an analysis of the assumptions according to which these objections are or would be relevant. His concerns in this analysis are chiefly epistemological (i.e., Kant's question addresses how we could have any insight into the relationship between "necessary existence" and a "supremely perfect being"). We could have such insight, Kant allows, if we could reason by analogy from propositions about triangles to propositions about God. Appropriately enough, it is entirely within the context of this analogy that Kant considers the traditional objections.

Nearly one half of the chapter "On the impossibility of an ontological proof of God's existence" treats specifically of Thomistic arguments. Since the overriding concerns, however, involve his inquiry into the limits of human cognition, Kant is able to expose quite easily the dependence of these classic objections on problems of human knowledge. His initial worry is that the notion of a necessary being is unintelligible,[22] and the Thomistic objections arise only upon analysis of the metaphor commonly employed in attempts to explain the concept in question. Kant's assumption that analogy is necessary in order to comprehend the attribution of God's existence is a prejudice he derives as much from Baumgarten as from any explicit arguments of his own. Granted, Kant's view could find equal justification in at least the language of either the *Fifth Meditation* or the *Discourse on the Method*.[23] It is only Baumgarten, though, who goes as far as to claim, in dramatic contradiction to seventeenth-century metaphysicians like Spinoza or Malebranche, that the absolute necessity of God's existence is analogous to the hypothetical necessity of judgments.[24] In his context, then, it appears obvious to Kant that our alleged comprehension of God's necessary existence depends upon the fatal triangle analogy.

Kant's criticism of the analogy appropriately begins with an introduction to the modal objection, and his analysis highlights the connection between this objection and the Thomistic. He first distinguishes the "necessity of judgments" from the "necessity of things," a distinction that is equivalent to the distinction between hypothetical and absolute necessity. In regard to the analogy with geometry, he remarks that geometrical propositions assert only hypothetical necessity; the analogy with the triangle and the sum of its sides refers only to a conditionally necessary judgment.[25] If I think of the triangle, then I am forced to make certain judgments about the three angles. The necessity of such a judgment, however, does not imply the necessity of the thing about which it is a judgment. Kant thus writes: "the above proposition does not say that the three angles are absolutely necessary, but rather that under the condition that a triangle exists (is given), three angles also exist (in it) necessarily."[26]

The reapplication of the analogy quickly leads to the Thomistic objection in its second formulation. The existential judgment is supposed (by acceptance of the analogy) to be as necessary as the predication of certain properties of a triangle. Since, however, the modal objection holds for the geometrical judgments (i.e., geometrical judgments are only hypothetically necessary), it should likewise prevail over the theological judgment. A characteristic of hypothetically necessary judgments is that they require the existence of their subjects to be separately and antecedently established. Transfer of this condition to the claim that "God exists" thus requires that the subject of this claim also be presumed to exist, so that the assertion of this instance of hypothetical necessity appears question-begging. In other words, since the predication of the properties of the triangle presupposes that the triangle itself exists, so should the predication of God's existence presuppose that he exist. Kant correctly concludes that I can with necessity infer God's existence only "under the condition that I posit this thing as given (existing)."

The point here is that necessity in thought differs from necessity of the thing, or logical necessity is different from ontological necessity, so that no analogy from the former can aid the comprehension of the latter.[27] The geometrical propositions are necessary judgments, or in them the combination of subject and predicate is necessary for thought. The geometrical entity (the triangle), however, is not ontologically necessary. The triangle does not necessarily exist. A general rule comparable to the second Thomistic objection is thus apparent: what is logically necessary is also ontologically necessary *provided that* the object in question exists. In other words, the angles exist necessarily *if* the triangle exists. Analogously, God exists necessarily if he exists. Kant explains the application of this rule to God:

> Nevertheless the illusion of this logical necessity has proved so powerful that when one has made a concept a priori of a thing that was set up so that its existence was comprehended within the range of its meaning, one believed that one could infer with certainty that because existence necessarily pertains to the object of this concept, i.e., *under the condition that I posit this thing as given (existing)*, its existence can also be posited necessarily (according to the rule of identity), and this being itself, therefore, is necessarily, because its existence is assumed arbitrarily and under the condition that I posit its object.[28]

The subsequent paragraph reveals further difficulties in the analogy, and it also serves to illuminate the intention of the entire discussion. The claim "God exists" is considered as an identical judgment. Such a judgment yields a contradiction when the predicate is "cancelled" and the subject remains. This holds evidently of our geometric example: "to posit a triangle and cancel its three angles is contradictory." If we reapply the analogy, then a contradiction should likewise ensue for the claim of God's existence; the statement "God is not" should produce a contradiction. Kant, however, retreats from this under the assumption that nothing is left to be contradicted: "If you cancel its existence, then you cancel the thing itself with all its predicates; where then is the contradiction supposed to come from?"[29]

The intention of the passage is to place the cogency of the analogy into question. The claim that "'God is not' is contradictory" is not in itself absurd. It is also not, however, strictly analogous to claim that "'the triangle does not have three angles' is contradictory." Kant, of course, establishes this only by assuming that "exists" posits "the subject together with all its predicates" and is to that extent to be distinguished from predicates such as "having three angles = 180 degrees" or "omnipotence." In other words, Kant's analysis of the claim "God exists" as an identical statement has to a certain extent already assumed the empirical objection.[30]

Kant's treatment of Clarke's objection

Clarke's objection reappears in the context of Kant's discussion of the Thomistic objection. Although this objection is not Thomistic, Kant's employment of it highlights its affinity with the scholastic objections. The objection arises among the possible answers to what for Kant is the decisive question concerning the ontological argument, viz., the question of the general status of existential propositions. The problem is posed at B 625: "I ask you: is the proposition, *this or that thing exists*—is this proposition, I say, an analytic or a synthetic proposition." The first option is considered, with the result that the claim is either tautologous or is subject to Clarke's objection:

> if it is the former, then with existence you add nothing to your thought of the thing; but then either *the thought that is in you must be the thing itself*, or else you have presupposed an existence as belonging to possibility, and then inferred that existence on this pretext from its inner possibility, which is nothing but a miserable tautology. (My emphasis.)

The latter disjunct concerns the possibility objection, and will be discussed below accordingly. Of immediate concern is the former claim: "the thought that is in you must be the thing itself." The ontological argument, according to Kant, confuses (or identifies)[31] our thought of God with God himself. The implicit reasoning is as follows. In an analytic claim the predicate states only what is already contained in the subject.[32] The claim "God exists" is, by assumption, an analytic claim. The grammatical predicate "exists" thus adds nothing to the subject "God." Kant makes one further (very revealing) assumption before drawing his conclusion: the subject term designates only our thought of the thing. With this we can validly conclude: "then with existence you add nothing to your thought of the thing."

Just as in the case of the Thomistic objections, the problem here does not concern the inference from "God" to "God exists"; it has been granted with the assumption of analyticity that the latter follows immediately from the former. The problem concerns rather the inference from *our thought of God* to God's existence. According to the Thomistic objection, it follows from our idea of God only that we must think of God as existing; i.e., the Thomistic objector allows only the inference from the thought of God to the thought of his existence, or from the thought of the subject to the thought of the predicate. The objection in question proceeds, however, in the reverse manner. Kant begins with the intended conclusion "God exists," and attempts to trace this back to the idea of God. The conclusion ("God exists") follows analytically from the subject itself ("God"); the desired result, however, is that it follow from our mere thought of the subject. The ontological argument would thus be valid only if this idea is the same as the subject itself.[33] In other words, God's existence would follow from our idea of God only under the condition that our idea is the same as the thing itself.

The affinity of this argument to the Thomistic objections is now evident. According to the first formulation of the latter, the ontological argument contains a confusion of existence-in-thought with real existence. Clarke's objection differs primarily in its presentation; the ontotheologian is said to have failed to distinguish the thought of God from the thing itself. The confusion is placed in the subject term, rather than, as in the Thomistic objection, in the predicate term. This difference, however, is negligible with respect to the proposition in question, since the predicate and subject terms are assumed to be indistinguishable.

This objection nonetheless poses a different metaphysical challenge to the proponent of the argument, which is why it does not fall under the rubric "Thomistic." The rationalist dogma concerning the reality of predication serves as an adequate response only to Aquinas's objections, but not to Clarke's. The latter's objection implies, correctly, that the ontological proof assumes (in addition to the reality of predication) some form of identity between our thought of God and the thing itself. This suggests yet a further systematic requirement for the proponents of the argument, one which was met with several adequate replies: there must be some mediation between God and our idea of him. We have seen how the inclusion of the human mind within God's nature (in Geulincx, Malebranche, Cudworth, and Spinoza) addresses just this problem.[34] It is just as true, however, that that the subjectivism of Descartes' position and the "dogmatism" of the eighteenth-century academic philosophy exposed certain versions of the ontological argument also to this objection[35]; in yet another case one of Kant's criticisms has a valid *local* application.

It is worth noting that, due primarily to the polemical nature of his text, Kant raises this objection in a form that is essentially inferior to Clarke's statement of the same objection. While Kant exceeds Clarke both in the clarity of his expression and in his placement of the objection in the context of the other objections, Clarke is more generous in that he notices that the objection does not necessarily cite a fallacy in the ontological argument, but rather a mere pedagogical shortcoming. In other words, Clarke's point is that the ontological argument, as he is familiar with this (probably via More's *Antidote*), does not suffice to explain why the subjective idea of God is also a "real idea"; he does recognize, however, that this equation is part of the intention of the argument. He seems open to a solution like the one offered by Malebranche, or the one that appears in Spinoza's philosophy, although he does not appear to recognize that the relevant doctrines serve as solutions to the problem he raises. Kant, on the other hand, insists on the subjective nature of the idea of God ("the thought that is *in you*"), and thus seems less aware that an adequate reply to the objection is possible. In other words, Kant does not seem to allow that we can have an idea that is not merely subjective; he assumes (or at least he pretends to assume) instead that the subject term of *any* proposition refers to a mere thought.[36]

The empirical objection in the First Critique

The entire discussion of the Thomistic objections proceeds upon the assumption that the claim "God exists" is analytic. The structure of Kant's argument is hypothetical: if, as the proponents of the ontological argument believe, an existential proposition can be analytic, then a number of logical difficulties ensue. In the *Critique* Kant argues (in direct contradiction to Reflection 3706) that Thomistic objections would be fatal to the argument, if it were granted that an existential proposition could be analytic. Kant's own view, however, is that every existential proposition is synthetic, i.e., that "exists" can never follow by direct implication from any subject. The preceding discussion of the Thomistic objections, then, amounts to nothing but an analysis of the consequent of a false hypothesis. The direct critique of the ontological argument properly begins with the proclamation of the self-evidence of the general rule of existential propositions:

> But if you admit, as *every rational person* in all fairness must, that every existential proposition is synthetic, then how will you claim that the predicate of existence cannot be negated without contradiction?[37]

Well aware that he is now arguing from an assumption that his opponents do not grant, Kant elaborates the Gassendian theory of existence in the final paragraphs of his chapter. He explains the traditional complaint that "existence is not a perfection" in terms of his distinction between real and logical predicates. A logical predicate is anything that can occupy the predicate position in a proposition. A real predicate, however, is "a concept of something that could add to the concept of a thing." The intention of his objection is to show that "existence" does not add any particular attribute to the content of the concept of a thing, a point that he illustrates with his well-known example of the "hundred dollars."

It is especially ironic that this example contributed to the fame of Kant's criticism, since Kant simply borrowed the example from a relatively unknown philosopher, Johann Bering.[38] Both Bering and Kant employ the example to the same end: the logical predicate "exists" adds nothing to the concept of a subject such as "one hundred dollars." In other words, the hundred dollars evidently do not increase (quantitatively) by their existing. Kant elaborates this point by claiming that the indifference to existence that the content of every concept possesses is essential to the idea that we think of anything real at all: i.e., if the existent and conceived contents were not the same, it could not be said that the concept was *of* those hundred dollars. In the traditional metaphysical terminology Kant's claim would read: existence does not belong to the essence of the hundred dollars; i.e., existence does not belong to the essence of any (finite) entity, a proposition that even the proponents of the ontological argument have always accepted as a general rule.

It would be unfair to accuse Kant of patent question-begging. He is not merely overlooking the fact that the intention of the argument is to assert that necessary existence is a unique predicate of God. He had rather dealt with this hypothesis in the first part of the chapter and concluded that, in its analytic form the argument (1) seems to fall victim to the Thomistic objection due to its dependence upon analogy and (2) without these fatal analogies the concept of a necessary entity is unintelligible. His overall strategy is thus to attack the ontological argument on multiple levels (Thomistic, empirical, epistemological) in order to leave the proponent of the argument with no escape.[39] His advocacy of the empirical objection should not be taken in isolation (and it is only in isolation that the objection is question-begging) but as one move within a more sophisticated critical strategy.

Included within this strategy is also a tentative effort at justifying the prejudice that underlies the empirical objection. Although Kant does restrict the application of "existence" to "objects of experience," his claim is not merely definitional like Hobbes's stipulation concerning that term. Although he was certainly impressed by the fact that Crusius also includes spatio-temporality in the definition of "existence," Kant surpasses his colleague from Leipzig by providing an argumentative background to this definition.[40] The latter begins, not with nominal definitions, but with an analysis of experiential knowledge. He then traces this back to its "transcendental conditions," which includes certain general propositions. Among the general propositions belonging to the "transcendental conditions of knowledge of experience" is the rule of the synthetic nature of existential claims. Kant, unlike Gassendi, Hobbes, or Crusius, allows that "an existence outside this field" (i.e., the field of common experience) is possible in principle.[41] His claim is only that assertions about such existence are not justifiable on his (Kant's) account of human knowledge in general.

Analogy and Equivocation: Kant's Theological Position

Like any empirical objector, Kant considers God under the category of a "thing" in general, although he relates his ontology to a novel theory of human knowledge. The crux of the objection, in any case, is that there is no exception to the empirical rule that the essence of a thing is distinct from its existence. Kant's version of this differs from those of his predecessors only in the placement of this doctrine within a theory of human cognition; his formulation of the essential point is still Gassendian. What is common to all empirical objectors is that they disallow the (apparently arbitrary) theological claims (1) that cognition of God is an absolute exception to all epistemic rules, and (2) that assertions about his attributes (including "existence") are not analogous to claims about the characteristics or existence of other entities. In other words, the empirical objection appears in opposition to the doctrine of equivocal attribution, since it consists of a consideration of assertions about God in terms of a general rule of predication. Conversely, the objection dissolves upon acceptance of this doctrine.

There is little evidence that Kant was aware of the importance for modern philosophy of the doctrine of equivocal attribution.[42] His reliance upon contemporary German textbooks acquainted him rather with the Thomistic doctrine of theological analogy.[43] Although Maimonides was read by some of his contemporaries, this was done mainly by those, like Mendelssohn, who were fluent in Hebrew. Kant does possess some knowledge of Spinoza, but even this was mediated by eighteenth-century interpreters like Wolff.[44] The overt emphasis on the doctrine of analogy that appears in the

Critique is a response only to the natural theologies of the German rationalists; his assertion (in his notes on Baumgarten) that "in 'natural theology' we cognize the highest being only in relation to the world, and thus not according to the absolute predicates of this being"[45] indicates his recognition of the inadequacy of analogy for a speculative theology, and an immense degree of credit is due him for his critique and revision of that theological position. That this was not the only prevalent position, however, is something that does not appear to have occurred to him.

Just as Kant's attack on the ontological argument is an attack on the eighteenth-century version of the argument, then, so is his broader attack on theology an attack on the doctrine of theological analogy; his attack on speculative theology is an attack on the theology of Wolff, Baumgarten, and Eberhard, and it does not extend to all possible (and actual) types of philosophical theology. This is easily discernible if the "Transcendental Dialectic" is read with an eye to the problem of divine predication. In the concluding passage to his "Antinomy," for example, he claims that "ideas of reason" consist of nothing more than analogies with objects of experience.[46] More importantly, in every case he is interested in the "ideas of reason" only to the extent that they serve some purpose in the organization of knowledge of experience (i.e., that they are considered only in relation to empirical concepts). When, in his subsequent *Critiques*, Kant advocates a kind of moral theology, he does so precisely by revising the doctrine of theological analogy.[47]

That we construct concepts of intelligible entities "by analogy" from concepts of experience is the theme of the traditional "transition objection." Kant's version of the latter, to be sure, differs greatly from the accusations of a Gassendi or a Hobbes, since Kant incorporates a modification of the doctrine of innate ideas (viz., the Cartesian reply to that objection) into his transition argument. Those seventeenth-century critics put forth the transition objection as if it were a mere psychological peculiarity of man (or at least certain men) that we form concepts like that of a "God," a necessary existent, etc. Kant, on the other hand, treats the transition as itself something like innate, and thus attempts a synthesis of the positions of innatists like Descartes with materialists like Gassendi. On his telling, it is the "natural course of human reason" that we form the idea of a necessary being, and our only mistake lies in ascribing "reality" to such ideas.[48]

It is enlightening to compare other aspects of his critique with the related theological positions, such as the notion of divine simplicity that goes hand-in-hand with the doctrine of equivocation. One passage relevant to this theme appears in the penultimate paragraph of the chapter on the ontological argument. In addition to the rule of the synthetic character of existential claims, Kant articulates a general rule for the relation of the various predicates of a thing: "the connection of all real properties in a thing is a synthesis about whose possibility we cannot judge a priori." According to this view, the conjunction of the attributes of each thing is a synthesis. The problem here should be apparent enough at this point. God, namely, has been traditionally understood (by the proponents of the ontological argument) as simple. In other words, the connection of God's properties is not synthetic but rather immediate. The various attributes of God are said to be indistinguishable insofar as they inhere in God.[49]

On this point Kant cannot plead ignorance. There is abundant evidence that Kant is aware of the doctrine of divine simplicity. First, unlike equivocal attribution, this doctrine belongs also to Wolff and his followers.[50] Second, he even proposes this doctrine in his writings of the 1760s. In Reflection 3733, for example, he writes that "the necessary being is a simple entity."[51] Finally, even in the *Critique* he recognizes this point as central to theological understanding: "the ideal of the original being must also be thought of as simple."[52] Kant is indeed aware that the idea of God does not correspond to his own description of what constitutes the nature of a concept of any "thing," but he takes this as evidence against the validity of the idea of God, rather than (which is equally plausible) against the appropriateness of his own metaphysics.

Kant's point in formulating the rule of synthetic connection of predicates, as is the case with the empirical objection, derives ultimately from his analysis of experiential knowledge. The most that can be ascertained from this decision of his, then, is that according to the theological doctrine of divine simplicity our comprehension of God fails to meet the criteria for knowledge that he (Kant) determines to be absolute. These criticisms are thus relevant to philosophical theology only under the assumption that the limits of "experiential" knowledge are the absolute limits of human knowledge, an assumption Kant takes himself already to have established in the *Critique*.[53]

A third criticism of the doctrine of theological analogy appears in Kant's chapter "The Transcendental Ideal." Unlike the materialists of the seventeenth and early eighteenth century, Kant does not think that the idea of an entity that enjoys all perfections is "a mere figment of the brain." He rather accepts that this notion is necessary in the context of an explanation of our experiential knowledge, but objects only to the hypostatization of this concept in spec-ulative theology. For Kant the hypostatization of the concept of a "God" occurs when we think of the ideal of reason (the *omnitudo realitatis*) as "a par-ticular being" or an "individual thing."[54] Here again his concern lies with our imagining the concept of God by analogy with "empirical reality." Previous philosophers who reject this analogy, however, also reject the notion that God is a particular being or individual thing, so that these criticisms of Kant's both are consistent with the claims of those philosophers (like Malebranche) and fail to endanger their ontological arguments. Two avenues for avoiding the subsumption of "God" under the general category of "things" were traversed by the seventeenth-century defenders of the ontological argument. The first was Malebranche's denial of God's particularity; the second was Spinoza's monism.[55] Kant's ignorance of these positions qualifies his entire critique of the ontological argument. He again attacks only the positions of Wolff, Baum-garten, and Leibniz.

Kant's Critique of the Possibility Argument

Gassendi was shown to have recognized that the intention of the ontological argument is to make a unique assertion about God, one that is not analogous to any empirical claim. He thereby implicitly acknowledges the ultimate futility of objections like the empirical. Kant likewise grants a small recogni-tion to the status of God as an exception to any rule of empirical knowledge, and an interesting objection to Leibniz and his followers arises in this context. The brief acknowledgement reads as follows:

> Against all these general inferences (which no human being can refuse to draw) you challenge me with the one case that you set up as a proof through the fact that there is one and indeed only this one concept for which the non-being or the cancelling of its object is contradictory within itself, and this is the concept of a most real being.[56]

Kant is thus not guilty of entirely ignoring the thought of God as such. He recognizes that the proponents of the argument had not simply mistaken, in his terms, a logical for a real predicate. They had rather asserted that the log-ical predicate "to exist" is in one unique and singular instance also a real pred-icate. This exceptional instance pertains to the metaphysical concept of God as *ens realissimum*, or supremely real entity. Kant himself reviews a version of the ontological argument based on this concept:

> It has, you say, all reality, and you are justified in assuming such a being as possible ... now existence is also comprehended under all reality: thus existence lies in the concept of something possible. If this thing is cancelled, then the internal possibility of the thing is cancelled, which is contradictory.[57]

Two criticisms of the argument follow. One of these is directed at the premise, the other at the inference:

> I answer: you have already committed a contradiction when you have brought the concept of its existence, under whatever disguised name, into the concept of a thing which you would think merely in terms of its possibility. If one allows you to do that, then you have won the illusion of a victory, but in fact you have said nothing; for you have committed a mere tautology.[58]

The argument in question is, according to Kant, partly contradictory and partly tautological. These objections are addressed to the argument from the premise: if the being to whose possibility existence belongs is possible, then that being exists. Kant is right to label the inference tautological; the consequent follows from the antecedent by the law of identity alone. The objection of contradiction, however, aims not at the inference but at the antecedent itself. The inclusion of existence in the definition of a being is said to be contradictory. Such a definition, however, is problematic, not in itself, but together with the consideration of the entity "merely in terms of its possibility." In other words, the contradiction rests in considering an entity in terms of its possibility while *simultaneously* denying that its possibility is separable from its existence.[59]

In this case there is evidence that Kant is not aware of alternatives to the eighteenth-century argument he is criticizing. If he had been so aware, he would likely also acknowledge that his position here is in full conformity with the view of the seventeenth-century proponents of the argument.[60] Those philosophers had also recognized that the assertion of necessary existence (understood as sameness of essence and existence) in the minor premise of the ontological argument precludes any prior analysis of possibility. This insight explains the emphasis upon the intuitive (Malebranche, Spinoza) or subjective (Descartes) nature of the argument in that century.

THE "CRITICAL" OBJECTION: THE CONTEXT OF EPISTEMIC REFUTATION

The analysis of the ontological argument in the chapter devoted to that proof appears in the context of a broader account of the constituent concepts of the minor premise (viz., "God" and "necessary existence"). On this point Kant follows the tradition that dates back to Gassendi, Huet, Cudworth, and Leibniz's middle period in asserting that the minor premise (which is mistaken for the entire argument) conjoins two essentially distinct concepts without any demonstration of their relation. The proof procedures of Leibniz's Vienna period and Wolff's *Theologia naturalis* are thus decisive for Kant's architectonic. Like his German predecessors, he claims that the concept of a necessary being derives initially from a cosmological argument, and that the problem at the core of the ontological argument lies in determining whether the concept of "God" (borrowed, at least in Wolff's exposition, from another division of philosophy) refers to the same entity to which the concept of a "necessary being" refers. Kant's most important objection to the ontological argument aims at exposing the impossibility of establishing this point.[61]

For Kant the idea of a necessary being arises in the solution of the "fourth conflict" of the "antinomy of pure reason." The conflict consists in the fact that reason has the need both (thesis) to infer the existence of something necessary and (antithesis) to exclude the idea of a necessary being either as an entity within the world or a temporal cause of the world.[62] The solution to the antinomy lies in the compatibility of the idea of a necessary being that is "merely intelligible" with the rule that "all things in the world of sense are completely contingent."[63] Kant's point is that it is valid to assume a "nonempirical condition" of the entire series of empirically conditioned, contingent beings, but that this nonempirical condition is a mere idea that, like all ideas (in his sense of this term), is incapable of being represented concretely.[64]

The concept of a God or highest being arises in a different yet analogous context. From the fact that "everything existing is thoroughly determined" in relation to every pair of opposed, possible predicates, it follows that in order to completely comprehend any given individual we would have to comprehend "everything possible and determine the thing through it."[65] Our understanding of empirical things as "thoroughly determined" thus requires that we assume the idea of a "sum total of all reality" (*omnitudo realitatis*) or "storehouse from which all possible predicates of things can be taken."[66] This is precisely the idea that Baumgarten identifies with the Cartesian notion of an *ens perfectissimum*.[67] Kant's interpretation of that traditional concept, then, is that it is an "idea" that must necessarily be assumed in the account of empirical knowledge, but that, like the idea of a necessary being, it can never appear in the sequence of representations and thus its "objectivity reality" can never be confirmed.

The problem at the core of establishing the existence of God (either ontologically or cosmologically) is to show that necessary existence belongs to the nature of an *ens perfectissimum* or, conversely, that the divine perfections belong to any being that is absolutely necessary.[68] On Kant's reading, the justification of these two ideas lies in their usefulness for empirical knowledge; they are the result of inferences that reason necessarily makes in providing an account of the unity of empirical knowledge. There is no justification, however, in the assertion of the "existence" or objective reality of an entity corresponding to either concept;[69] further, there is no good reason to infer that the *omnitudo realitatis* or God is the being to whom necessary existence belongs.[70]

Only because *both* concepts are necessary assumptions of reason are philosophers prone to conclude that a supremely perfect being possesses necessary existence. In other words, if it were not necessary to assume the idea of a necessary being, no one would be fooled into concluding that the *omnitudo realitatis* is an actual (necessary) entity:

> reason notices the ideal and merely fictive character of such a presupposition much too easily to allow itself to be persuaded by this alone straightway to assume a mere creature of its own thinking to be an actual being, were it not urged from *another source* to seek somewhere for a resting place in the regress from the conditioned. . . .[71]

Kant's argument thus aims at the minor premise, or the claim that necessary existence belongs to the nature of God. According to his view, the premise contains two distinct concepts whose necessary relation requires demonstration.[72] The argument, in outline, is an old one. Gassendi formulates it in essence, while Leibniz and Wolff oblige the request by actually attempting the requested demonstration. Kant's position, however, is innovative on this point. His conclusion is that such a demonstration is *in principle* impossible for humans, since it would constitute an operation of pure reason and an extension of this beyond its rightful boundaries (viz., the organization of empirical knowledge). He allows that each of the constituent concepts of the premise has its place in the account of rational comprehension of empirical reality, but insists that these ideas are "mere ideas" that do not otherwise refer to entities the reality of which we could confirm. His intention is not to deny "necessary existence" to the "supremely perfect being" (i.e., he does not assert that an objective formulation of the minor premise is in fact false). Rather, he claims that the attribution of necessary existence to God is something into which human reason has no insight.[73]

This is the background for his discussion of the ontological proof. The Thomistic, empirical, epistemological, and possibility objections are subordinate to the "Critical," to the extent that the former represent only the detailed criticism of the relation between "God" and "necessary existence." In other words, the traditional objections serve only to illuminate the problems implied by the desired connection between the *ens necessarium* and the *ens perfectissimum*. The superseding Critical objection maintains that the endeavor to conjoin these concepts is doomed from the start, since the proper function of both ideas is limited to the regulation of empirical knowledge.

In this case it is the priority granted to empirical knowledge that conditions Kant's emphasis on analogy. The concept of a necessary being, Kant allows, is nonempirical. But this *non*-empirical concept remains only *relative* to the empirical, so that the purpose of the former is understood to be its usefulness for the latter. The fate of the ontological argument, then, hinges ultimately upon the possibility of a nonempirical knowledge of an existent, which possibility Kant seems to preclude as a matter of principle. This preclusion results from Kant's assumption (1) that our knowledge of a "merely intelligible" entity arises only by analogy to sensible entities and (2) that we can have no knowledge that is not explicable by such analogy. Descartes and his successors had proceeded from a very different assumption. They understand all assertion of the existence of finite entities to represent an equivocation on the only real entity, namely, God. Moreover, sensible entities are defined precisely by their dependence upon a nonempirical, whether this be expressed according to the scholastic formula of *ens creatum* or by Spinoza's theory of modes.[74]

One final observation should be noted as a corollary to the Critical objection, as far as the adoption of the two-concept thesis and the interpretation of the minor premise as synthetic is concerned. It has been correctly observed that, viewed from the Critical standpoint, two distinct concepts are conjoined in the premise as if this conjunction were self-evident.[75] This problem, however, follows only upon the acceptance of the two-concept thesis, i.e., the thesis that the ideas of "God" (*ens perfectissimum*) and "necessary existence" (*ens necessarium*) have diverse origins. That thesis is overtly contradicted by the common metaphysical doctrine that God is *the same* as his existence, as well as the Cartesian claim that we first discover the concept of necessary existence in the investigation of the metaphysical concept of God. The position of at least some of the proponents of the ontological argument is thus that any demonstration of the connection in question would be superfluous and/or misleading; they hold not only that "necessary being" and "perfect being" refer to the same entity, but also that these have the same basic meaning. Whether these are two concepts or just one is precisely the question begged on both sides of the debate (i.e., to the two-argument critic it appears that the proponents of the ontological proof conflate two concepts, or at least identify them without justification). To the proponents, however, critics like Kant demand a synthetic account of an idea that is essentially simple, and they do so only on the basis of the contested assumption of the priority of empirical knowledge.

THE *CRITIQUE* QUALIFIED: MENDELSSOHN'S *MORGENSTUNDEN*

Although he fails to highlight any internal fallacy in the more consistent versions of the ontological argument, Kant nonetheless succeeds in momentarily removing the a priori proofs from philosophical discussion. He accomplishes this mainly by imposing dramatic changes on the aims and methods of philosophical discourse. In the decades following the publication of the *Critique of Pure Reason*, the old rationalist philosophy loses its appeal, and the ontological argument becomes as outdated as the textbooks of Wolff and Baumgarten. Philosophy in Germany, at least for many, takes a new direction. Kant requires of it, no longer a dry catalogue of the various entities in and beyond the world, but an inquiry into the subjective conditions of experience. Various subjective idealisms arise in a collective effort to complete what Kant is believed to have begun.[76] This story, the story of German idealism, ends ironically enough with a return to the ontological argument. Before Hegel reintroduces the a priori proof into the idealist context, however, German philosophy sees one final defense of the ontological argument of the Wolffians.

Kant's close friend and contemporary Moses Mendelssohn responds to *Critique of Pure Reason* with an informative summary and defense of the a priori proof, one that highlights certain shortcomings of the principal objections, but nonetheless fails to place the argument in a context convincing enough to avert Kant's influence. Mendelssohn (1729–1786) belongs to a later generation than Wolff or Baumgarten, and, like other philosophers of the middle of the century, he discovers a more compelling presentation of his philosophy than the text-book form of his predecessors. His philosophy, however, has much in common with the school philosophy, and he agrees with them on matters as essential as the possibility of mathematical demonstration of philosophical knowledge. Among his many noteworthy works is his engaging treatise on natural theology entitled *Morgenstunden* or "Morning Hours."[77] The work appears first in 1785, or several years after Kant's *Critique of Pure Reason*. In it Mendelssohn undertakes an intelligent, if not completely successful, defense of the ontological argument (although he does not follow Kant in employing this name).

Mendelssohn's explanation of the problem of an ontological argument, as well as his knowledgeable summary of its history, ranks among the best short texts on the argument. Most notable is his awareness of the uniqueness of the claim in the traditional forms of ontological argument. Mendelssohn makes this point more clearly and powerfully than any of his predecessors, although he recognizes it as their intention and he attributes the strength of the point to them. It is his perceptiveness on the matter of the exceptional status of the argument that allows him to expose the shortcomings of some of Kant's objections. Specifically, Mendelssohn notices, perhaps partly as a result of his familiarity with Maimonides and other Hebrew theologians,[78] that Kant's criticisms depend on some theory of analogy. The emphasis on the uniqueness of the ontological inference thus pervades his exposition: "In the entire sphere of human cognition there is not a single example of this type of inference."[79] Mendelssohn is clearly aware, then, that it does not suffice to raise as objections general rules that apply to every other inference.

Unlike Kant, Mendelssohn does not take the exceptional status of the ontological inference to speak against its validity: "this peculiarity (*Seltenheit*), or rather this uniqueness, should not alone give us any pause, since it is in this case the very mark of truth."[80] He is thus able to perceive quite clearly the inadequacy of the empirical objection, and he explains how, in the case of an ontological argument, the matter rests only on the difference between God and finite entities, and not at all on whether "existence" is taken as a perfection, as the *complementum essentiae* of Baumgarten, or, with Gassendi and Kant, as "*Position*":

Even if actual existence is not a predicate, but rather the positing (*Position*) of all the predicates of a thing, or whether it is otherwise something inexplicable, but of which we are all well aware; *no matter*, I can think of (any given) contingent thing without this position. I can omit "existence" from the idea of any contingent thing, without cancelling the idea. It remains a concept without instantiation (*Begriff ohne Sache*). This is not the case, however, with the necessary being. I cannot separate existence from this idea, without destroying the idea itself. I must think the thing (*Sache*) along with the concept, or simply let go of the concept. *The whole matter rests on this important distinction*, and the distinction in no way rests on a merely nominal (*willkuerlich*) definition.[81]

This impressive summary of the central problem of the ontological argument places Kant's criticism in perspective: Kant's infamous "hundred dollars" example, together with the rejection of "being" as a predicate, fails *in isolation* as a critique of the a priori proof. That proof rests, and has always rested, on the absolute difference between the infinite and the finite, and no general theory of "existence," of predicative propositions, or of laws of demonstration, can alone provide any relevant criticism. Even Kant's most enthusiastic supporter with respect the ontological argument, Dieter Henrich, admits that whoever limits the critique of the ontological argument to platitudes like "being is not a predicate" "would have to be persuaded (by the ontological argument) solely from reading Mendelssohn's *Morgenstunden*."[82] The historical effectiveness of Kant's criticisms lies only in his having convinced so many that he had discovered the limits of human thought. By contrast, Mendelssohn's reply in defense of the argument does not appear to have been widely read, a fact that can in no way speak against its philosophical value. The ontological argument, in 1785, is still not the object of any directly successful critique. Its temporary disappearance is a product only of the belief that humans are incapable of obtaining any genuine cognition beyond the field of "experience," as this term is defined in the opening chapters of the *Critique of Pure Reason*. Kant's successors, however, undertake a criticism of him on this very point.

NOTES

1. See Kant's 1763 essay "The One Possible Basis for a Demonstration of the Existence of God in Kant's Gesammelte Schriften," ed. Akademie der Wissenschaften, Berlin 1910 (hereafter "AA"), vol. II, pp. 63–163.

2. AA 1 394. Translations from the *Nova dilucidatio* and other pre-Critical texts are my own. For the relevant definition of God, see Wolff's *Theologia naturalis* II #24.

3. This argument is already a frequent theme in the *Objections and Replies* to the *Meditations*. Arnauld and Caterus anticipate much of what Kant says here and subsequently. See AT VII 207–14; CSM II 145–50 and Descartes' reply at AT VII 237–47; CSM II 165–72.

4. Kant (AA 1 394): "The concept of the cause is by nature prior to the concept of the caused, and the latter is posterior to the former: the *causa sui* would thus be both prior and posterior to itself, which is absurd." Arnauld (AT VII 210; CSM 147): " it is absurd to think of a thing's receiving existence yet at the same time possessing that existence prior to the time when we conceive that it received it. Yet this is just what would happen if we were to apply the notion of cause and effect of the same thing in respect to itself.... The notion of a cause is essentially prior to the notion of an effect."

5. Consult the passages listed in the previous notes; see also Hegel's development of Descartes' arguments (chapter seven below).

6. Much of Kant's terminology in the dissertation is that of Crusius's "Ontologie." See *Sketch* numbers 84–85 for this particular example.

7. *Metaphysica* #823: "The opposite of the divine existence is impossible," where "impossible" has been previously defined as "self-contradictory."

8. "This impossibility of the opposite is a ground of our knowledge of the existence, but an antecedent determining cause is simply lacking" (AA I 394).

9. See Wolff's *Theologia naturalis* II, #24.

10. AA 1 394–95 (my translation).

11. Henrich (p. 181 n.2), and Josef Schmucker ("Die Gottebeweise beim vorkritischen Kant," in *Kant Studien* 74, 1983, pp. 445–63) read the text in this way.

12. *Metaphysica* #810 and #823; Kant's vocabulary is taken from this text, not from Leibniz or Wolff.

13. AT VII 67–68; CSM 46–47.

14. Henrich suggests (p. 182) that Kant could have encountered the empirical objection in either Johann Mosheim's *Cudworthi systema intellectuale* (dissertation, Jena, 1733) or Crusius's *Sketch*. These are improbable speculations, however, given that both Crusius and Cudworth accept the predication of "existence" in the case of God. It is more likely that Kant imagined himself an innovator in respect to the empirical objection, since his only real predecessor in this regard is Gassendi.

15. As Martin Schoenfeld (*The Philosophy of the Young Kant*, Oxord, 2000, p. 293, n. 30) notes in correction of Henrich and others that Crusius considers existence to be a predicate. See *Sketch* #46: "existence is the predicate of a thing according to which it is to be encountered outside the mind in some specific time and place."

16. Reflection 3706 (AA 17, 240); cf. Henrich's (p. 9) discussion of this note.

17. E.g., Reflection 3731 (AA 17, 272)

18. Crusius objects to the derivation of the principle of sufficient reason from the principle of contradiction, and so he disallows any use of the latter in justifying existential claims (see *Sketch* #234).

19. Reflection 3736 (AA 17, 276)

20. For a recent review of this problem in Kant, see Kenneth R. Westphal's "Epistemic Reflection and Cognitive Reference in Kant's Transcendental Response to Skepticism" in *Kant Studien* 94 (2), 2003, pp. 135–71.

21. Henrich's (p. 9) overstatement of his case is a mere reaction to comments like those by Hegel (see chapter seven, I): "In (Kant's) Critical work there is not a single passage that suggests he opposes ontotheology in the manner of Saint Thomas." In his chapter on Hegel, Henrich (p. 194ff.) seems to contradict this prefatory statement of his by arguing, again contra Hegel, that Kant's employment of the Thomistic objection does not represent a mere assumption. In the course of the argument Henrich of course concedes that Kant ultimately assents to the Thomistic claim.

22. KrV B 620–21. I cite the *First Critique* by page number of the B edition; except where otherwise noted, I use the Cambridge translation by Paul Guyer and Allen Wood (Cambridge, 1997).

23. In the *Discourse* (AT VI 36–37; CSM I 129) Descartes limits himself to the analogical presentation.

24. *Metaphysica* #827.

25. KrV B 621: "all the alleged examples are taken only from judgments, but not from things and their existence."

26. Ibid.

27. This distinction was prevalent in twentieth-century discussions of the argument (see, e.g., John Hick's "A Critique of the 'Second Argument,'" in *The Many Faced Argument*, eds. Hick and McGill, Macmillan, 1967, pp. 341–56).

28. KrV B 622 (my emphasis).

29. In Reflection 4659 (AA 17 628) Kant relates this argument to the claim in #823 of Baumgarten's *Metaphysica*: "if a supremely perfect being were to not exist, nothing would be lacking to it, since the being itself would be lacking."

30. It is well documented in the literature that Kant's argument in this paragraph is question-begging. See, e.g., Charles Nussbaum, "Did Kant Refute the Ontological Argument?" in *Southwest Philosophy Review* 10(1), 1994, pp. 147–56. See also Nicholas Everitt, "Kant's Discussion of the Ontological Argument," in *Kant-Studien* 86, 1995, pp. 385–405, and Herbert Nelson, "Kant on Arguments Cosmological and Ontological," in *American Catholic Philosophic Quarterly* 67 (2), 1993, pp. 167–84.

31. Kant directly attributes only an *identification*, but the context of the argument suggests that it is rather a *confusion* (i.e., the identification, Kant suggests, is an error).

32. KrV B 10.

33. Identity is certainly too strong here, but it is what Kant asserts.

34. Descartes provides the mediation at best indirectly. In *Meditation III*, it is proved that God causes our idea of him, so that there is some relation of the sort required. Spinoza, Malebranche, Geulincx, and others improve upon this reply by incorporating the "idea" of God within God's nature. Their ontological arguments are not subjective. Hegel, however, brings the notion to its extreme consequence: our knowledge of God is ultimately God's self-knowledge. On this, see chapter seven.

35. Passages like the one from the *Regulae* (AT X 373; CSM I 17) that assert the divinity of the human mind suggest we could exempt him from this charge, since they suggest his affinity to post-Cartesian rationalists.

36. Kant's rhetoric in the *Critique of Pure Reason* is extremely strong, and can cause the unfortunate and misleading impression that he is naïve about so many points regarding the history of metaphysics. Regarding the idea of God and the relation of this to the human mind, some of his notes indeed suggest a more careful and sympathetic position. See, for instance, Reflection 6048 (AA 18 433).

37. KrV B 626, my translation. In an effort to conceal the *ad hominem* nature of Kant's argument, Guyer and Wood omit the expression "rational person" (perhaps "reasonable person") from their translation of the text.

38. Bering's *Pruefung der Beweise fuer das Dasein Gottes aus den Begriffen eines hoechstvollkommenen und notwendigen Wesens* (*Examination of the Proofs for the Existence of God from the Ideas of a Supremely Perfect and a Necessary Being*, Giessen, 1780) appeared just prior to the *First Critique*. For an analysis of this work and its influence on Kant, see Henrich, pp. 115–23. For an alternative thesis concerning the history of the example, see Sebastien Charles's "De l'utilisation critique d'un exemple monetaire en philosophie: Kant en face a Buffier," in *Kant Studien* 91 (3), 2000, pp. 356–65.

39. I owe some thanks to Reinhard Schaeffer and Michael Wladika of the University of Heidelberg for encouraging this approach to Kant's chapter.

40. See *Sketch* #44–#45.

41. KrV B 629.

42. One apparent piece of evidence is Reflection 4732 (AA 17 690): "we do not wish to think of the *ens extramundanum* through *predicata mundana*" (Kant mixes these Latin phrases with his German). Kant's intention in this note, however, is to criticize theological analogy; he recognizes the need for equivocation but does not seem aware of the prevalence of the requisite doctrine.

43. See *Metaphysica* #826–#827. Baumgarten (#826) actually distinguishes three modes of predication that apply in natural theology (analogy, eminence, and reduction) but claims (#827) that the hypothetical necessity of judgments is similar to the absolute necessity of the divine existence, so that our knowledge of the divine existence is indeed analogical. The doctrine of eminence most closely resembles the doctrine of equivocation, since "eminence" implies the lack of an analogy with experiential quali-

ties. For Kant's discussion of this see Reflection 6041ff. (AA 18 431). Kant's later discussions of divine attribution appear in the context of his debate with Eberhard. See Reflections #6286 and #6300–#6301. Some of Kant's remarks on this issue appear in the *Lectures on Philosophical Theology*, ed. Allen Wood and Gertrude Clark, Cornell, 1978, pp. 52–54.

44. For an example of how Spinoza was read during the years of Kant's education, see the German translation of and commentary on the *Ethics* that appears among Wolff's collected works.

45. Reflection 4732 (AA 17 690).

46. B 594/A 566: : "... nothing is left for us but the analogy by which we utilize concepts of experience in making some sort of concept of intelligible things, with which we have not the least acquaintance as they are in themselves."

47. For a detailed discussion of Kant's theory of analogy, see Jerry H. Gill's "Kant, Analogy, and Natural Theology," in *International Journal for Philosophy of Religion* 16 (1984), pp. 19–28, and Paul E. Stroble's "'Without Running Riot': Kant, Analogical Language, and Theological Discourse" in *Sophia* 32 (3), 1993, pp. 57–72.

48. On the appropriateness of the Cartesian doctrine of innateness, see the notes in AA 18 555ff.

49. Ch. 17 of the *Monologion* is entitled: "The supreme being is so simple that whatever things can be predicated of its essence are one and the same thing in it." In *Mediation III* Descartes writes: "... the unity, simplicity or inseparability of all the attributes of God is one of the most important of the perfections which I understand him to have." In a passage from his *Second Replies* he claims that we imagine these separately only by "a defect in our understanding" (AT VII 137; CSM II 98).

50. *Theologia naturalis* I #47

51. AA 17 275.

52. KrV B 607.

53. Kant is very ambiguous about what his argument is for this "restriction thesis." Kant scholars accordingly fail to locate his proof that knowledge has definite limits. For an attempt at this see Paul Guyer's "Thought and Being: Hegel's Critique of Kant's Theoretical Philosophy," in *The Cambridge Companion to Hegel*, ed. Frederick C. Beiser, Cambridge, 1993, pp. 171–210.

54. KrV B 608, B 611.

55. See the discussions of this point above, chapter 3 and especially chapter 4.

56. KrV B 624.

57. Ibid.

58. KrV B 625.

59. In Kant's terminology "essence" and "possibility" are nearly interchangeable, as they are for Leibniz.

60. See above, chapter 5, section I B.

61. For a very detailed discussion of the following argument, see Henrich, pp. 137–87.

62. KrV B 480–83

63. KrV B 588–89/A 560–61.

64. KrV B 596/A 567.

65. KrV B 601/A 573. The doctrine of "thoroughgoing determination" is Leibnizian in origin, but Kant's version of it derives from Baumgarten, *Metaphysica* #148.

66. KrV B 603–604/A 575–76.

67. See *Metaphysica* #812, #823.

68. On the convertibility of these propositions and the mutual dependence of the ontological and cosmological arguments, see KrV B 637/A 608. See also Reflection 3733 (AA 17 274–75).

69. In the case of the *omnitudo realitatis*, Kant makes this point (KrV B 660–61) by alleging that the proofs for God's existence conflate distributive and collective unity.

70. Kant accepts that, if we were compelled to choose a being that possesses necessary existence, the *omnitudo realitatis* would be the best candidate. His contention is that we cannot actually know that this is the case (i.e., we cannot have insight into the fact that "God possesses necessary existence").

71. KrV B 611–12/A 583–84.

72. Kant's clearest exposition of this point appears in the section (KrV B 611–19) on "The grounds of proof of speculative reason for inferring the existence of a highest being."

73. On Kant's view, "we merely flatter ourselves" (KrV B 615) that we can make the required inference.

74. See *Principles of Philosophy* I 52 (AT VIIIA 24; CSM I 210).

75. Henrich (pp. 152–53) writes that Descartes "makes this connection as if it were self-evident."

76. For a detailed account of the directions philosophy takes in Germany in these years, see Frederick Beiser's *The Fate of Reason: German Philosophy from Kant to Fichte* (Harvard, 1987).

77. Citations from this work are from the Reclam paperback edition (1979). Translations are my own.

78. In 1760 Mendelssohn wrote (in Hebrew) a commentary on Maimonides' *Logical Terms*. See his *Gesammelte Schriften*, Akademie-Verlag, Berlin, v. II, pp. 197–230.

79. *Morgensstunden*, p. 170.

80. Ibid.

81. Ibid., p. 175 (my emphasis).

82. Henrich, p. 139.

Chapter Seven

HEGEL'S RECONSTRUCTION
OF THE ARGUMENT

I n the several decades after the appearance of *The Critique of Pure Reason* the ontological argument suffers one of its longest silences since its discovery by Anselm. Although Mendelssohn's *Morgenstunden* provides a vigorous defense, this text does not have nearly the level of influence on the next generation of philosophers as does the *Critique*. The a priori proof cannot even be said to be among the key remnants of the school philosophy that the last of the Wolffians attempt to salvage.[1] It is not until the 1820s that the argument reemerges into the forefront of philosophy, this time in the context of Hegel's lectures on the philosophy of religion. Hegel's defense of the argument in these later lecture courses, however, represents the culmination of over twenty years of development of the central ideas that underlie the Cartesian argument. Hegel's system is, among other things, a resurrection of the entire context of that argument, so that the stage is completely set when his ontological argument finally enters the scene.

Although he never produces a separate treatise devoted solely to the ontological argument, this proof is one of Hegel's most lasting preoccupations. At no point does he seem to have shared the majority opinion that Kant had refuted the argument. Even his earliest writings convey a longstanding conviction that Kant had completely misunderstood the Cartesian proof. References to the argument appear in almost every conceivable context, and he treats the proof at least in passing in almost every work from his Jena essays to his last lectures, when it finally becomes a central theme for him.[2] In most cases he portrays his advocacy of the argument as evidence of his affinity to a metaphysical tradition including Descartes and Spinoza. Just as often he cites the argument as an illustration of the difference between Kant's philosophy and his own, so that establishing the validity of the argument is central to the end of securing his position in relation to that philosopher.

Hegel's role as defender of the Cartesian argument has been the subject of mischaracterization. In the few existing English-language accounts of the history of this argument Hegel's contribution has simply been overlooked, due mainly to the fact that many anglophone philosophers have been unable to appreciate his philosophical contributions.[3] The more thorough accounts of the history of the argument have appeared in Germany, where Hegel's affinity to prominent "pre-Kantian" philosophers has been dramatically underestimated.[4] While it is true, as Henrich writes, that Hegel equals Kant in the tenacity of his criticism of the mathematical exposition of seventeenth- and eighteenth-century philosophy, it is not the case that his advocacy of the ontological argument represents an absolute break from the positions of those writers. His defense of the argument is in fact in agreement on nearly all the principal points with the primary seventeenth-century proponents of the proof.

The parallels between Hegel's ontological argument and its seventeenth-century form are indeed striking. He opposes the Thomistic, empirical, and possibility objections in ways closely related to the Cartesian replies to those complaints. He develops a theory of the relation of human consciousness to divine consciousness that is in some respects an elaboration of Spinoza's view of the matter. He follows Malebranche in defining God as "being," and he offers an intricate argument relating this conception to the other definitions of God such as *causa sui* and *ens necessarium*. His arguments in defense of these last concepts are consistent with some Cartesian arguments. He also develops a theory of the cognition of God that would explain why the a priori arguments do not receive assent from all parties, and on this point he is again in agreement with the predominant trends of the argument's history.

The notion that Hegel's defense of the argument should represent a radical break from previous rationalists is a product of the belief that the argument was in fact convincingly refuted by Kant and his followers. Kant's success, however, was more local than most historians of philosophy have been prone to imagine. His objections aim primarily at an eighteenth-century form of the ontological argument that differs in significant ways from the seventeenth-century versions of the proof. His critique of the doctrine of theological analogy, his equation of "essence" with "possibility," and his insistence that the concepts of "necessary existence" and of a "supremely perfect entity" have diverse origins stem from the limited context within which he operated. Kant was simply unaware of the more consistent forms of the ontological argument, and even his most original criticisms apply only to his immediate predecessors.

In order to "restore the proofs of God's existence to a position of honor,"[5] then, Hegel has only to indicate the shortcomings in Kant's critique. In this regard there is no doubt that he overstates his case. Although Hegel bases his defense of the ontological argument on an awareness of its history, he fails to draw the appropriate distinctions among the "pre-Kantian" proponents of the proof, and he frequently writes as if Kant had committed nothing but a gross misunderstanding. At the same time, however, his theory of the history of philosophy prevents him from being able to discard Kant's contribution as utterly useless.[6] In some passages he thus represents himself as achieving a synthesis of ontotheological and critical positions. His "absolute idealism," for instance, although in its conclusions is closely related to the rationalist epistemologies of the seventeenth century, concedes some points to Kant's analysis of finite consciousness. His argument for the inclusion of "necessary existence" within God's nature likewise accepts a qualified two-concept thesis, although he alleges to overcome the duality with the help of his notion of a "speculative concept."

HEGEL THE CARTESIAN

The Thomistic objection: a referee for an age-old dispute

Several commentators have remarked that Hegel often mistakes the Thomistic objection for Kant's full criticism of the argument.[7] While it is true that Hegel is less than thorough in his account of his predecessors, the priority given to the Thomistic objection does not stem from a failure to notice that Kant had raised other objections.[8] Rather, the objection in question serves, for Hegel, as a focal point of the difference between his own system and Kant's. The Critical philosophy, on Hegel's interpretation, arrives at the basic conclusion that "being" is distinct from the "concept." By contrast, he frequently describes his own philosophy as an attempt to demonstrate that being is a characteristic of the concept, or to prove in general the "unity of thought and being." If Hegel puts seemingly unjust emphasis on this first objection, then, it is not because he interprets Kant in such a way that the objection would serve, *for Kant*, as the central point of criticism. Rather, it is because he interprets the difference between Kantian and Hegelian philosophy in such a way that Aquinas's objection condenses the most basic point of dispute between these approaches.

If the purpose of the Thomistic objection is to stipulate a general distinction between "what is merely thought" and "what is," then Kant's philosophy indeed represents a full-scale attempt to establish the universal applicability of this objection. The culmination of Kant's criticism of "dogmatic metaphysics" is that the most fundamental ideas of human reason, such as "necessary existence," represent *mere* ideas to which no reality corresponds (at least as far as we could ever confirm); he also argues that metaphysical categories (substance, cause, etc.) apply only within the realm of human experience. These "Critical" positions occasion his assent to an otherwise apparently crude formulation of the Thomistic objection. In one colorfully condescending expression of the claim, he insists that existence cannot be "plucked" (*ausgeklaubt*) from the idea of a thing. This passage becomes the subject of a running joke with which Hegel makes dozens of references to the ontological argument and its critique.[9]

The "dogmatic" metaphysicians who serve as the targets of Kant's criticism, nearly all of whom are proponents of the ontological argument, argue instead for what Hegel calls a "unity of thought a being." By this expression Hegel means that for these philosophers the categories of thought are also the categories of extramental entities.[10] In other words, what we predicate of the objects of experience belongs to those things independently of our experiencing them. The major premise of the Cartesian argument establishes precisely this point: anything we perceive to belong to a thing, under certain ideal epistemic conditions (viz., clarity and distinctness), really belongs to that thing. Other proponents of the ontological argument likewise claim that ideal epistemic conditions (real definitions, the analysis of possibility, etc.) provide the justification for direct inferences from thoughts to realities.

If Hegel at times appears to reduce the history of the ontological argument to a conflict of assumptions concerning the difference or identity of thought and being, then, the basic claim is not for that matter inaccurate.[11] The dispute between the proponents and the critics concerning the Thomistic objection is describable in those terms, and even Kant's position consists largely in the criticism of doctrines like the one asserting the reality of predicates. Peculiar is only Hegel's claim that the history of philosophy offers nothing more than unjustified assumptions on this point. In his opinion the rationalists assert the unity of thought and being only in unproven axioms;[12] he likewise claims that Kant fails to prove the difference between the concept and being.[13] Scholars have appropriately considered these allegations unfair; the only basis for the claims is that Hegel imports a standard of what counts as a "proof" that is foreign to the philosophers to whom he is referring.[14] His frequent complaints regarding the lack of proof of traditional philosophical claims conditions his own attempt to claim for himself the honor of being the first to justify his position on the ontological argument. Remarks along these lines must be taken with a grain of salt, without their thereby diminishing the value of his actual contributions.

Hegel sees himself as the first to accept the task of "proving" the identity of thought and being. In doing so he ultimately sides with the rationalists in his conviction that the categories of thought possess metaphysical applicability, hence his equation of "logic" with "metaphysics." He nonetheless understands himself to provide a more thorough and convincing argument for the rationalist thesis. His argument is supposed to be more thorough as a result of his appropriation of critical doctrines within his idealist framework. He does not present his "absolute idealism" as an outright refusal of the Thomistic position; he argues instead that "thought" is *both* the same as *and* different from "being," so that his position is supposed to represent a compromise between the rationalists and Kant. The former, he claims, merely assert doctrines like the reality of predication, and they claim to possess immediate knowledge of metaphysical reality. In Hegel's view the ontological argument is and always has been valid, but it requires recognition that "being" is the opposite of thought, while at the same time being proceeds from thought.[15]

The Referee Chooses Sides: God in the Human Mind

Hegel becomes aware of Clarke's objection to the ontological argument through the writings of both Kant and the German skeptic Gottlob Ernst Schulze. In regards to this objection he also offers another extremely general portrayal according to which each of his predecessors stands in either one of two camps. The rationalist philosophers and defenders of the ontological argument consider the human mind to participate in the divine intellect, while the objectors deny this important claim. In an early essay Hegel writes as if there is no explanation for the duality of positions on this issue; later, in his lectures on the philosophy of religion, he claims to synthesize the two views in question by arguing that the finite, human intellect is both in union with and in separation from the infinite, divine intellect. His actual position is in fact entirely consonant with the view held by the seventeenth-century proponents of the ontological proof.

In response to Schulze's massive two-volume work, *Critique of Theoretical Philosophy*, Hegel composes his 1803 essay "The Relationship of Skepticism to Philosophy."[16] As the article makes clear, the young Hegel already expresses frustration with the disrepute of the ontological argument among the followers of Kant. The first discussion of Schulze's criticism of the ontological proof refers to the "supremely simple joke" that Kant had discovered, namely, that "being" is something different from "the concept."[17] The ensuing passages foreshadow all of Hegel's later remarks on the Kantian criticisms of the ontological argument, replete with jokes and the use of the term "*herausklauben.*"

Following Kant, Schulze begins his discussion of the ontological argument by distinguishing logical from ontological necessity. This simple distinction is supposed to reveal "the illusion and empty hairsplitting of the ontological argument."[18] In greater detail than any of his predecessors Schulze identifies this Thomistic objection with both Clarke's objection and the metaphysical doctrine that serves as a reply to the latter: if the transition from a necessary judgment to an existent is possible, the human intellect must possess some relation to the divine intellect.[19] Schulze (unlike Kant or Clarke) recognizes that Plato, Descartes, Spinoza, and Leibniz each describe versions of this relationship and that the objection in question thus has no efficacy that is internal to their philosophies. Hegel offers the following summary of Schulze's summary of this "theosophical" tradition:

> It is explained in the "Remark" that according to Plato the ideas and principles that are inborn in the soul in our present life, through which alone we are able to know the actual as it is, and not as it appears to the senses, these ideas and principles are mere recollections of the intuitions in which the soul participated during its contact with God. Descartes appeals, in this matter, to the truthfulness of God. For Spinoza, our ideas are true because they consist of God's representations and cognitions, to the extent that God comprises the essence of our mind. These cognitions, since they are in God, must be in complete agreement with their objects. Cognition and object must be, in this case, one and the same. According to Leibniz, the a priori

principles of our minds, as well as our representations generally, possess truth and reality because they are images of the concepts and truths that are in God's intellect. The latter truths are the principle of possibility, existence and creation of all real things in the world.[20]

This summary of the reply to Clarke's objection represents an unusual recognition, by a critic, of the consistency of the defense of the ontological argument. Schulze nonetheless rejects that argument by attacking the doctrine of the divine character of human reason. Assuming the skeptical distinction between subjective concepts and their corresponding realities, he asks how it could be shown that the former accurately apply to the latter. The answer lies, of course, in the indicated relationship of the human mind to the mind of God. But our knowledge that there is such a relationship, Schulze notes, derives only from our innate ideas, or from the subjective concepts themselves. The appeal to God thus involves circular reasoning, since our ideas about our relationship to God must be true if this relationship is to guarantee the truth of our ideas. Schulze accuses the entire metaphysical tradition of a version of the Arnauld circle.

Hegel acknowledges the broad applicability of this problem, but objects only to the skeptical starting point of Schulze's argument. For the rationalists there is no circularity in arguing from the divinity of our understanding to the truth of our concepts; rather, the truth of our concepts is nothing different from the divinity of our understanding. Conversely, to say that our understanding possesses a divine character is to say nothing more than that we have true concepts.[21] It must be conceded, on the other hand, that if the distinction between "subjective concepts" and "reality" is accepted as a starting point, then only circular arguments can be raised against the skeptic. Any appeal to the divine character of reason would first presume the truth of at least one idea, viz., the idea that reason is divine, and would thereby contradict the accepted distinction. *If* the distinction is accepted, there is no noncircular solution to the dilemma it poses.[22] The assertion that reason is divine, however, presupposes in turn the nullity of the distinction between subjective concepts and reality, so that the objector is left only with the illusion of a victory, having introduced a premise foreign to his opponent, the "dogmatic metaphysician." Hegel concludes, in a passage whose irony makes it difficult to interpret, that there are simply two "races of consciousness" corresponding to the two basic positions on the status of human reason:

Nothing remains, then, apart from the need to accept that there are two races of consciousness: one race that is conscious of this relationship [to God's nature] and one that explains such consciousness to be theosophical charlatanism (*theosphische Grille*).[23]

This amusing passage represents another instance of Hegel classifying the entire history of philosophy in terms of a basic disagreement. In 1803 Hegel is content to leave the issue unresolved; two decades later, in the *Lectures on the Philosophy of Religion*, he claims to have "resolved the opposition" by synthesizing the diverse positions (i.e., he asserts the divinity of human reason while recognizing that subjective concepts differ from their corresponding realities). In fact, however, his position is in entire agreement with those of the pre-Kantian rationalists. His arguments that reason must be understood as divine resonate with a number of passages from Descartes' *Regulae*.[24] His "synthesis" consists primarily in his recognition of finite consciousness as a "moment" differentiable from our participation in the infinite intellect, with the subsequent doctrine that this consciousness is illusory. The position here is consistent with even Geulincx's metaphorical statement of the defense against Clarke's objection. Geulincx claims that we are "*both* in and out of God," not simply that our mind is within the divine intellect.[25] Spinoza likewise allows for an apparent distinction between our mind and God's, and his interpretation of this difference in terms of the theory of modes has more in common with Hegel's concept of "moment" than the latter ever admits.

Walter Jaeschke has correctly noticed that the introduction of the unity of human and divine reason as a theme is what ultimately distinguishes Hegel's "philosophy of religion" from the "natural theology" of the Wolffian metaphysics.[26] Hegel's position thus appears original at least in the context of eighteenth- and nineteenth-century German philosophy. His emphasis on the role of this relationship (between the finite mind and God) in the ontological argument, however, represents an accurate interpretation of the Cartesian form of that argument. Descartes' argument is, unlike Baumgarten's or Wolff's, not merely about God but rather our perception of him. For Descartes our understanding of our relationship to God determines even our awareness of our own existence.[27] Hegel's innovation lies in his completion of this argument: first, he claims that God's relationship to the human intellect is essential also to his (God's) nature, not merely to ours; second, he relates our religious awareness of God to the philosophical perception of him.[28]

For Hegel it is essential to God that he appear to both a religious community and rational inquiry.[29] In other words, the appearance to the religious community belongs to God's essence, as does his being comprehended in philosophical thought. With respect to both philosophy and religion Hegel employs an essentialist interpretation of history in order to relate the nature of God to his comprehension in the human mind. Both the history of religion and the history of philosophy demonstrate the process of reunification of God with man after an initial separation. The aim of Hegel's account of these histories is to show that the historical and factual difference between the human and divine intellects is ultimately overcome; man is and has been separate from God, but the knowledge brought about by Christian history and catalogued in Hegel's philosophical system eventually achieves a unification with God.

Our recognition of God simultaneously represents the overcoming of our own finitude and our reconciliation with him. Since Hegel holds that our knowledge of God brings about a reunion with him, he is in a position to agree with Malebranche in accepting the classical objection of the anti-Cartesians that it could not be by finite, human reason as such that God is known. His position implies instead that we come to know God only by "the mind of God in man."[30] To the extent that human consciousness possesses knowledge of God, it is the divine in the human that possesses this knowledge. To that same extent, then, the divinity constitutes the intellect, and our knowledge of God is God's self-knowledge, a point that Spinoza also raises in the context of his discussion of "intellectual love of God."[31] God's self-knowledge is, of course, not substantially distinct from its object, so that the Kantian objection "the thought that is in you must be the thing itself" finds affirmation in Hegel's metaphysics. It would indeed follow from our idea of God that he exists *if our idea of God were God's idea of himself.*

"Descartes . . . Does Not Speak of 'One Hundred Dollars'"

In the wake of Kant's *Critique of Pure Reason* it was the empirical objection that enjoyed an especially distinguished reputation. For that very reason it is also the object of Hegel's most unforgiving scorn. Kant's popularization of Gassendi's objection appears to Hegel to signal a victory for unphilosophical consciousness: in it God suffers comparison with a small sum of money. Hegel's opposition to this objection is accordingly less qualified than his rejection of the Thomistic and Clarkean quibbles; in this instance he does not portray his defense of the ontological argument as a synthesis of previous positions. He instead considers it sufficient to highlight the intention of the Cartesian argument, and his comments on the empirical objection demonstrate his affinity to both Cartesian and post-Cartesian positions. In the *Lectures on the History of Philosophy* his defense of Descartes appears in the chapter on Kant:

> I can imagine whatever I want, and it does not for that matter exist. It depends, though, on *what* I represent to myself: if I think or comprehend the subjective and being, then there is a transition. Descartes expressly asserts this unity only of the concept of God (for exactly this is God), and he does not speak of "one hundred dollars."[32]

In the *Science of Logic* he accordingly emphasizes the importance of the difference between God and finite entities, and he claims (contra Leibniz) that this distinction is prior to any difference between a thing (i.e., its essence) and its existence.[33] The priority of the distinction between God and creatures serves, in the history of the argument, also as the response to the modal objection; Hegel stands in agreement with the pre-Leibnizian rationalists in his conviction that the gap between a definition and the existence of the definiendum cannot be generalized to include also the definition of God, since the differences among definienda affect the criteria for the definitions. Hegel frequently expresses this point by claiming that the distinction between a concept or definition and an existence belongs to definition of finitude, whereas the definition of God is "the unity of thought and existence."[34]

Hegel follows Descartes in the modal specification of the distinction between the "existence of God" and all other instances of "existence." He justifies his concept of necessary existence, however, neither axiomatically in the manner of Descartes (in which case the relationship between "contingent" and "necessary" would remain unclarified), nor through a proof *e contingentia mundi* in the manner of Leibniz and Wolff (in which case our knowledge of necessity derives from our knowledge of contingency). His rejection of the standard cosmological proof demonstrates his kinship rather to Spinoza; both philosophers shun the proof because it inverts the order of knowing and the order of being. The incongruity between *what* the argument proves and *how* it is proved lends that argument to the misconception that the necessary exists because the contingent exists. Hegel proposes a revision of the traditional cosmological argument that expresses the monistic thesis: the proof should instead show that "contingent existence" is something false.[35] The revised conclusion reads: "The absolutely necessary *exists*, not because the contingent exists, but rather because the contingent is a non-being, only an appearance. The existence of the contingent is not truly actual. The absolutely necessary is its being and its truth."[36]

Although Hegel thus stands in agreement with the Spinozistic view that ascribes reality in the pre-eminent sense only to God, he attempts to differentiate his version of this claim by rejecting the traditional version of the doctrine of equivocal attribution. If we say particular things "exist," for both Hegel and the Cartesians, we employ this term in a different, borrowed sense.[37] Unlike the latter, however, Hegel thinks this borrowed sense of "exist" is not entirely distinct from the genuine sense of "existence," which is applicable only to God. He criticizes the Spinozistic doctrine of equivocation because he takes that view to lead to "acosmism," or the denial of the reality of all finite entities.[38] By contrast he attempts, in his *Science of Logic*, to interpret the notions of "contingency" and "necessity" such that these modalities serve as "moments" of a single concept of existence.

In defense of the classical version of the ontological argument Hegel undertakes an attack on Kant's interpretation of "essence" and "existence" to the extent that the latter lends ontological priority to individual objects of experience. His arguments to this effect are reminiscent of Spinoza's reply to the empirical objection. Both philosophers take aim at the notion that finite entities possess independent reality. For Kant, according to Hegel, the concept of "essence" implies precisely this independence, since that philosopher employs the term to designate the describable content of a thing considered in isolation from its context. The "existence" of a thing, by contrast, refers to the thing's "position" in relation to a percipient subject and to other items in the field of experience. The difference between the essence of a finite thing and the existence of the same is thus the difference between an isolated content and its relation to everything else. Kant's empirical objection, on this reading, amounts to nothing more than the assertion that the content "one hundred dollars" is the same content whether or not it enters into relationship with the state of my fortune.[39]

Even in the case of a finite entity, however, the indifference of a thing to its "existence" persists only to the extent that it is *considered* in isolation from its relations. Hegel's objection to Kant centers on the fact that the latter remains fixated on the finite content and assumes this to be something real apart from its relations. By contrast, Hegel defends an ontological thesis that is shared by both Leibniz and Spinoza, viz., that a thing's relations are essential to it. The hundred dollars are related to my fortune even when I do not possess them; an imagined hundred dollars are related negatively to my fortune, to the extent that I lack them. Further, the content is related to the economy in general, to what can be bought with them, etc. Apart from this broad context the expression "one hundred dollars" is meaningless. The deception involved in the empirical objection thus lies at least partly in the apparent self-sufficiency of the content of a finite thing (a point that motivates Spinoza's monism). If I imagine the hundred dollars I abstract them from every relation. But even as imagined they are related to me, my fortune, etc. Since the content as imagined consists in nothing but the separation of this from its context, it is a spurious and illusory concept. It does not actually possess the independence that I attribute to it; the independence is instead "a borrowed form attached to it by the subjective understanding."[40]

Both Spinoza and Malebranche disarm the empirical objection and avoid the analogy between God and finite things by limiting the extension of the notion of "thinghood." Descartes' definition of God as an *ens perfectissimum* indeed encourages the misunderstanding that God is subsumable (alongside creatures) under the species "thing." Although this confusion is nearly impossible in the context of post-Cartesian rationalism, where God is either defined as "being" simpliciter or as the only substance, the eighteenth century saw the predominance of empirical argumentation against theology. In post–Kantian philosophy, however, the concept of God again precludes the subsumption necessary for an empirical objection. Schelling's notion of "the unconditioned" (*das Unbedingte*, literally "the non-reified thing") led Hegel to the insight that God does not fall under the general category of "entity."[41] In this matter Hegel overlooks his fraternity with the post-Cartesians, and he understands his contemporaries to have made progress over the rationalists.[42]

The final defense against the empirical objection lies in the designation of a privileged standpoint. Descartes qualifies his minor premise with the reminder that only those who have "made a sufficiently careful investigation of what God is," or those who have freed themselves from "preconceived notions" can attain to the observation that a special species of existence is uniquely ascribable to God. The standpoint of Cartesian philosophy is achieved in the first two *Meditations*, or in the first seven sections of the *Principles*. Hegel's philosophy likewise establishes a privileged standpoint. The presupposition of the system includes, like in the case of the *cogito*, awareness of the unity of thought and being, and thus a transcendence of other forms of consciousness. The text describing the ascent to the proper standpoint is, famously, the *Phenomenology of Spirit*.[43] The system of logic, and thus the ontological argument, is intelligible only after the standpoint has been achieved.[44]

Possibility, God, and the Organization of Metaphysics

Both Kant and Descartes reject Leibniz's claim that the possibility of the concept from which the ontological argument departs requires demonstration prior to the conclusion that God exists. Kant argues that the Leibnizian proof contradicts its own commitment to the analysis of possibility by defining existence into possibility. It is contradictory to *at once* consider an entity "merely" in terms of its possibility *and* to include existence within this possibility. Spinoza, Malebranche, and in some instances even Descartes, however, demonstrate the existence of God with greater consistency by limiting the concept of "possible existence" to finite entities.[45] Any prior inquiry into the "possibility" of the notion of God illicitly transfers a property of finitude (viz., possible existence) into the infinite. Hegel raises this same point in reference to the Leibnizian demonstration of the existence of God.

In his 1829 lecture series on the proofs for the existence of God Hegel takes issue with the structure of the Wolffian *Theologia naturalis* and thereby attacks the proof procedure of the entire Leibnizian school. Following Leibniz, Wolff begins with an analysis of the concept of God, and then proceeds to prove the existence of a corresponding entity and, finally, to derive its attributes. Hegel intends to show this "activity of the understanding" in separating God's nature from his existence, and these from his attributes, to be an inadequate procedure. The inadequacy of the division is revealed by the very concept of God. If God "cannot be thought except as existing," then no analysis of the thought of God can precede the proof of his existence.[46] Hegel notes that such a concept precludes a purely logical analysis of "possibility": if God can only be thought as existing, "then the concept should not be thought in isolation from being, since this concept possesses no truth apart from being."[47] The definition of God from which the ontological argument proceeds does not permit of any prior analysis in terms of mere possibility.

Although Hegel agrees with the Cartesians in his conviction that it is contradictory to speak of God as possible, his own rejection of the Leibnizian/Wolffian arguments is not limited to this point. A preliminary proof of God's possibility or noncontradictoriness is unnecessary not only because "God" as a specific object of investigation is exempt from such a requirement. *Any* isolated demonstration of possibility rests, for Hegel, on mistaken assumptions.[48] Prior consideration of a concept as possible (noncontradictory) presupposes that something contradictory is impossible, or incapable of existing. Descartes expresses the axiom in question thusly: "all self-contradictoriness resides solely in our thought . . . it cannot occur in anything which is outside the intellect."[49] Only upon acceptance of this axiom would a proof of a thing as possible bear any importance in relation to the thing's existence. Hegel rejects the axiom, which he takes to be common to both Kant and the rationalists, by claiming that every "thing" is an "existing contradiction."[50]

THE DEFINITIONS OF GOD AND THE TWO-CONCEPT THESIS

The speculative concept and God

In his universal rejection of the analysis of possibility Hegel criticizes a form of reasoning he takes to be common to both the ontotheologians and the objectors, while at the same time he intends to correct a flaw in the form of the ontological argument that had contributed to its misunderstanding. His predecessors, he claims, had mistaken the "abstract thought" of God for the *concept* of God.[51] The first point involved in reformulating the ontological argument, then, concerns distinguishing the "abstract thoughts" or "formal concepts" of God from the genuine, or in Hegel's terms, the "speculative" concept of God. The argument in the *Science of Logic* aims at demonstrating the speculative concept of God to incorporate a series of "abstract" notions of the deity. Since his ultimate claim is that the many traditional notions of God (*ens necessarium*, *ens perfectissimum*, etc.) belong to a single dialectical "concept," the main argument in the *Logic* serves as a response to the two-concept thesis.

The analysis of possibility pertains only to abstract thoughts considered in isolation, since possibility designates nothing more than noncontradictoriness or, as Hegel calls it, "formal self-identity." In contrast to the formal concept, the speculative concept is *concretely identical*, which means that it represents a unity of apparently diverse determinations or "moments." The speculative concept encompasses and incorporates whatever can be derived from it by a dialectical argument.[52] Hegel's conclusion, and thus his refutation of the two-concept thesis, is that, although "necessary existence" and "perfect being" designate distinct *thoughts*, if a dialectical argument is constructed linking one to the other then these thoughts are thereby shown to be merely distinct moments of a single *concept*.

The concept of God in the speculative sense of "concept" is a dialectical unity of the many predicates or determinations of God. The predicates of God are infinity, omniscience, perfection, necessity, etc. These are not to be taken as distinct definitions of God, corresponding to the "concepts" of an *ens necessarium*, *ens perfectissimum*, etc., but rather as "moments of one and the same concept."[53] There can thus be no problem of showing that the *omnitudo realitatis* is the *ens necessarium*, as if two absolutely distinct concepts were designated by these terms. What is instead necessary is to show that these two "abstract thoughts," viz., the thought of necessity and the thought of a unity of all perfections, are moments of a single concept of God. Since the abstract thoughts or predicates of the subject "God" correspond to the moments or categories of the *Logic*, the proof that the categories of logic mutually imply one another also amounts to a proof that the various determinations of God do in fact constitute a single concept.[54]

OMNITUDO REALITATIS AND PURE BEING

Hegel begins his deduction of the various "definitions of the absolute" with the notion of "pure being."[55] In the history of the ontological argument it is Malebranche who offers this notion as an interpretation of the Cartesian *ens perfectissimum*. Hegel's argument attributes special weight to the Malebranchean reading, and he considers this to be the only consistent interpretation of the relevant definition of God. In his various remarks on the pre-Kantian natural theology he identifies the Baumgartian definition of an *omnitudo realitatis*, which he translates into German as *Inbegriff aller Realitaeten* ("sum of all realities"), with the abstract notion of pure being.[56] This identification appears to be a curious oversight with respect to the historical development of the idea of God. In fact it represents an implicit critique of eighteenth-century ontology and, by extension, of the prevalent version of the ontological argument.

Hegel's first objection to the concept of an *omnitudo realitatis* or *unio perfectorum* is that the requirement of the simplicity of the realities or perfections (and hence the entire argument for possibility) also implies that the realities should be indistinguishable from one another. For Hegel, any qualitative difference leads inevitably to contradiction, so that an enumeration of genuinely diverse attributes is incompatible with noncontradictoriness.[57] The Leibnizians seem blind to this consequence, and they insist instead upon a plurality of simple perfections; Leibniz's claim that the simple perfections possess nothing with which they could contradict each other begs the question of how a given perfection could differentiate itself from the others. Likewise, Baumgarten's nod to the simplicity of the realities is incompatible with his account of their plurality.[58] It was only the seventeenth-century metaphysicians who offered a consistent conception of God as a perfect being, since on their interpretations the perfections are indeed indistinguishable within his nature.

The doctrine of equivocation is a direct consequence of the simplicity and indistinguishability of the perfections. If God's "justice" is a simple characteristic, then this has little or nothing to do with "justice" as we employ this term in other instances.[59] Hegel's claim is that the proponent of the concept of an *omnitudo realitatis*, or any interpretation of the Cartesian concept of God, is committed to the doctrine of equivocal attribution. In fact he criticizes Leibniz for attempting to disguise this consequence with the notion of the "temperance" of the attributes.[60] What is less clear is whether Hegel understood that the seventeenth-century proponents of the concept of an *ens perfectissimum* accepted and elaborated this consequence. In any case, Hegel's argument suggests that the notion of a sum of all predicates implies the notion of God as simple and as a possessor of attributes only in an equivocal sense. If he is wrong, historically speaking, to identify Baumgarten's definition of God with Malebranche's,[61] this does not damage the significance of his claim: the philosophical consequence of Baumgarten's definition is that his concept of God is equivalent to the notion of abstract being.[62]

Ens Necessarium, Causa Sui,
and the Concept of the Concept

The abstract notion of "being" or "sum of all realities" that the rationalists equated with the concept of God stands at the very beginning of an argument in which the other categories of logic are shown to follow by a, perhaps loose, dialectical implication.[63] Included in this chain of categories are the basic concepts of traditional metaphysics, which Hegel subsumes under the general category of "essence." The "Doctrine of Essence" incorporates logical concepts such as identity and contradiction, modal concepts like necessity and contingency, and relational concepts like wholes and parts, cause and effect, etc. Hegel's primary intention is to demonstrate the dependence of these concepts upon one another; the meaning of each category is implicitly related to the meaning of the others. The categories thus comprise a single web of concepts, or, in Hegel's terms, of "thought-determinations" of a single concept.

Hegel's second aim is to demonstrate the relationships of each constellation of concepts within a given general category. In his chapter on modalities, for instance, Hegel attempts to show that it is not the case that "contingency," "possibility," and "necessity," represent utterly distinct modalities.[64] The particular modalities are instead diverse moments of a single, unifying concept of modality (viz. "absolute necessity"). His argument proceeds by analysis of the individual concepts, and he alleges to prove not only that these concepts imply one another, but also that the differences among them are "illusory."[65] By this he means only that the distinctions (between, e.g., contingency and necessity) do not apply absolutely, but rather each distinction is relative to an entire set of distinctions.

This method of dialectical argumentation gives rise to two theological consequences. First, to the extent that each stage of logic includes an inference from a finite category to an infinite one, each stage represents a version of the traditional a posteriori proofs of God's existence.[66] In the first division of the *Logic*, for instance, Hegel argues that the notion of finitude implies the notion of infinity.[67] In the "Doctrine of Essence" a similar inference departs from the notion of "contingency" and concludes that this implies ("finds its truth in") the notion of "absolute necessity."[68] Each a posteriori proof of this type indicates the appropriateness of one traditional "concept" or attribute of God, such as infinity or necessity; Hegel's analysis of modality and of the relation of the notion of "contingency" to "necessity" is also a justification of the traditional notion of an *ens necessarium*.[69]

While each stage of the *Logic* corresponds to the traditional proofs of a given attribute, the larger argument of the work relates the traditional notions of God (i.e., his attributes) to one another, and thus serves as Hegel's solution to the problem of the relation of the divine attributes.[70] The dialectical inference from "being" to "essence," and within "essence" from "identity" to "causality," provides a justification for the traditional theological claims that, e.g., the *omnitudo realitatis* is an infinite being. Proceeding further along the logical chain, Hegel claims also that "the infinite being is a necessary being" and that "the necessary being is a *causa sui*."

In demonstrating the appropriateness and connection of the traditional "thoughts" of God, Hegel assumes positions on both the question of the intelligibility of God's nature and the problem of divine predication. Like Spinoza, Hegel takes God's nature to be thoroughly cognizable, if only by "the mind of God within us" (which corresponds only to our ability to comprehend the inferences or "transitions" of the *Logic*). Unlike Spinoza, however, he does not understand the predicates of God to possess an utterly different sense than those we predicate of other entities. Instead he places the attributes of God in relation to common concepts of causality, necessity, etc., and this enables him to give a more accessible explanation of the concept of God. With respect to the concept of cause, for instance, Hegel does not rest content with the claim that in the case of God we employ an utterly distinct sense of causality. Instead he criticizes the rule that "every cause is distinct from its effect" more thoroughly than Descartes had done. The rule in question holds only "to the extent that the causal relation is abstracted from them."[71] The causal relation, by contrast, actually involves the negation of the distinction between the two entities.[72] The theological notion of *causa sui* expresses the "truth" of the causal relation as this relation appears among finite phenomena, since "causality" indicates the extent to which two given things are identical. For Hegel there is a sense in which every cause is a *causa sui*.

A similar development serves to justify the notion of an *ens necessarium*. Against the rationalists of the seventeenth century who understand the concepts of contingency and necessity to define absolutely different modes of existence (interpreted respectively as difference and identity of "essence" and "existence"), Hegel understands these concepts to refer ultimately to a single logical moment. "Contingency" describes the fact that a given entity is both considered in isolation from its context and nonetheless entirely dependent upon that context.[73] Later in his 1829 *Lectures on the Proofs for the Existence of*

God Hegel shows the same contradiction to characterize the concept of necessity.[74] Contingency and necessity are merely apparently diverse modalities of a single entity, viz., the "absolute" or God.

The "Doctrine of Essence" closes with, on the one hand, the identification of modality and causality (e.g., the necessity of a thing lies in its causality, the *ens necessarium* is the *causa sui*), but also of the identification of these metaphysical notions with "the concept." Since Hegel understands the notion of self-causality to express the truth of causality, he interprets the concept of cause as the "sublation" of the apparent difference between cause and effect. "Causality" expresses the unity of two diverse substances, a cause and an effect. While it is true that every cause is distinct from its effect, no difference between the cause and the effect is identifiable within the causal relation. The concept of causality is the concept of the removal of apparent difference. The same content constitutes the content of "the concept" in its speculative sense, and this leads Hegel to identify the concept of a *causa sui* with the concept of the concept.

HEGEL'S SYSTEM AND THE *FIRST REPLIES* SYLLOGISM

According to the two-argument thesis, the problem involved in the Cartesian minor premise concerns the identification of the notion of an *ens necessarium* or *causa sui* with the representation of God as an *ens realissimum* or *omnitudo realitatis*. An elaboration of the premise should thus read "the *omnitudo realitatis* is the *ens necessarium*" or, in English, "the sum of all realities necessarily exists." If the necessary being is the concept as such, the premise reads "the sum of all realities is the concept." The initial equivalence from the *Logic* completes the restatement of the minor premise: the notion of a "sum of all realities" or *omnitudo realitatis* is the abstract thought of "being." The assertion that "the sum of all realities is the concept" can thus be stated: being is the concept. This last claim is the explicit thesis of the *Logic*, so that that text comprises one large argument for the Cartesian minor premise.[75]

Like the Cartesian minor premise, Hegel's *Logic* argues only that the *concept* of a perfect being implies the concept of necessary existence. A separate premise is required in order to prove that the necessity of our perceiving God's existence implies the real necessity of his existence. In the Cartesian schema, this role is played by the predication thesis and the doctrine of clear and distinct ideas that supports that thesis. Hegel's solution is considerably more elaborate: prior to the *Logic* lies the phenomenological proof that the reality of consciousness is also the reality of its object. The notion of "absolute knowledge" with which the *Phenomenology of Spirit* concludes replaces the less direct assurance that what we predicate of a thing really belongs to that thing. Just as the argument in the *Fifth Meditation* appeals to clarity and distinctness, so does the argument of the *Logic* presuppose the epistemological idealism established in the *Phenomenology*.[76] If the *Logic* provides only the requisite argument for the Cartesian minor premise and the first detailed reply to the two-concept thesis, then it is the *Logic* and *Phenomenology* together that provide the full elaboration of the *First Replies* syllogism.

A second consideration validates the *Logic* as a claim of real predication independently of any reference to the *Phenomenology*. Part of the argument for "absolute idealism" involves the trivialization of existential claims. To say that something "is" or exists, for Hegel, is to say virtually nothing about that thing. Thomistic and empirical objectors presuppose, on the contrary, a definite concept of "being" and thereby distinguish being that is merely thought (*in apprehensione intellectus*) from real being (*in rerum natura*). Related to this distinction is the prejudice, exemplified by Hobbes, that "existence" means primarily corporeal existence. Even Kant is under the influence of a similar prejudice. Although his interpretation of existence as "objective reality" and his definition of this in terms of "appearance" represents a novel justification of classical empiricist prejudices, his critique of theology nonetheless ultimately concludes with the same point as Hobbes's apparently less sophisticated claim. Kant's point is that the ideal of reason (i.e., the idea of God) cannot possess confirmable objective reality (i.e., it cannot appear in the field of common external experience). This is quite obviously a loose analog to the claim that God is not corporeal, and neither version of the claim succeeds as a negation of the theological claim that "God exists."[77]

Hegel addresses this problem by lending the notion of "being" a much more general and trivial meaning. In the *Logic* he interprets "being" as the emptiest possible concept. Its place at the beginning of the chain of logical deduction also implies that it is predicable of every subsequent notion.[78] The concept "is" simply because being determines itself into essence, which subsequently determines itself into the concept. If the inferences from one category to the next are all valid, in which case the dialectical progression from "being" to the "idea" is justified, then the claim that the concept as the "absolutely necessary entity" *is* or *exists* is not only inevitable and correct, it is also a trivial and "superfluous" observation.[79] To say "God is" would be to say very little about God.

Hegel consistently attributes "being" in such a broad and trivial fashion. Anything that is identifiable exists, in some sense of this term. Whether or not the existence is "real" is a secondary question. It is justifiable to ask what kind of existence God, or anything else possesses, but to ask whether it "really exists" or exists merely conceptually is to open the door to manifold misunderstandings. In general, nothing less could be said of a thing than that it "is," and everything that could be talked about possesses being:

> That a given thing *is* constitutes the very least and the most abstract thing that could be said of it. Even if it is only something subjective like knowledge or belief, being nevertheless belongs to it. The objects as well, that only *are* in belief or knowledge, possess a kind of being.[80]

If it is permissible to predicate a kind of "being" even to objects of fantasy, then it would seem uncontroversial to predicate a kind of being to God:

> We might well say that it would be very odd if spirit's innermost core, the concept, or even if I, or above all the concrete totality that God is, were not rich enough to contain within itself even so poor a determination as *being* is—for being is the poorest and most abstract one of all.[81]

HEGEL CONTRA KANT: GOD IN RELIGION AND THE CRITICAL OBJECTION

The Critical and epistemological objections express the suspicion that the idea of God from which the ontological argument begins is an arbitrary and/or subjective construction. The connection between God and his existence, the objector alleges, is a fabrication of thought that possesses at best a merely subjective necessity. The proponents of the ontological argument respond to this objection in a manner that partly concedes its point: the idea of God, and specifically the incorporation of existence within this, is indeed a matter that pertains only to thought. In the Cartesian exposition of the argument this criticism is deflected by the reference to the immediacy and evidence of the perception of God's necessary existence; the Cartesian argument is essentially a claim about our perception. Subsequent philosophers develop this point more completely by modifying the concept of God. Malebranche and Geulincx in particular define God as "the place of minds," and so attribute to God an essentially conceptual existence. In his *Lectures on the Proofs of the Existence of God* Hegel elaborates precisely this point: "God is intellect, and exists only for the intellect, and only for the pure intellect, i.e., for thought."[82] His more complete response consists in a development of two traditional concerns: God possesses an "existence" other than empirical existence; and from the fact that something occurs only in thought it does not follow that it is arbitrary or fictional.

Hegel's lectures on the philosophy of religion develop a number of themes that address the contention that the intellectual nature of the proof is suggestive of fictitiousness. Among these themes is Hegel's defense of the antecedent relation between the human and divine intellects, and this provides the groundwork for his response to Schulze's restatement of Clarke's objection. A similar theme furthers the defense of ontotheology in the face of the Critical objection: what the proofs for the existence of God ultimately express is a subjective movement that Hegel calls "the elevation of the mind to God."[83] The structure of the *Logic* provides a glimpse into this movement: in mediating between God (the sum of all realities) and his necessary existence (the concept) the *Logic* moves from an abstract thought to the complete concept of the divinity.

That God's existence is designated by the term "concept" already implies that God does not possess an existence apart from thought. The objection that the metaphysical proofs do not demonstrate anything beyond an operation of reason is thus both correct and ineffective; in dealing with "God" we are essentially concerned with a rational entity: "the object, with which (metaphysical proof) is concerned, is essentially in thinking."[84] The concept is grasped only by thought, and in proving God's existence we are supposed to be doing nothing other than "grasping the concept."

Hegel directs this thesis to the apparent objection that *God is only in religion*, and he associates this claim, perhaps too hastily, with Kant's thesis that the existence of God is a "postulate" of reason. That there is no God apart from religion (or moral reflection, for that matter), however, does not imply that religion is a pursuit with no object. On the contrary, Hegel's point is that it belongs to God's nature to reveal himself to the human intellect through religion, and this distinguishes Hegel's claim from the contention that God is a mere postulate or belief:

> ... *that God is only in religion* has the weighty and true meaning that it belongs to God's perfect self-sufficiency ... to exist *for the human intellect* ... this is a completely other sense (of the expression) than the one previously discussed, according to which God is only a postulate or belief.[85]

Similarly, to object that the metaphysical arguments establish their truths only within the rational is to state something both correct and trivial. Error ensues, on the part of the objector, only to the extent that something "merely rational" is assumed to be for that very reason untrue.[86] On these points Hegel reverts to the same distinctions anticipated by Descartes. The latter asserted that an "idea" differs from a fictitious construction. The fact that I can *imagine* a "necessarily existing lion" does not imply that my idea of a "necessarily existing God" is equally fictional. Everything hinges on distinguishing "true ideas" like the latter from fictions like the former. This same procedure of distinguishing true from fictitious thought carries over into the process of "elevation" that Hegel intends to inspire with his dialectic.[87]

THE EXPERIENCE OF GOD AND THE PROBLEM OF INTUITION REVISITED

Hegel's defense of the *First Replies* syllogism involves a reduction of the proof of the necessary entity to a proof of the necessity of a certain train of thought; God's existence is nothing but "the elevation of the mind to God," or the transcendence of the finite and subjective mode of thinking.[88] The elevation is an "internal experience" and is thus capable only of the same kind of demonstration as any other experience: it is justified only in actually having the experience. To the extent that anyone has this experience, that person intuits the "existence of God" according to the meaning that this last expression has been given. The fate of the ontological proof hinges upon the reality of a certain kind of cognition, or of a certain cognitive experience. On this point Hegel once again opposes himself to Kantian "Criticism," and specifically to the claim that knowledge of "experience" (in the narrow sense) is the only kind of knowledge. Aside from the value of any positive claim on the part of Kant, the claim that a given species of knowledge is beyond human capacity is difficult to defend.[89] At any rate, the actuality of the cognition in question would serve as a decisive disproof of Kant's or any analogous claim. Hegel thus alleges to refute Kant "through the very fact" of the experience of "elevation":

> Assurance has been granted to the claim that this form of cognition, which is incapable of higher truth, is the single, exclusive manner of cognition . . . (however) what we intend to observe is the liberation of this cognition from its one-sidedness and thereby to demonstrate by our very act (*durch die Tat*

zu zeigen) that there exists a kind of cognition other than the one that is considered to be the only kind.[90]

On Hegel's view, then, it is incumbent upon each philosopher who engages in the inquiry concerning the ontological argument to enact the elevation of the mind to God, from which standpoint the premise attributing necessary existence to God should appear as an obvious truth.[91] By "elevation" Hegel intends nothing more than the subjective act involved in the comprehension of the inferences that comprise the transitions from one logical category to the next. Whoever "grasps" or comprehends that "being is the concept," i.e., whoever gazes from the summit of absolute knowledge and thereby understands the inferences of Hegelian logic, also perceives the existence of God via participation in God's self-knowledge.

This doctrine of "elevation," at least as he outlines it in these lectures,[92] signals a striking admission on Hegel's part: the reader cannot be persuaded by Hegel's claims in the manner in which one is persuaded by an argument that proceeds according to antecedently accepted laws of inference. In other words, Hegel cannot demonstrate the existence of God in any sense of "demonstrate" that involves convincing someone who initially rejects the conclusion; he cannot show that anyone who disagrees is in error. What his arguments actually prove is considerably less than one might hope. The supports he offers for the Cartesian argument thus contains the remnants of the principal shortcomings of the seventeenth-century argument. The objection of philosophers like Cudworth, viz., that no one will be converted by this argument, applies to Hegel's *Logic* as well as to Spinoza's *Ethics*. Likewise, Huet's complaint concerning the credibility of anyone who alleges to have a special type of knowledge applies also to the Hegelian reformulation of the argument. In the end, Hegel, like Descartes, must leave it to each philosopher to "elevate" his or her own mind and thereby to prove "*durch die Tat*" *for him- or herself* that God exists.

A Postscript to the Ontological Argument in Modern Philosophy

Hegel's system represents the philosophical culmination of the defense of the *ratio Anselmi* in the context of modern metaphysics. By no means, however, does he represent the chronological end of this movement; on the contrary, a century after his death Collingwood defended the Hegelian version of the argument and rightfully claimed that this had never met with refutation on the part of anyone who understood it.[93] Two striking facts lend this last statement a tenor of irony. First, the list of people who claimed to understand Hegel's ontological argument was a very short one.[94] Second, and more importantly, what Hegel accomplishes is as little subject to refutation as it is to demonstration.

The Hegelian context of the ontological proof nearly translates into principle what appears only as a fact in the early modern debates over the argument. Early modernity indeed struggled with both the irrefutability and the indemonstrability of the argument. On the one hand, the traditional objections to the proof failed to provide an adequate and decisive refutation of the consistent forms of the argument; on the other hand, even the best formulations of the proof suffered from an incapacity to persuade anyone not predisposed to accept the conclusion. These problems pervaded the debates in question, however, in only the most sincere possible sense. The philosophers of the seventeenth and eighteenth centuries vigorously attacked or defended the ontological proof with the intention either of refuting it or demonstrating its soundness. Hegel's case seems unique in that he openly accepts the indemonstrability of God's existence by reducing the notion of "proof" to the description of a cognitive process. To that extent he offers what could be considered the most complete version of the modern argument, although he fails to free it from its most basic difficulties.

In providing the principles underlying the ontological proof with more detail Hegel at the same time, perhaps inadvertently, exposes their relative insignificance. Whereas the early modern rationalists appealed to an intelligible (if indefensible) theological position concerning the relation of the human mind to God, Hegel makes God into an act of the human mind. Whereas the early moderns combat the Thomistic and empirical objections by indicating that the existence of God differs dramatically from the existence of creatures, Hegel extends this point by reducing any assertion of "existence" to a triviality. The intention of these doctrines was to "preserve the truth" of the basic claim in the argument, and it should not be denied that he made steps toward accomplishing this. His arguments serve as further evidence that the Cartesian argument does not involve any easily identifiable fallacy, but that the proof is one whose usefulness is severely limited.

In light of this curious fact it makes considerable sense that in some arenas (e.g., seventeenth-century English philosophy) the ontological argument was dismissed due to its inutility. Cases are indeed rare in which individuals have cited such an argument as their reason for belief in God, and history seems to be without example of the argument's success in persuading someone to accept the existence of God as a truth. The ontological argument, in its modern form, at least, seems incapable of demonstrating what it purports to show, where "demonstrate" implies proving from premises that are accessible to those who do not initially accept the conclusion. At the same time, however, the argument appears to be unassailable, and history is not much richer in examples of successful refutations of ontological proofs. This problem goes a long way toward explaining why, on the one hand, the legacy of Anselm's argument has been so lasting, while on the other hand the argument has, for most of its nine hundred years, remained somewhat marginal.

This problem with the argument, however, does not unequivocally represent a weakness in the proof. Even in the case of Anselm, the purpose was not to persuade the "fool," but rather to expose the fool for just that. Anselm intended to show that the fool or atheist could not understand his/her own statement "God does not exist."[95] In modernity the fool becomes a skeptic; this problem is most evident in the case of Descartes and More, who intend to show that whoever denies the existence of God is committed to the denial of all knowledge claims whatsoever. In an important sense, then, Hegel's admission that the "argument" is a mere "description" does no injustice to these earlier forms of the proof. The appearance of an "argument," as this term is frequently taken, has always been at least slightly misleading.

One recent study of the ontological argument has considered the implications of this problem beyond what is possible in an historical study. In his book *Ontological Arguments and Belief in God*, Graham Oppy examines the proof in terms of its "dialectical effectiveness" (i.e., its capacity to persuade people).[96] It should be no surprise that he concludes that the argument possesses no such effectiveness. Oppy, however, takes this fact for a fatal flaw in the proof, since (he assumes) today it no longer seems reasonable to accuse every atheist or agnostic of complete skepticism. "Given that there are reasonable agnostics and atheists," he writes, "there can be no ontological argument that provides them with a reason to change their views."[97] The above analyses show that this claim indeed holds of the modern argument, but that we should rather make the initial clause hypothetical. The early modern proponents of the argument deny precisely that there are "reasonable agnostics and atheists," and the purpose of the ontological argument has always been to show that atheists are *eo ipso* unreasonable. Part of the value of studying the argument is thus that it requires us to ask precisely whether and how it could be reasonable to deny the claim "God exists."

NOTES

1. Henry Allison's *The Kant-Eberhard Controversy* (Johns Hopkins, 1973) recounts one of the key episodes in the defense of rationalism against Kantianism.

2. The following is a partial bibliography of Hegel's comments on the ontological argument. I will cite mainly from the Suhrkamp edition of his works (*Werke*, 20 vols., ed. Eva Moldenhauer and Karl Markus Michel, 1970), and will provide pages numbers to English translations where possible. All translations in the text or notes, however, are my own. Suhrkamp 5, pp. 85–92 (*Science of Logic*, trans. A. V. Miller, Humanities Press, 1959, hereafter "SL," pp. 84–90); Suhrkamp 5, pp. 119–20, SL, pp. 111–14; Suhrkamp 6, pp. 125–28, SL 481–84; Suhrkamp 6, pp. 249–69, SL, pp. 580–96; Suhrkamp 2, pp. 251–62; Suhrkamp 20, pp. 359–64 (*Lectures on the History of Philosophy*, trans. Haldane and Simson, London 1892–96, hereafter "HS," pp. 451–57); Suhrkamp 20, pp. 256–58, HS, pp. 131–41; Suhrkamp 8, pp. 135–36 (*Encyclopedia Logic*, trans. Harris, Suchting and Geraets, Hackett, 1995, hereafter "EL," pp. 98–100); Suhrkamp 8, pp. 165–66, EL, pp. 122–23; Suhrkamp 8, pp. 183–84, EL, pp. 137–39, Suhkamp 8, pp. 232–34, EL, pp. 175–78.

3. Hartshorne's (pp. 234–37) unsympathetic treatment of Hegel is all-too-typical.

4. Henrich's (pp. 189–219) view is characteristic of many German historians of philosophy, who too frequently imagine all philosophy prior to 1781 to have been a mere prelude to the "Golden Age" of German philosophy.

5. Rel III 310. Citations from Hegel's lectures on the philosophy of religion will be from the Felix Meiner edition (ed. Walter Jaeschke, 1995) and will be referenced by "Rel" with volume and page number. The English translation by Peter Hodgson (*Lectures on the Philosophy of Religion*, 3 vols., University of California Press, 1984) includes Jaeschke's pagination.

6. Defenders of Kant have, with a certain degree of appropriateness, understood Hegel's position on the ontological argument to be at odds with his theory of history (see Henrich, pp. 203ff.).

7. Both Rohls (pp. 373ff.) and Jaeschke (*Reason in Religion: The Foundations of Hegel's Philosophy of Religion*, trans. Peter Hodgson, University of California Press, 1990, pp. 20–28) assume Henrich's (p. 196) claim concerning this point.

8. The discussion of Kant's critique of the cosmological argument that is inserted in the 1829 lectures (Suhrkamp 17, pp. 421–39) provides ample evidence that Hegel is aware of the other objections, including especially the two-concept thesis.

9. KrV B 631: "Es war etwas ganz Unnatuerliches und eine blosse Neuerung des Schulwitzes, aus einer ganz willkuerlichen Idee das Dasein des ihr entsprechenden Gegenstandes selbst *ausklauben* zu wollen. (It was an entirely unnatural innovation of scholastic subtlety to try to pluck the existence of an object from a completely arbitrary idea)." As Hodgson has noted (*The Lectures on the Philosophy of Religion* vol. 1, ed. Peter Hodgson, University of California Press, 1984, p. 435, n. 156) that the English translators of the *Critique*, including Guyer and Wood as well as Kemp Smith, unfortunately soften the expression by translating "extract." The result is that one of Hegel's favorite jokes is lost on the English reader, since Hegel employs the term "*ausklauben*" or its near equivalent "*herausklauben*" dozens of times in humorous reference to this passage.

10. See Suhrkamp 8, pp. 93–106 (EL, pp. 65–76)

11. A typical summary of the history of the ontological argument in terms of the Thomistic objection runs: "The ontological argument begins with the absolute concept; the transition is made from thought to being: such is the case with Anselm, Descartes and Spinoza; all accept the unity of thought and being. Kant says, however, that just as little reality can be assigned to this Ideal of Reason; there is no transition from the concept to being, the latter cannot be derived from the concept" (Suhrkamp 20, p. 360).

12. "The identity of the concept and objectivity has appeared in two forms in the history of philosophy . . . either with the presupposition of the absolute diversity and self-sufficiency of the concept for itself and likewise of objectivity for itself . . . or as the absolute identity of the two realms. The latter has been the ground of each and every philosophy, either as an unexpressed thought . . . or as a presupposed definition or axiom" (*Heidelberg Encyclopedia* #139; see his *Gesammelte Werke* vol. 13, ed. Klaus Grotsch and Wolfgang Bonsiepen, Felix Meiner, 2000). I owe thanks to Dieter Henrich for this reference.

13. Rel III 114–15.

14. Cf. Henrich, pp. 197ff.

15. Rel III 115: "The first thing is, that the determination of being be shown to be affirmatively contained within the concept; this is then the unity of thought and being. Secondly, they are nonetheless different, so that their unity is the negative unity of both. . . . The distinction must also be expressed, and the unity should be produced in accordance with this distinction. It belongs to logic to demonstrate precisely this. That the concept is this movement, to determine itself as being, is this dialectic, this movement, to determine itself as its opposite, *that logical aspect is a further development that is not given in the ontological argument. The shortcoming of the argument is its failure to provide this development*" (my italics).

16. Suhrkamp 2, pp. 213–72; Schulze's *Kritik der theoretischen Philosophie* (Hamburg 1801) has been reprinted in Aetas Kantiana (Culture et Civilisation, Brussels, 1973).

17. Suhrkamp 2, p. 252.

18. Suhrkamp 2, pp. 258, 252: "das Blendwerk und die leere Spitzfindigkeit des ontologischen Beweises."

19. Schulze departs from the ontological argument at this point, and addresses instead Leibniz's justification for the doctrine of innate ideas. The objection he raises, however, is the same with respect to either the doctrine of innate ideas or the theological proofs. When applied to the doctrine of innate ideas, the Thomistic objection claims that if there are innate ideas, they are not for that matter true, since truth implies a relation to something beyond the mind.

20. Suhrkamp 2, pp. 262–63.

21. "It was, however, not necessary to separate the truth and reliability of the so-called innate ideas from . . . the eternal and real cognitions in God . . . rather *both are one and the same*; there is no matter of a proof of the former by means of the latter; all circularity therefore disappears, and nothing remains except the observation . . . that reason, according to Leibniz, is divine" (Suhrkamp 2, pp. 264–65).

22. As discussed in the first chapter, Descartes indeed accepts this distinction and thus the Thomistic objection (the major premise notwithstanding). In resolving the dilemma, then, he faces the difficulty that Schulze points out. Arnauld raises precisely this point in the *Fourth Set of Objections* (AT VII 214; CSM II 150). Descartes does not seem to have an adequate reply to the charge of circularity (see AT VII 245–46; CSM II 171). There is a considerable literature on this problem in the context of Descartes' philosophy (see especially Willis Doney's "The Cartesian Circle," *Journal of the History of Ideas* 16, 1955, 324–38; Harry Frankfurt's "Memory and the Cartesian Circle," in Moyal, ed. *Descartes: Critical Assessments*, vol. II, Routledge, 1991, pp. 354–61, and John O. Nelson's "In Defense of Descartes: Squaring a Reputed Circle," in Moyal, pp. 362–70).

23. Suhkamp 2, p. 265.

24. Rel I 46: ". . . it is to be pointed out that there cannot be two kinds of reason and two kinds of spirit (*Geist*). There cannot be a divine reason and a human one, a divine intellect (*Geist*) and a human one that would be simply diverse, and which would have opposed essences. Human reason, and the spiritual consciousness of this, the consciousness of its essence, is reason in general. This is the divine in the human; and the intellect (*Geist*), to the extent that it can be called the divine intellect, is not merely beyond the stars or beyond the world. God is rather present and omnipresent, and God, as mind (*Geist*), is present in the intellect (*Geist*)." Compare Descartes' *Regulae*: "For the human mind has within it a sort of spark of the divine, in which the first seeds of useful ways of thinking are sown, seeds which, however neglected and stifled by studies which impede them, often bear fruit of their own accord" (AT X 373; CSM I 17).

25. See chapter three.

26. Jaeschke (*Reason in Religion: The Foundations of Hegel's Philosophy of Religion*, trans. Michael J. Stewart and Peter Hodgson, University of California Press, 1990, p. 231) discusses this point at length.

27. Consider the argument in *Mediation III* (AT VII 45–46; CSM II 31): "my perception of God is prior to my perception of myself. . . ."

28. Hence his frequent references to Anselm (see Suhrkamp 17, pp. 350ff.).

29. Rel I 229: "A God that does not appear is an abstraction." Cf. ibid., p. 237: "A relationship to consciousness belongs to the essence (*Sein*) of God; only as an abstraction does God lie beyond consciousness."

30. Suhrkamp 17, p. 385.

31. EVP36: "The mind's intellectual love of God is the very love of God by which God loves himself . . ." (*Opera* II 302; Curley, p. 612).

32. Suhrkamp 20, p. 362; HS, p. 454.

33. Suhrkamp 5, p. 92 (SL, p. 89): "Although it is nonetheless correct that being is distinct from the concept, God is even more distinct from the hundred dollars and other finite things."

34. Continuation of previous quote: "It is the *definition of finite things*, that concept and being are distinct in them . . . the abstract definition of God is, on the contrary, precisely that his concept and his being are not separate and are inseparable." Cf. Rel. I 329.

35. In reference to Kant's monetary example, Hegel writes: "such an existence is only a disappearing moment" (Suhrkamp 20, p. 362; HS, p. 454).

36. Suhrkamp 17, p. 464.

37. *The Lectures on the Philosophy of Religion*, more than any of Hegel's other works, frequently express an acosmism: "If we ascribe existence (*Sein*) to particular things, that is only a borrowed existence, only the semblance of an existence, not the absolutely independent existence that God is" (Rel I 268).

38. On Hegel's critique of Spinoza, see esp. Suhrkamp 20, pp. 157–96. Among the many articles on this topic, the best is probably Kenneth L. Schmitz's "Hegel's Assessment of Spinoza," in *The Philosophy of Baruch Spinoza*, ed. Richard Kennington, Catholic University of America Press, 1980.

39. See Suhrkamp 6, pp. 125–26 (SL, pp. 249–50).

40. Suhrkamp 5, p. 90; SL, pp. 88. Hegel distinguishes terminologically between the "concept" of a finite content and a concept in the more important sense by designating the former as *representation*. Something like "one hundred dollars" is "no concept at all, only a determination of the content of my consciousness" (Rel I 325–26).

41. See e.g., Rel I 34. For Schelling's use of this idea, see his *Vom Ich als Princip der Philosophie, oder ueber das Unbedingte in menschlichen Wissen*, in his *Saemtliche Werke*, ed. K. F. A. Schelling, Stuttgart, J. G. Cotta, 1856–61, vol. I, pp. 29–244.

42. Consider the following amusing remark on Kant's chapter on the "transcendental ideal": "...*these days* God is *no longer* considered as a thing, and no one pokes around among 'all possible things' in order to determine which one best fits the concept of God" (Suhrkamp 17, p. 425; my emphasis).

43. The *Phenomenology*, although in many respects an unprecedented text, plays essentially the same role as the first two *Meditations* or Spinoza's *Treatise on the Emendation of the Intellect*. Each text leads the reader through the forms of unscientific/prephilosophical consciousness with the intention of removing/transcending them. In other words, each text is designed to aid the student in reaching the standpoint from which the subsequent philosophical truths are valid. What is of interest here is simply that such an endeavor is essential to the ontological argument, since this argument is evidently invalid from an everyday/prephilosophical standpoint.

44. Henrich sees this as a shortcoming of the ontological argument, since it implies that the *objections* to the argument maintain a kind of validity: "the opponents of ontotheology would be dissuaded from their objections only if they were forced to occupy the standpoint of absolute knowledge" (p. 218). He is perhaps right to point out that Hegel has no *compelling* argument for why anyone must seek absolute knowledge. The decision to philosophize would then be a presupposition of Hegel's system, as well as of the others. The passage, however, tacitly implies that the ontological argument *is* valid from the absolute standpoint, which Henrich nowhere else admits. It also presupposes that the burden of proof is on the ontotheologian. Hegel, however, accepts this burden in at least two ways, and does attempt to provide an explanation of why the absolute standpoint is or should be adopted. First, he offers several hypothetical arguments that suggest that philosophy and/or religion require a standpoint like his own. Second, his more risky argument derives from a teleological interpretation of history that has made absolute philosophical knowledge its necessary result.

45. "Geometrical Demonstration," AT VII 166; CSM II 117.

46. Suhrkamp 17, p. 393; in a typical conflation of pre-Kantian philosophers, Hegel attributes Spinoza's (EID1) definition of God to Wolff.

47. Suhrkamp 17, p. 393.

48. "There should be no talk in philosophy of proving *that something is possible*, or *that something else* is *possible* too; and that something, as people also say, is 'thinkable'" (Suhrkamp 8, p. 282). This translation is from the Hackett edition.

49. AT VII 152; CSM II 108.

50. Among Hegel's many discussions of this point, the best occurs in the *Logic*, where Hegel summarizes his view by claiming that "all things are in themselves contradictory;" Suhrkamp 6, p. 74; SL, p. 439.

51. Suhrkamp 17, p. 395: "It can be added that what is here called the *concept* of God and of his possibility should only be called a *thought*, and even an abstract thought."

52. Ibid. Cf.: "... such a unity of determinations ... is not to be taken as a subject to which many predicates would be attributed, in which case the predicates would only have their connection in a third, but would otherwise be opposed to one another. The unity of the predicates is rather essential to the predicates themselves. In other words, the unity is such that it is constituted by means of the determinations, and vice versa, and that these diverse determinations are themselves this: to be inseparable from one another, to translate themselves into the others and to have no meaning at all without the others. ..."

53. Ibid., p. 397.

54. This theological reading of the logic is strongly suggested by the entirety of the 1829 lecture series on the proofs for the existence of God (Suhrkamp 17, pp. 347–535).

55. Suhrkamp 8, p. 231 (EL, p. 175).

56. Suhrkamp 5, pp. 119–20 (SL, pp. 111–14); Suhrkamp 8, pp. 183–84 (EL, pp. 137–39).

57. Suhrkamp 5, p. 121 (SL, p. 113); on the following page Hegel refers to Spinoza's dictum *omniis determinatio negatio est.*

58. *Metaphysica* #840.

59. Suhrkamp 5, p. 120 (SL, p. 112).

60. Ibid.

61. Henrich's objection (p. 200) to this identification is based on the fact that he, inverting Hegel's move, wishes to reduce the Malebranchean view to the Baumgarten.

62. Suhrkamp 5, p. 120 (SL, p. 112): "Reality, if it is taken in the same manner as in this definition of God, as transcending its determination, ceases to be reality; it is transformed into abstract being. God as the purely real in every real thing or as the sum of all realities is the same indeterminate, formless entity as the absolute in which all is one." In the subsequent paragraph Hegel writes: "this reality in every real thing, the being (Sein) in every being (Dasein), that the notion of God purports to express, is nothing other than the abstract being which is the same as nothing." Cf. Suhrkamp 6, pp. 284–85 (SL, p. 609); Rel III 196.

63. On the nature of the inferences in Hegel's Logic, see J. N. Findlay's *Hegel: A Re-examination*, Allen and Unwin, 1958.

64. See especially Suhrkamp 6, p. 190 (SL, p. 532).

65. I am using "illusory" in reference to Hegel's concept of "*Schein*" as he employs this throughout the "Doctrine of Essence."

66. Suhrkamp 17, p. 419: "Each stage through which (the logical progression) passes contains the elevation (*Erhebung*) of a category of finitude into its infinity; each stage thus also contains a metaphysical concept of God, and to the extent that the necessity of the elevation is grasped, each stage contains ... a proof of God's existence." Cf. Rel. I 318.

67. Suhrkamp 5, pp. 156ff. (SL, pp. 143ff.).

68. Suhrkamp 6, p. 215 (SL, p. 552).

69. In his lectures on the philosophy of religion Hegel uses "necessity" and "necessary entity" interchangeably, despite his warning in the *Logic* that the categories should not be reified. Cf. Rel I 34.

70. For an insightful treatment of this problem in early modern philosophy, see Jean-Marie Beyssade "The Idea of God and the Proofs of His Existence," in *The Cambridge Companion to Descartes*, ed. John Cottingham, Cambridge, 1992, pp. 174–99). See also Suhrkamp 17, p. 419.

71. Suhrkamp 8, p. 298 (EL, pp. 228–29).

72. In both the greater *Logic* and the *Encyclopedia* Hegel employs an amusing example referring to "rain" in order to illustrate this point. See Suhrkamp 6, p. 226 (SL, p. 560) and Suhrkamp 8, p. 298 (EL, p. 228).

73. Suhrkamp 6, pp. 205–206. George di Giovanni ("The Category of Contingency in the Hegelian Logic," in *Art and Logic in Hegel's Philosophy*, ed. Steinkraus and Schmitz, Humanities Press, 1980, pp. 179–200) offers an enlightening commentary on these passages.

74. Suhrkamp 17, p. 453: "We can see that there are two opposed determinations that are required for the necessity of something: its self-sufficiency, but in this respect it is individuated and indifferent to whether or not it exists; and its being grounded and contained within a complete relation to everything surrounding it, but in this respect it is not self-sufficient."

75. Cf. Henrich, pp. 214–16.

76. Surhkamp 5, pp. 42–43 (SL, pp. 48–49). In the early twentieth century this claim of Hegel's was challenged by his German commentators on the grounds that the arguments in the *Phenomenology* presuppose a fully developed speculative logic. See Nicholai Hartmann's *Die Philosophie des deutschen Idealismus*, Berlin-Leipzig 1929, and Wolfgang Albrecht's *Hegel's Gottesbeweis: eine Studie zur ,Wissenscheaft der Logik,'* Duncker und Humblot, Berlin, 1958. Henrich (pp. 208ff.) borrows this view.

77. Hegel provides an amusing discussion of this point in the introductory section of his "Doctrine of the Concept." Suhrkamp 6, pp. 256ff. (SL, pp. 586ff.)

78. Surhkamp 5, p. 165 (SL, p. 149): "It is nevertheless superfluous when dealing with concrete concepts to repeat prior and more abstract categories such as 'reality.' . . . Such repetitive claims like 'essence is real' or 'the idea is real' are occasioned only by the fact that the most abstract categories, e.g., being, existence, reality, or finitude, are the most available (*Gelaeufigste*) to uneducated persons."

79. The notion that it is superfluous to predicate a given category of its subsequent categories arises in the final chapters of the *Logic*.

80. Suhrkamp 17, p. 369.

81. Suhrkamp 8, p. 136 (EL, p. 99); I have here used the translation from the EL.

82. Suhrkamp 17, p. 356. The appearance of the word "thought" (Gedanken) justifies the translation of "Geist" in this instance as "intellect."

83. Suhrkamp 17, pp. 356–57; 17, pp. 379–80; 17, p. 386; 17, pp. 400–401; 17, p. 471; 17, p. 479.

84. Suhrkamp 17, p. 390.

85. Ibid., p. 383. In these passages Hegel is thinking of the arguments in *The Critique of Practical Reason*, bk. II, chap. 2, trans. Lewis White Beck, Macmillan, 1956, see esp. p. 132.

86. See note 77.

87. Suhrkamp 17, p. 391: "there is a pressing yet externally imposed need to examine this elevation and to bring to consciousness the various acts and determinations that are contained within it. This is done in order to purify the elevation of every contingency and especially of the contingencies of thought."

88. Rel I 312: ". . . the proofs are *nothing more than* a description of the self-elevation to God" (my emphasis).

89. Hegel criticizes Kant's thesis (that there is a clearly delineable limit to human knowledge) with his "Scholasticus" joke. See Suhrkamp 8, pp. 53–54. See also Justus Hartnack's "Categories and Things-in-Themselves," in Stephen Priest, ed., *Hegel's Critique of Kant*, Oxford, Clarendon Press, 1987, pp. 77–86), and W. H. Walsh's "The Idea of a Critique of Pure Reason," ibid. pp. 119–34.

90. Suhrkamp 17, p. 365.

91. Hegel sometimes emphasizes the ease with which the existence of God is inferred from his essence (see Suhrkamp 17, p. 427).

92. For an interesting interpretation of this doctrine, which would rescue Hegel from my criticism of him, see Robert M. Wallace's *Hegel's Philosophy of Reality, Freedom, and God*, Cambridge, 2005.

93. *Essay on Philosophical Method*, Oxford, Clarendon Press, 1933.

94. This is not to mention that to "understand" the Hegelian argument would be to enact the elevation and thus to experience God, so that anyone who understands the proof necessarily assents to its conclusion. Hegel's detractors are in turn forced to argue that neither they nor the Hegelians understand anything by expressions like "elevation of the mind to God."

95. *Proslogion* IV.

96. Cambridge, 1995.

97. P. 116.

GLOSSARY OF TERMS, ARGUMENTS, AND POSITIONS

Aristes paradox: although it belongs to human knowledge to perceive God qua being immediately, we perceive only "that" being is, not "what" it is. This we do despite our awareness that for God essence ("what") and existence ("that") are indistinguishable.

Cartesian rule (for truth): whatever I clearly and distinctly perceive is true.

Clarke's objection: the ontological argument confuses the idea of God for the object of that idea. Alternatively: the conclusion follows only if the "thing" whose existence is asserted is the same as the idea "in my mind."

Critical objection: justifiable employment of the constituent concepts of the conclusion ("God necessarily exists") extends only to the organization of empirical knowledge.

empirical objection: the proof makes illicit use of "existence" as a predicate. Existence is not a "perfection," or is not among the properties that can belong to the definition or essence of a thing.

finitude objection: a finite being cannot perceive the infinite.

First Replies syllogism: That which we clearly understand to belong to the true and immutable nature, or essence, or form of something, can be truly asserted of that thing. But once we have made a sufficiently careful investigation of what God is, we clearly and distinctly understand that (necessary) existence belongs to his true and immutable nature. Hence we can now truly assert of God that he does exist.

inconceivability objection: God is by his very nature unknowable.

intuitionist objection: The argument makes an unreliable appeal to the private intuition of an individual philosopher. There is no reason why anyone should lend credence to claims about the metaphysician's private experience.

major premise: see "predication thesis."

minor premise: existence belongs to the idea, nature, or essence of God.

modal objection: the premise of the argument asserts existence hypothetically or conditionally, whereas the conclusion asserts existence absolutely. Alternatively: the necessity of the premise is hypothetical, whereas the necessity of the conclusion is absolute.

perfection argument: God is a being who possesses all perfections; existence is a perfection; therefore God exists.

persuasiveness problem: since the ontological argument proves ineffective in convincing infidels, it is useless for any practical purpose. [N.B.: The defender of this claim assumes that the value of an argument lies at least partly in its persuasiveness, or that persuasiveness is a necessary criterion of a good argument.]

possibility objection: versions of the argument illegitimately assumes the non-contradictoriness of the idea of God.

possibility argument (or "possibility syllogism"): if God is possible, God exists; God is possible; therefore, God exists.

predication thesis: whatever I clearly and distinctly believe to belong to a thing really belongs to that thing.

Thomistic objections: these consist in claims that inferences from an idea or definition to an existential proposition are in principle invalid. The objection has two closely related forms, which their founder and namesake carefully distinguishes:

> *First version*: the argument conflates "real" existence (*existentia in rerum natura*) with existence "in thought" (*in apprehensione intellectus*). In that case, the meaning of "existence" in the premise differs from its meaning in the conclusion; the argument thus commits the fallacy of four terms (equivocation).

> *Second version*: The conclusion ("God exists") follows only if it is granted that a perfect being actually exists. In other words, the conclusion of the argument appears among the premises. Anselm's argument is a *petitio principii*.

Transition objection: the idea of God is a construction developed by analogy or transition from the ideas of other objects. Alternatively, the ideas of the attributes of God are formed by transition or indefinite extension from finite and genuinely intelligible qualities (e.g., the notion of "omniscience" is a mere extension or multiplication of the idea of human knowledge).

two-concept thesis: the minor premise of the argument conjoins the concepts of "perfection" and "necessity" without appropriate demonstration.

two-argument thesis: separate arguments are required to prove the existence of a necessary being and a supremely perfect being respectively.

BIBLIOGRAPHY

PRIMARY SOURCES

Anselm. *Monologion, A New, Interpretive Translation of St. Anselm's Monologion and Proslogion*. (bilingual edition) Ed. Hopkins, Jasper. Arthur J. Banning Press, Minneapolis 1986.

———. *Proslogion*. In *A New, Interpretive Translation of St. Anselm's Monologion and Proslogion*. (bilingual edition) Ed. Hopkins, Jasper. Arthur J. Banning Press, Minneapolis 1986.

Aquinas, Thomas. *Summa theologicae*. McGraw Hill, 1963.

Baumgarten, Alexander Gottlieb. *Metaphysica*. Halle, 1779 (originally 1739).

Bering, Johann. *Pruefung der Beweise fuer das Dasein Gottes aus den Begriffen eines hoechstvollkommenen und notwendigen Wesens*. Giessen, 1780.

Clarke, Samuel. *A Demonstration of the Being and Attributes of God and Other Writings*. Ed. Ezio Vailati, Cambridge, 1998 (1738 edition).

———. *A Demonstration of the Being and Attributes of God*. Frommann Verlag Stuttgart, 1964 (1705 edition).

———. *G. W. Leibniz and Samuel Clarke. Correspondence*, edited by Roger Ariew, Hackett, 2000.

Collingwood, Robin George. *Essay on Philosophical Method*. Oxford, Clarendon Press, 1933.

———. *Essay on Metaphysics*. Oxford, Clarendon Press, 1940.

Crusius, Christian August. *Entwurf der notwendigen Vernunftwahrheiten*. Leipzig, 1745.

Cudworth, Ralph. *True Intellectual System of the Universe*. First American Edition, Andover, 1839 (originally 1678).

Descartes, René. *Descartes: Philosophical Letters.* Trans. Anthony Kenny, Oxford, 1970.

————. *Discourse on the Method,* in CSM I, AT I; *Meditations on First Philosophy* and *Objections and Replies,* in CSM II, AT VII.

————. *Oeuvres de Descartes.* Eds. Adam and Tannery. Paris/Vrin, revised edition, 1964–76 ("AT").

————. *The Philosophical Writings of Descartes.* (CSM) Eds. John Cottingham, Robert Stoothoff, and Dugald Murdoch.

————. *Principles of Philosophy,* in CSM I, AT VIIIa.

Duns Scotus, John. *The* De primo principio *of John Duns Scotus.* Ed. and trans. Evan Roche. St. Bonaventure, 1949.

Gassendi, Pierre. *Disquisitio metaphysica seu dubitationes et instantiae adversus Renati Cartesii Metaphysicam, et responsa, ou, Doutes et instances contre la Metaphysique de R. Descartes et ses reponses.* Ed. and trans. Bernard Rochot. Paris, J. Vrin, 1962.

————. *The Selected Works of Pierre Gassendi.* Ed. and trans. Craig B. Brush. Johnson Reprint Corporation. New York, 1972.

Geulincx, Arnold. *Opera philosophica.* Ed. J. P. N. Land. Martinus Nijhoff, 1892.

Hegel, G. W. F. *Enzyklopaedie der philosophischen Wissenschaften I.* Suhrkamp 8. English edition: *The Encyclopedia Logic.* Trans. Geraets, Suchting, and Harris. Hackett, 1991.

————. "Glauben und Wissen," in *Jenaer Schriften 1801–1807.* Suhrkamp 2, pp. 287–433.

————. "Verhaeltnis des Skeptizismus zur Philosophie. Darstellung seiner vershiedenen Modifikationen und Vergleiching des neuesten mit dem altesten." Suhrkamp edition ("Suhrkamp"), v. 2, pp. 213–73.

————. *Vorlesungen ueber die Geschichte der Philosohie III.* Suhrkamp 20. English edition: *Lectures on the History of Philosophy,* trans. Haldane and Simson, London, 1892–96.

————. *Vorlesungen ueber die Philosophie der Religion I & II.* Suhrkamp, 16 & 17.

————. *Vorlesungen ueber die Philosophie der Religion 1 & 3.* Felix Meiner, 1995 ("Rel. I" and "Rel. III"). English edition: *Lectures on the Philosophy of religion.* Trans. Peter Hodgson, University of California Press, 1984.

————. *Wissenschaft der Logik.* Suhrkamp 5 & 6. English edition: *Science of Logic.* Trans. Miller, A. V. Humanities Press, 1959.

Hobbes, Thomas. *Leviathan.* Ed. J. C. A. Gaskin. Oxford University Press, 1998.

————. *Thomas White's* De mundo *Examined.* Trans. Harold Whitmore Jones, Bradford University Press, 1976.

Huet, Pierre-Daniel. *Censura philosophiae cartesianae,* Paris, 1689. English edition: *Against Cartesian Philosophy.* Trans. Thomas M. Lennon, JHP Book Series, Humanity Books, 2003.

Jaquelot, Isaac. *Dissertation sur l'existence de Dieu.* Hague, 1697.

Kant, Immanuel. *Kritik der reine Vernunft.* AA 3–4. English edition: *Critique of Pure Reason.* Trans. Allen Wood and Paul Guyer, Cambridge, 1997.

———. *Kritik der praktischen Vernunft.* AA 5. English edition: *Critique of Practical Reason.* Trans. Lewis White Beck. Macmillan, 1956.

———. *Lectures on Philosophical Theology.* Ed. Allen Wood and Gertrude Clark. Cornell, 1978.

———. *The One Possible Basis for a Demonstration of the Existence of God,* Gordon Treash, New York: Abaris, 1763.

———. *Principorum primorum cognitionis metaphysicae nova dilucidatio.* In *Kant's gesammelte Schriften.* Ed. Prussian Academy of the Sciences, Walter de Gruyter, 1926 ("AA"), vol. 1.

———. *Reflexionen zur Metaphysik,* AA 17, 18.

Leibniz, G. W. "Against Descartes on the Existence of God," (1700) G IV 401.

———. *Arguments sent to me by Mr. Jaquelot in defense of Descartes' controversial proof of the existence of God, together with my replies.* (1702) G III 442–48.

———. *Briefwechsel zwischen Leibniz und Christian Wolff.* Ed. Gebhardt, Hildesheim, 1963 (originally Halle, 1860).

———. *Briefwechsel zwischen Leibniz, Eckhard, und Molanus.* G I 235ff.

———. *Die mathematischen Schriften von Gottfried Wilhelm Leibniz.* Ed. Carl Immanuel Gerhardt. Berlin, Weidmann, 1849–55 ("GM").

———. *Die philosophischen Schriften von Gottfried Wilhelm Leibniz.* Ed. Carl Immanuel Gerhardt. Berlin, Weidmann, 1849–55 ("G").

———. *Discourse on Metaphysics.* G IV 427–65.

———. *G. W. Leibniz and Samuel Clarke. Correspondence.* Ed. Roger Ariew. Hackett, 2000.

———. "Letter to Duchess Sophia" (1680) G IV 294–96.

———. "Meditations on Knowledge, Truth and Ideas." G IV 422ff.; Loemker, pp. 292–93.

———. *Monadology.* G VI 607–23. Trans. Nicholas Rescher. Pittsburgh University Press, 1991.

———. *New Essays on Human Understanding.* Trans Jonathan Bennet and Peter Remnant, Cambridge, 1981.

———. "On Nature's Secrets" (1690) G VII 310–12.

———. *Philosophical Papers and Letters.* Ed. Leroy Loemker. 2nd ed. Riedel, 1969.

———. "Principles of Nature and Grace, Based on Reason." (1686) G VI 598–606.

———. *Quod ens perfectissimum existit.* (1676) G VII 261.

———. *Saemtliche Schriften und Briefe.* Berlin Academy, 1923 ("A").

———. *Theodicy: Essays on the Goodness of God, the Freedom of Man and the Origin of Evil.* Open Court Press, 1985.

Locke, John. *Essay Concerning Human Understanding.* Oxford, 1975.

Malebranche, Nicholas. *Dialogues on Metaphysics and on Religion.* Trans. Morris Ginsberg, George Allen and Unwin, 1923. Oeuvres XII.

———. *Oeuvres Completes de Malebranche.* Ed. Henri Gouhier. J Vrin, Paris, 1958. ("Oeuvres").

———. *Search after the Truth.* Trans. Thomas Lennon and Paul Olscamp. Ohio State University Press, 1980. Oeuvres II & III

Mendelssohn, Moses. *Morgenstunden. oder, Vorlesungen über das Dasein Gottes.* Ed. Dominique Bourel. Stuttgart, 1979.

More, Henry. *Antidote against Atheism* (1652). In the *Philosophical Writings of Henry More.* Ed. Flora Mackinnon, Oxford University Press, 1925.

———. *Henry More's Refutation of Spinoza.* Hildesheim, New York, 1991.

Mosheim, Johann. *Cudworthi systema intellectuale.* Dissertation, Jena, 1733.

Revius, Jacobus. *Methodi cartesianae consideratio theological.* Leiden, 1648.

———. *A Theological Examination of Cartesian Philosophy.* Ed. Aza Goudriaan. Brill, Leiden, 2002.

Schelling, F. W. J. *Vom Ich als Princip der Philosophie, oder ueber das Unbedingte in menschlichen Wissen,* in his *Saemtliche Werke.* Ed. K. F. A. Schelling. Stuttgart, J. G. Cotta, 1856–61, vol. I, pp. 29–244.

Spinoza, Benedict. *The Collected Works of Spinoza.* Ed. Edwin Curley. Princeton University Press, 1985.

———, *Descartes' Principles of Philosophy* with the *Cogitata metaphysica,* Curley, pp. 221–346, *Opera* I.

———. *Ethics.* Curley, pp. 408–617, *Opera* II.

———. *Letters.* Ed. Samuel Shirley, Hackett, 1995.

———. *Short Treatise on God, Man and His Well-Being.* Curley, pp. 61–146, *Opera* I.

———. *Spinoza Opera.* Ed. Gebhart, Heidelberg, 1925.

———. *Treatise on the Emendation of the Intellect.* Curley, pp. 7–45, *Opera* II.

Wolff, Christian. *Theologia naturalis.* Ed. Jean Ecole, Georg Olms, 1978 (originally Leipzig 1736).

———. *Ontologia, Theologia naturalis.* Ed. Jean Ecole, Georg Olms, 1978 (originally Leipzig, 1736).

SECONDARY SOURCES

Aaron, Richard. *John Locke,* Oxford, 1965.

Albrecht, W. *Hegels Gottesbeweis, eine Studie zur 'Wissenschaft der Logik.'* Berlin, 1958.

Allison, Henry. "We can only act under the idea of freedom," Pacific Division APA Presidential Address, in *Proceedings and Addresses of the APA,* no. 2, pp. 39–50.

Allison, Henry. *The Kant-Eberhard Controversy.* Johns Hopkins, 1973.

Alston, William P., "The Ontological Argument Revisited," in *Descartes: A Collection of Critical Essays.* Ed. Willis Doney. Anchor books, 1967, pp. 278–303.

Ameriks, Karl. "Hegel's critique of Kant's theoretical philosophy" in *Philosophy and Phenomenological Research* 46(1), 1985, pp. 1–35.

Armour, Leslie. *Logic and Reality: An Investigation into the Idea of a Dialectical System.* Assen, Humanites Press, 1972.

Baillie, James Black. *The Origin and Significance of Hegel's Logic: A General Introduction to Hegel's System.* Macmillan, 1901.

Balaban, Oded, and Avshalom, Asnat. "The Ontological Argument Reconsidered," in *Journal of Philosophical Research* 15, 1990, pp. 279–310.

Baptist, Gabriella. "Ways and Loci of Modality," in *Essay's on Hegel's Logic.* Ed. George DiGiovanni. SUNY, 1990.

Bausola, Adriano. "Die Moeglichkeit des volkommensten Wesens und der ontologische Gottesbeweis: die Position von Leibniz," in *Studia Leibnitiana* 13, 1981, pp. 1–24.

Beck, Lewis White. *Early German Philosophy.* Harvard, 1969.

Beiser, Frederick. *The Fate of Reason: German Philosophy from Kant to Fichte.* Harvard, 1987.

Beyssade, Jean-Marie. "The idea of God and the Proofs of His Existence," in *The Cambridge Companion to Descartes.* Ed. John Cottingham, Cambridge, 1992, pp. 174–99.

Blaha, Ottokar. *Die Ontologie Kants.* Munich, 1967.

Blumenfield, David. "Leibniz's Ontological and Cosmological Arguments," in *The Cambridge Companion to Leibniz.* Ed. Nicholas Jolley, Cambridge 1995, pp. 353–81.

Bonansea, Bernardino. "The Ontological Argument: Proponents and Opponents," in *Studies in Philosophy and the History of Philosophy.* Ed. John K. Ryan, Catholic University of America Press, 1973.

———. "Duns Scotus and St. Anselm's Ontological Argument," in *Studies in Philosophy and in the History of Philosophy.* Ed. John K. Ryan, Catholic University Press, 1969.

Bossart, William. "Is Philosophy Transcendental?" in *Monist* 55, 1971, pp. 293–311.

Broad, C. D. *Kant: An Introduction.* Cambridge, 1978.

Brodeur, Jean-Paul. "Quatenus: de la contradiction en philosophie," in *Dialogue* 16, 1977, pp. 22–67.

Brundell, Barry. *Pierre Gassendi: From Aristotelianism to a New Natural Philosophy.* Kluwer, 1987.

Buckley, Michael J. *At the Origins of Modern Atheism.* Yale University Press, 1987.

Burbidge, John. "The Necessity of Contingency," in *Art and Logic in Hegel's Philosophy.*

Ed. Warren E. Steinkraus and Kenneth I. Schmitz, Humanities Press, 1980, pp. 201–18.

——. *On Hegel's Logic: Fragments of A Commentary.* Humanities Press, 1981.

Burkhardt, Hans. "Modalities in Language, Thought and Reality in Leibniz, Descartes and Crusius," in *Synthese* 75, 1988, pp. 183–215.

Calton, Patricia Marie. *Hegel's Metaphysics of God: The Ontological Proof as the Development of a Trinitarian Ontology.* Ashgate, 2001.

Cargile, James. "The Ontological Argument," in *Philosophy* 50, 1975, pp. 69–80.

Carnes, Robert. "Descartes and the Ontological Argument," in *Philosophy and Phenomenological Research* 24, 1964, pp. 502–11.

Carr, Spencer. "Spinoza's Distinction between Rational and Intuitive Knowledge," in *The Philosophical Review* 87, 1978.

Chaffin, Deborah. "A Reply to Gabriella Baptist's 'Ways and Loci of Modality,'" in *Essays on Hegel's Logic.* Ed. George Di Giovanni. SUNY, 1990.

Charles, Sebastien. "De l'utilisation critique d'un exemple monetaire en philosophie: Kant en face a Buffier," in *Kant Studien* 91(3), 2000, 356–65.

Cress, Donald. "Does Descartes Have Two 'Ontological Arguments?'" in *International Studies in Philosophy* 7, 1975, pp. 155–66.

——. "Does Descartes' 'Ontological Argument' Really Stand on its Own?" in *Studi Internazionali di Filosofia* 5, 1973, pp. 127–36.

Crichlow, Harold. "Kant and Hegel: Their Religious Philosophies Compared," in *Bulletin of the Hegel Society of Great Britain* 33, 1996, pp. 87–102.

Curley, Edwin. *Behind the Geometrical Method.* Princeton, 1988.

——. "Experience in Spinoza's Theory of Knowledge," in *Spinoza: A Collection of Critical Essays.* Ed. Marjorie Grene. Anchor Books, 1973, pp. 25–59.

——. "Hobbes versus Descartes," in *Descartes and his Contemporaries.* Ed. Roger Ariew and Marjorie Greene. University of Chicago Press, 1995, pp. 97–105.

——. "'I durst not write so badly' or, How to Read Hobbes' Theological-Political Treatise," in *Hobbes e Spinoza.* Ed. Daniela Bostrenghi. Naples, 1992, pp. 497–593.

——. "Spinoza's Geometric Method," in *Studia Spinozana* 2, 1986.

Devine, Philip. "'Exists' and Anselm's Argument," in *Grazer Philosophische Studien* 3, 1977, pp. 59–70.

Dickey, Lawrence. "Hegel on Religion and Philosophy," in *The Cambridge Companion to Hegel.* Ed. Frederick C. Beiser. Cambridge, 1993, pp. 301–47.

Di Giovanni, George. "The Category of Contingency in the Hegelian Logic," in *Art and Logic in Hegel's Philosophy.* Ed. Warren E. Steinkraus and Kenneth I. Schmitz. Humanities Press, 1980, pp. 179–200.

Domke, Karl. *Das Problem der metaphysischen Gottesbeweise in der Philosophie Hegels.* Dissertation, Leipzig, 1940.

Doney, Willis. "The Cartesian Circle," in *Journal of the History of Ideas* 16, 1955, pp. 324–38.

———. "Descartes' Argument from Omnipotence," in *René Descartes: Critical Assessments Volume II*. Ed. Moyal, Routledge, 1991, pp. 371–80.

———. "Did Caterus Misunderstand Descartes' Ontological Proof?" in *René Descartes: Critical Assessments, Volume II*. Ed. Moyal Routledge, 1991.

———. "The Geometrical Presentation of Descartes' A Priori Proof," in *Descartes: Critical and Interpretive Essays*. Ed., Michael Hooker. Johns Hopkins University Press, 1978, pp. 1–25.

———. "Spinoza's Ontological Proof," in *The Philosophy of Baruch Spinoza*. Ed. Richard Kennington. Catholic University of America Press, 1980, pp. 35–52.

D'Oro, Giuseppina. "On Collingwood's Rehabilitation of the Ontological Argument," in *Idealistic Studies* 30 (3), 2000, pp. 173–88.

Dougherty, M. V. "The Importance of Cartesian Triangles: A New Look as Descartes' Ontological Argument," in *International Journal of Philosophical Studies* 10 (1), 2002, pp. 35–62.

Dutton, Blake. "The Ontological Argument: Aquinas's Objection and Descartes' Reply," in *American Catholic Philosophic Quarterly* 67 (4), 1993, pp. 431–50.

Earle, William. "The Ontological Argument in Spinoza," in *Philosophy and Phenomenological Research* 11, 1951, pp. 549–54.

———. "The Ontological Argument in Spinoza: Twenty Years Later," in *Spinoza: A Collection of Critical Essays*, ed. Marjorie Grene. Anchor Books/Doubleday, 1973, pp. 220–26.

Everitt, Nicholas. "Kant's Discussion of the Ontological Argument," in *Kant-Studien* 86, 1995, pp. 385–405.

Ferber, Rafael. "Das Normative 'Ist,'" in *Zeitschrift fuer philosophische Forschung* 82, 1988, pp. 371–96.

Findlay, J. N. *Hegel: A Re-examination*. Allen and Unwin, 1958.

Fischer, Kuno. *Geschichte der neuern Philosophie*. Heidelberg, 1867–78.

Forgie, William. "The Caterus Objection," in *International Journal for the Philosophy of Religion* 41, 1990, pp. 81–104.

———. "Existence Assertions and the Ontological Argument," in *Mind* 83, 1974, pp. 260–62.

———. "Kant on the Relation Between the Cosmological and Ontological Arguments," in *International Journal for Philosophy of Religion* 44, 1993, pp. 1–12.

Forster, Eckart. "Die Bedeutung von SS 76, 77 der Kritik der Urteilskraft fuer die Entwicklung der nachkantischen Philosophie," in *Zeitschrift fuer philosophische Forschung* 56 (3), 2002, pp. 321–45.

Frankfurt, Harry. "Memory and the Cartesian Circle," in *Decartes: Critical Assessments, Vol. II*. Ed. Moyal. Routledge, 1991, pp. 354–61.

Gabbey, Alan. "*Philosophia cartesiana triumphata*: Henry More and Descartes, 1646–71," in *Problems in Cartesianism*. Ed. T. M. Lennon et al. Kingston and Montreal: Queens McGill University Press, 1982, pp. 171–249.

Gale, Richard. "'A priori' Arguments from God's Abstractness," in *Nous* 20, 1986, pp. 531–43.

Garber, Daniel. "J. B. Morin and the *Second Objections*," in Ariew and Grene, pp. 63–82.

Garrett, Don. "Spinoza's Ontological Argument," in *Philosophical Review* 88, 1979, pp. 198–223. Reprint in Genevieve Lloyd, ed. *Spinoza: Critical Assessments*, Routledge, 2001.

Gill, Jerry H. "Kant, Analogy, and Natural Theology," in *International Journal for Philosophy of Religion* 16, 1984, 19–28.

Girard, Louis. *L'argument ontologique chez Saint Anselme et chez Hegel*. Rodopi, Amsterdam, 1995.

Gotterbarn, Donald. "Leibniz's Completion of Descartes' Proof," in *Studia Leibnitiana* 8, 1976, pp. 105–12.

Goudriaan, Aza. "Die Erkennbarkeit Gottes in der Philosophie Claubergs," in *Johannes Clauberg and Cartesian Philosophy in the Seventeenth Century*. Ed. Theo Verbeek. Dordrecht, 1999.

Gouhier, Henri. "La prevue ontologique de Descartes," in *Revue Internationale de Philosophie* VII, 1954, pp. 295ff.

Graeser, Andreas. "Hegel ueber die Rede vom Absoluten—Teil I: Urteil, Satz und Spekulative Gehalt," in *Zeitschrift fuer philosophische Forschung* 44 (2), 1990, pp. 175–93.

Grier, Michelle. *Kant's Doctrine of Transcendental Illusion*. Cambridge, 2001.

Griffiss, James. "The Kantian Background of Hegel's *Logic*," in *New Scholasticism* 43, 1969, pp. 509–29.

Guerolt, Martial. *Descartes selon l'ordre des raisons*, English: *Descartes' Philosophy Interpreted According to the Order of Reasons*. Trans. Roger Ariew. Minnesota 1985.

———. *Spinoza I: Dieu (Ethique, I)*. Hildesheim, 1968.

Gutterer, Dietrich. "Der Spekulative Satz," in *Kodikas-Code* 1, 1979, pp. 235–47.

Guyer, Paul. "Thought and Being: Hegel's Critique of Kant's Theoretical Philosophy," in *The Cambridge Companion to Hegel*. Ed. Frederick C. Beiser, Cambridge, 1993, pp. 171–210.

Haight, David. "Is Existence an Essential Predicate," in *Idealistic Studies*, 1977, pp. 192–97.

Harnischmacher, Iris. *Der Metaphysische Gehalt der Hegelschen Logik*. Fromann-Holzboog, 2001.

Harris, E. E. "Mr. Ryle and the Ontological Argument," in *The Many Faced Argument*. Eds. John Hick and Arthur McGill. Macmillan, 1967, pp. 261–68.

Harris, Errol. "Collingwood's Treatment of the Ontological Argument," in *Critical Essays on the Philosophy of R. G. Collingwood*. Ed. Michael Krausz. Oxford, Clarendon Press, 1972.

Harris, H. S. "The Legacy of Hegel," in *Monist* 48, 1964, pp. 112–28.

Hartmann, Klaus. "Hegel: A Non-Metaphysical View," in *Hegel: A Collection of Critical Essays*. Ed. Alasdair MacIntyre. Notre Dame, 1972, pp. 101–24.

Hartmann Nicholai. *Die Philosophie des deutschen Idealismus*. Berlin-Leipzig, 1929.

Hartnack, Justus. "Categories and Things-in-Themselves," in *Hegel's Critique of Kant*. Ed. Stephen Priest, Oxford, 1987. pp. 77–86.

Hartshorne, Charles. *Anselm's Discovery*. Open Court Press, 1965.

———. "What Did Anselm Discover?" in *Union Seminary Quarterly Review* 17, 1962, pp. 213–22. Reprint in *The Many Faced Argument*. Eds. Hick and McGill, pp. 321–34.

Hasker, W. "Is there a Second Ontological Argument," in *International Journal for the Philosophy of Religion* 13, 1982, pp. 93–102.

Heede, Reinhard. *Die goettliche Idee und ihre Erscheinung in der Religion*. Dissertation, Muenster/Westphalia, 1972.

Henrich, Dieter. *Der Ontologische Gottesbeweis*, Tuebingen, 1961.

———. "Hegels Logik der Reflexion. Neue Fassung," in *Die Wissenschaft der Logik und die Logik der Reflexion*, ed. Henrich, Bonn, 1978.

Herrschaft, Lutz. "'Das was ich mir vorstelle ist darum doch noch nicht': Der ontologische Gottesbeweis in der neueren Diskussion," in *Zeitschrift fuer philosophische Forschung* 47 (3), 1993, pp. 461–76.

Hick, John. "A Critique of the 'Second Argument,'" in *The Many Faced Argument*. Ed. Hick and McGill. Macmillan, 1967. pp. 341–56.

———. *The Existence of God*. Macmillan, 1964.

Hick, John, and Arthur McGill. *The Many Faced Argument: Recent Studies on the Ontological Argument for the Existence of God*. Macmillan, New York, 1967.

Hintikka, Jaakko. "Kant on Existence, Predication and the Ontological Argument," in *Dialectica* 35, 1981, pp. 128–46.

Hofstadter, Albert. "The Question of the Categories," in *Journal of Philosophy* 48, 1951, pp. 173–84.

Houlgate, Stephen. "Hegel's Critique of Foundationalism in the 'Doctrine of Essence,'" in *Bulletin of the Hegel Society of Great Britain* 39–40, 1999, pp. 18–34.

———. *Hegel, Nietzsche and the Criticism of Metaphysics*. Cambridge, 1986.

Humber, James. "Descartes' Ontological Argument as Non-Causal," in *New Scholasticism* 44, 1970, pp. 449–59.

———. "Spinoza's Proof of God's Necessary Existence," in *Modern Schoolman* 49, 1972, pp. 221–33.

Imlay, Robert. "Descartes' Ontological Argument," in *New Scholasticism* 43, 1969, pp. 440–48.

Ingram, David. "Hegel on Leibniz and Individuation," in *Kant Studien* 76, 1985, pp. 420–35.

Jaeschke, Walter. *Reason in Religion: The Foundations of Hegel's Philosophy of Religion.* Trans. J. Michael Stewart and Peter Hodgson. University of California Press, 1990.

Johnson, Paul Owen. *The Critique of Thought: a Re-examination of Hegel's 'Science of Logic.'* Brookfield, 1988.

Johnston, T. A. "A Note on Kant's Criticism of the Arguments for the Existence of God," in *Australasian Journal of Philosophy* 21, 1943, pp. 10–16.

Kalinowski, Georges. "Sur l'argument ontologique de Leibniz," in *Studia Leibnitiana* 17, 1985, pp. 94–97.

Kaufmann, David. *Geschichte der Attributenlehre in der jeudischen Religionsphilosophie des Mittelalters von Saadja bis Maimäuni.* Amsterdam Philosophical Press, 1967.

Kiteley, Murray. "Existence and the Ontological Argument," in *Philosophy and Phenomenological Research* 18, 1958, pp. 533–35.

Kreimendahl, Lothar. "Zur Geschichte des ontologischen Gottesbeweises," in *Philosophische Rundschau* 44 (1), 1997, pp. 44–51.

Ladic, Jean-Marie. "Malebranche et l'argument ontologique," in *Revue Philosophique de la France et de l'Etranger,* 1996.

Laura, Ronald. "God, Necessary Exemplification and the Synthetic / Analytic Distinction," in *International journal for the Philosophy of Religion* 4, 1973, pp. 119–27.

Leftow, Brian. "Individual and Attribute in the Ontological Argument," in *Faith and Philosophy* 7 (2), 1990, pp. 235–42.

———. "Is God an Abstract Object?" in *Nous* 24 (4), 1990, pp. 581–98.

Loeb, Louis. "The Cartesian Circle," in *The Cambridge Companion to Descartes.* Ed. John Cottingham. Cambridge, 1992, pp. 200–35.

Loewer, Barry. "Leibniz and the Ontological Argument," in *Philosophical Studies* 34, 1978, pp. 105–109.

Lomasky, Loren. "Leibniz and the Modal Argument for God's Existence," in *Monist* 54, 1970, pp. 250–69.

Longuenesse, Beatrice. "Point of View of Man or Knowledge of God: Kant and Hegel on Concept, Judgment and Reason," in *The Reception of Kant's Critical Philosophy: Fichte Schelling and Hegel.* Ed. Sally Sedgwick, Cambridge, 2000.

Mackie, J. L. "The Riddle of Existence," in *Aristotelian Society,* supplement 50, 1976, pp. 247–66.

Malcolm, Norman. "Anselm's Ontological Arguments," in *The Philosophical Review* 69 (1), 1960, pp. 41–62. Reprint in Hick and McGill, pp. 310–20.

Marion, Jean-Luc. *Cartesian Questions: Method and Metaphysics.* Chicago, 1999.

———. "Is the Ontological Argument Ontological?" in *Journal of the History of Philosophy* 30 (2), 1992, pp. 201–18.

———. *On Descartes' Metaphysical Prism.* Chicago, 1996.

Maritain, Jacques. "Il n'y a pas de savoir sans intuitivite," in *Revue Thomiste* 70, 1970, pp. 30–71.

Martinich, A. P. *The Two Gods of "Leviathan."* Cambridge, 1992.

Mason, Richard. *The God of Spinoza.* Cambridge, 1997.

Matthews, Gareth. "Aquinas on Saying that God Doesn't Exist," in *Monist* 47, 1963, pp. 472–77.

McGrath, P. J. "Does the Ontological Argument Beg the Question?" in *Religious Studies* 30 (3), 1994, pp. 305–10.

Miller, Robert. "The Ontological Argument in St. Anselm and Descartes," in *Modern Schoolman* 32, 1955, 341–49.

Moyal, Georges, ed. *Rene Descartes: Critical Assessments*, Routledge, 1991.

Mure, G. R. G. *A Study of Hegel's Logic.* Oxford, Clarendon Press, 1950.

Nelson, Herbert J. "Kant on Arguments Cosmological and Ontological," in *American Catholic Philosophical Quarterly* 67 (2), 1993, pp. 167–84.

Nelson, John O. "In Defense of Descartes: Squaring a Reputed Circle," in *René Descartes: Critical Assessments, Vol. II.* Ed. Moyal. Routledge 1991, pp. 362–70.

Nussbaum, Charles. "Did Kant Refute the Ontological Argument?" in *Southwest Philosophy Review* 10 (1), 1994, pp. 147–56.

Oppy, Graham. *Ontological Arguments and the Belief in God.* Cambridge, 1995.

Orenduff, J. M. "Existence Proofs and the Ontological Argument," in *Southwest Philosophical Studies* 5, 1980, pp. 50–54.

Parkinson, G. H. R. "Hegel, Pantheism, and Spinoza," in *Journal of the History of Ideas* 38, 1977, pp. 449–59.

———. *Spinoza's Theory of Knowledge.* London, 1954.

Pasternack, Lawrence. "The *ens realissimum* and necessary being in the *Critique of Pure Reason*," in *Religious Studies* 37 (4), 2001, pp. 467–74.

Pena, Lorenzo. "Essence and Existence in Leibniz's Ontology," in *Synthesis Philosophica* 12 (2), 1997, pp. 415–31.

Pinkerton, R. J. "Kant's Refutation of the Ontological Argument," in *Indian Philosophical Quarterly* 5, 1977, pp. 19–38.

Plantinga, Alvin. "Alston on the Ontological Argument," in *Descartes: A Collection of Critical Essays.* Ed. Willis Doney, Anchor Books, 1967, pp. 303–11.

———. *God and Other Minds.* Cornell, 1967.

———. "Kant's Objection to the Ontological Argument," in *Journal of Philosophy* 63, 1966, pp. 537–45.

———. *The Nature of Necessity.* Oxford, 1974.

Priest, Graham. *Beyond the Limits of Thought.* Cambridge, 1995.

Reardon, Bernard. *Hegel's Philosophy of Religion.* Harper & Row, 1977.

Remnant, Peter. "Kant and the Cosmological Argument," in *Australasian Journal of Philosophy* 37, 1959, pp. 152–55.

Richli, Urs. *Form und Inhalt in Hegel's "Wissenschaft der Logik."* Wien, 1982.

Richman, Robert. "A Serious Look at the Ontological Argument," in *Ratio* 18, 1976, pp. 85–89.

Rinaldi, Giacomo. "Die Aktualitaet von Hegels Logik," in *Jahrbuch fuer Hegelforschung*, pp. 1996, pp. 27–54.

Roed, Wolfgang. *Der Gott der reinen Vernunft.* C. H. Beck, Munich, 1992.

———. "Spinoza's Idee der scientia intuitiva und die Spinozanische Wissenschaftskonzeption," in *Zeitschrift fuer philosophische Forschung* 31, 1977.

Rohatyn, Dennis. "Kant's 'Disproof' of God," in *Sophia* 34, 1974, pp. 30–31.

Rohls, Jan. *Theologie und Metaphysik: Der ontologische Gottesbeweis und seine Kritiker.* Guetersloh, 1987.

Rome, Beatrice K. *The Philosophy of Malebranche.* Henry Regnery Company, Chicago, 1963.

Ryle, Gilbert. "Back to the Ontological Argument," in *The Many Faced Argument.* Eds. John Hick and Arthur McGill. Macmillan, 1967, pp. 269–74.

———. "Mr. Collingwood and the Ontological Argument," in *The Many Faced Argument.* Eds. John Hick and Arthur McGill. Macmillan, 1967, pp. 246–60.

Schaffer, Jerome. "Existence, Predication and the Ontological Argument," in *Mind*, 1962, pp. 307–25.

Schmitz, Kenneth L. "Hegel's Assessment of Spinoza," in *The Philosophy of Baruch Spinoza.* Ed. Richard Kennington. Catholic University of America Press, 1980.

Schmucker, Josef. "Die Gottebeweise beim vorkritischen Kant," in *Kant Studien* 74, 1983, pp. 445–63.

Schoenfeld, Martin. *The Philosophy of the Young Kant.* Oxford, 2000.

Secada, Jorge *Cartesian Metaphysics.* Cambridge, 2000.

Sedgwick, Sally, "Hegel, McDowell and Recent Defenses of Kant," in *Journal for the British Society for Phenomenology* 31 (3), October 2000, pp. 229–47.

Seifert, Josef. *Gott als Gottesbeweis: eine phaenomenologische Neubrgruendung des ontologischen Arguments.* Heidelberg, 1996.

Shur, E. "The Theory of the Concept, the Judgment, and Inference in Formal and Dialectical Logic," in *Philosophy and Phenomenological Research* 5, 1944, pp. 199–216.

Sievert, Donald. "Essential Truths and the Ontological Argument," in *Southwest Philosophy Review* 6 (1), 1990, pp. 59–64.

Silva, Jose. "A Criticism of Leibniz's Views on the Ontological Argument," in *Dialogos* 31 (68), 1996, pp. 183–92.

Sorley, W. R. *A History of British Philosophy to 1900*, 2nd ed., Cambridge, 1965, pp. 75–103.

Sorrel, Tom. "Hobbes's Objections and Hobbes's System," in Ariew and Grene, pp. 83–96.

Stroble, Paul E. "'without running riot': Kant, Analogical Language, and Theological Discourse," in *Sophia* 32 (3), 1993, pp. 57–72.

Tichy, Pavel. "Existence and God," in *Journal of Philosophy* 76, 1979, pp. 403–20.

Tomasoni, Francesco. "'Conjecture,' 'Conceivability,' 'Existence' between Henry More and Ralph Cudworth," in *The Return of Scepticism: from Hobbes and Descartes to Bayle*. Ed. Gianni Paganini. Kluwer, 2003, pp. 55–80.

Tooley, Michael. "Does the Cosmological Argument Entail the Ontological Argument?" in *Monist* 54, 1970, pp. 416–26.

Wahl, Russell. "The Arnauld-Malebranche Controversy and Descartes' Ideas," *Monist* 71, 1988, pp. 560–72.

Wallace, Robert M. *Hegel's Philosophy of Reality, Freedom, and God*. Cambridge, 1995.

Walsh, W. H. "The Idea of a Critique of Pure Reason," in *Hegel's Critique of Kant*. Ed. Stephen Priest. Oxford, 1987, pp. 119–34.

———. "Kant as Seen by Hegel," in *Hegel's Critique of Kant*. Ed. Stephen Priest. Oxford, 1987, pp. 205–20.

Walton, Douglas. "The Circle in the Ontological Argument," in *International Journal for the Philosophy of Religion* 9, 1978, 193–218.

Watson, Richard. "Malebranche and Arnauld on Ideas," in *Modern Schoolman* 71 (4), 1994, pp. 259–70.

Webb, Mark. "Natural Theology and the Concept of Perfection in Descartes, Spinoza and Leibniz," in *Religious Studies* 25 (4), 1989, pp. 459–75.

Werther, David. "Leibniz and the Possibility of God's Existence," in *Religious Studies* 32 (1), 1996, pp. 37–48.

Wertz, S. K. "Why Is the Ontological Proof in Descartes' Fifth Meditation?" in *Southwest Philosophy Review* 6 (2), 1990, pp. 107–109.

Westphal, Kenneth R. "Epistemic Reflection and Cognitive Reference in Kant's Transcendental Response to Skepticism," in *Kant Studien*, 94 (2), 2003, pp. 135–71.

Westphal, Merold. "Hegel's Theory of the Concept," in *Art and Logic in Hegel's Philosophy*. Ed. Warren E. Steinkraus and Kenneth I. Schmitz. Humanities Press, 1980, pp. 103–20.

Wilson, Margaret. "Spinoza's Theory of Knowledge," in *The Cambridge Companion to Spinoza*. Ed. Don Garrett. Cambridge, 1996.

Woelfle, Gerhard Martin. *Die Wesenslogik in Hegels "Wissenschaft der Logik."* Frommann Holzboog, Stuttgart, 1994.

Wolfhart, Gunter. "Das unendliche Urteil: zur Interpretation eines Kanpitels aus Hegel's *Wissenscheft der Logik*," in *Zeitschrift fuer philosophische Forschung* 39, 1985, pp. 85–100.

Wolfson, Harry. *The Philosophy of Spinoza*, Harvard, 1934.

Wood, Allen. *Kant's Rational Theology*. Cornell University Press, 1969.

Wundt, Max. *Die duetsche Schulphilosophie im Zeitalter der Aufklaerung.* Hildesheim (Olms), 1964.

Young, Michael J. "Kant on Existence," in *Ratio* 18, 1976, pp. 91–106.

Yovel, Yirmiyahu. "Spinoza, the First Anti-Cartesian," in *Idealistic Studies* 33 (2–3), 2003, pp. 121–40.

Zarka, Yves Charles. "First Philosophy and the Foundations of Knowledge," in *The Cambridge Companion to Hobbes.* Cambridge, 1996, pp. 62–85.

INDEX